The Day
the Pigs
Refused to
Be Driven to
Market

Robin Wight

THE DAY
THE PIGS
REFUSED TO
BE DRIVEN TO
MARKET

Advertising and the
Consumer Revolution

Random House, New York

Grateful acknowledgment is made to the following for permission to reprint previously published material:

Harvard University, Graduate School of Business Administration for the chart "Businessmen's Attitudes to Advertising" from *Advertising in America: The Consumer View*, by Raymond A. Bauer and Stephen A. Greyser. (Division of Research, Harvard Business School, Boston, 1968) Table III-1.

Reader's Digest Association Ltd: For a chart from Table 64 in *Survey of Europe Today*, Copyright The Reader's Digest Association Ltd. 1970.

Originally published in England by Hart-Davis, MacGibbon, London.

Library of Congress Cataloging in Publication Data

Wight, Robin.
The day the pigs refused to be driven to market:
advertising and the consumer revolution.

1. Advertising. 2. Consumers. I. Title.
HF5823.W49 1974 640.73 73-11432
ISBN 0-394-4780-7

Manufactured in the United States of America

9 8 7 6 5 4 3 2

To Julia

ACKNOWLEDGMENTS

Many people have helped with developing the arguments of this book, though none of them—of course—should be held responsible for anything I have written.

In particular, I would like to thank (in alphabetical order) Tony Crowther, Max Forsythe, Winston Fletcher, Terry Grimward, Derrick Hass, Robert Lacey, Raymond Lotthé, Chris Rainer and Laurie Rosenbaum. I am also grateful to Diana Cunliffe, Lindsay Clifford and Jill Retter for helping with the research.

In addition, no one can write about the subject of business and advertising without being indebted to the American magazines *Fortune, Business Week* and *Advertising Age,* and the British *Management Today, Campaign* and *Ad Weekly.* The following sources have also been of great assistance to me in the writing of this book:

The Affluent Worker in the Class Structure, by John H. Goldthorpe et al.; *America, Inc.,* by Jerry S. Cohen and Morton Mintz; "The Role of Crusader-Triggered Controversy in Technology Assessment," by Dennis W. Brezina, in a paper published by the George Washington University; "Government and the Market Economy," by Samuel Brittain (an Institute of Economic Affairs leaflet); *Future Shock,* by Alvin Toffler; *Managers and Their Wives,* by Drs. B. and J. Pahl; *Abundance for What? and Other Essays,* by David Riesman; "What One Little Ad Can Do," by Leo Bogart, Stuart Tolley and Frank Orenstein, which appeared in the *Journal of Advertising Research* (August 1970); *Occupation: Housewife,* by Helena Z. Lopata; *The Greening of America,* by Charles Reich; E. B. Weiss's columns in *Advertising Age*; and various research reports from J. Walter Thompson Ltd.

Finally, I would like to thank my British editor, Michael Dempsey, for suggesting I write this book in the first place. And my wife, Julia, for not divorcing me during the writing of it.

INTRODUCTION

In 1948, in a world of ration books and Cold War, George Orwell inverted the 4 and 8 to create 1984. This was to be the date by which, encased in blue overalls and numbed by Victory Gin, we awaited like Pharaoh's lackeys the instructions of Big Brother.

In 1974 we are over two thirds of the way, in time, to this future. And though few today accept the trend toward Orwell's Big Brother anywhere near the way it was accepted a quarter of a century ago, his basic assumption is still widely accepted: that as individuals we are increasingly under control of the state—or the corporate state, as it has now become. The "them" who stuff brown envelopes through our mail boxes to announce that our back garden is to become part of a thruway. The gentlemen in blue (sometimes not so gentle) who can hold us without a lawyer present pending a charge being made. The computers who can make us their slaves. And so on until one reaches a politico-technocratic tyranny equipped with all the modern conveniences.

Perhaps the most widely accepted part of this vision is the control over our lives exercised by the mass media, and in particular that part of it trying to separate us from our hard-earned pay checks; advertising and marketing.

First came Orwell, then Vance Packard, then Galbraith to preach the same gospel: that the predestination of persuasion had replaced the free will of perfect competition. And growing fat on this mythology were the golden-fingered admen who, whatever private doubts they may have had about these immense powers, were not going to repudiate this unsolicited testimonial to their skills.

The predictable result was that no company felt complete without its high-stepping agency pumping out the hard-hitting messages through the lines of NBC, CBS, ITV, or via the wide open spaces of the printed page. But instead of being White-Tornadoed into submission, the recipients of this bombardment responded in

ix

a way that anyone who studied either the bombing of Dresden or had made but a cursory study of social psychology could have foreseen. The worm started to turn. While the whiter-than-white miracle was being promised, the consumer discovered a truth that was several shades grayer, for equipped with new learning sensors and gifted with a new electronic sight, the consumer now had eyes that could see through things that his parents' vision might have bounced off. Little by little this growing disenchantment has swollen into a quiet, silent, bloodless revolution that is on the point of transforming our society as profoundly as did the granting of universal suffrage a century ago. This revolution has had no marches, no manifesto, no real leaders and few formal followers. Its organization (where it exists) is composed of equal mixtures of enthusiasm and inexperience. Yet it has already the strength to humble the biggest and most powerful corporation in the world, and none that it has challenged has emerged unchanged.

This book is about that revolution—how and where it grew, the ideologies that fueled its growth, the activities that formed its purpose, and the areas into which it can be expected to spread. It is a phenomenon whose existence will be traced both to profound changes within the structure of our society and to the unresponsiveness of the advertising industry to these changes—an unresponsiveness that has led them to worship false gods in a way that may yet involve the industry's ultimate self-destruction.

I am by no means the first reporter of some of the events described in this volume. Indeed, in one sense, there may be little that is totally new within these covers. (That so many of the facts reported here have been ignored or brushed aside by the advertising community on both sides of the Atlantic is one of the strongest criticisms to be made against them.) Much of this volume, indeed, is no more than a patchwork quilt of ideas that has been freely drawn from many existing sources. But by their juxtaposition these ideas, for me at least, form a pattern that is not readily apparent while they remain separate.

These ideas cover many fields—sociology, economics, psychology, anthropology and even history—in which I am not qualified to encroach. But in the full knowledge that a little learning is a dangerous thing, I have done so (if only to show these entrenched specialties that little breadth has its hazards, too). The price of this is that, no doubt, on some points of detail I shall have to stand corrected even though I have endeavored to minimize this by using established sources as support for my argument, and by having the benefit of certain specialist advisers.

But it is my hope that whatever slips time and my critics may reveal, they will not be used as a subterfuge for ignoring the central argument, for if it *is* true that the pivotal relationship of our society, between business and the consumer, is being transformed in ways that have neither been fully recognized nor fully understood, then those whose fortunes are built on that relationship—be they admen or businessmen—are heading for a fall. If this book helps in any way to break that fall and then helps to lead to the development of a new coincidence of self-interest between business and the consumer, it will have more than served its purpose.

R. W.

CONTENTS

xiii

The Day
the Pigs
Refused to
Be Driven to
Market

ONE

The Democracy of the Marketplace

●

I AM A GRASS ROOT
Lapel badge of George McGovern supporter
at 1972 Democratic National Convention

On November 23, 1969, a columnist in the Chicago *Daily News*, Mike Royko, put a coupon with five names at the bottom of his column. According to Royko, each of the names represented a potential candidate in the 1972 presidential election. The men listed were Ed Muskie, Hubert Humphrey, Ted Kennedy, George McGovern and Ralph Nader. Royko asked his readers to let him know which of these men should be the Democratic candidate in the forthcoming election. The vote from the readers of the *Daily News*, in the city that keeps that revolutionary figure Mayor Richard J. Daley in power tallied as follows: Muskie 7 percent, McGovern 2, Kennedy 2, Humphrey 0.5, and Nader 89 percent.

The fact that a man who five years previously had been an unknown young lawyer could rise to this level of public esteem, could attract forty times as many votes as a member of the Kennedy clan, purely on the basis of what he had done for consumers, was the final evidence to all who remained in doubt that something was stirring in the American marketplace.

In the Japanese marketplace, too, a similar phenomenon was at work. Here—in a society that had been one of the world's most hierarchical, where respect for superiors was a watchword of life—members of women's community associations boycotted the buying of color TV sets until the manufacturers agreed to reduce the price by $60 a set. And having done that, they joined with five other consumer groups to boycott the products of the world's third largest cosmetic company.

Western Europe has not been immune to all this, either. Germany, Sweden, France and even backward Britain have also felt pressures from the bottom of the pyramid. In Germany, for example, when a detergent called Dash was advertised with housewives saying, "No, I won't swap my box of Dash for two of another make," the company ran into unexpected trouble. Hundreds of housewives disconcerted Dash by offering to make the swap, and one indignant individual even offered to hand over one ton of Dash for two tons of Persil.

In Britain, it was forecast that the Trade Descriptions Act, one of the major pieces of consumer-protection legislation, would give rise to about 50,000 complaints a year. In actual fact there were 96,000 in the first year, 112,000 in the second and 120,000 in the third. Complaints are currently running at twenty-six times the rate of prosecutions, showing that the consumer is already a great deal fussier than the law.

These are but a few examples of the developments that have been making headlines in every advanced society in recent years.

Are they just that—headlines? Just products of the media looking for stories? Perhaps simply a political fashion, like Prohibition, which will soon fade away? Or if something real, then merely isolated incidents far from the real feelings of the silent majority?

Those who interpret these shock waves as no more than passing tremors make a grave error (as many, from the President of the United States downwards, have already discovered), for these "isolated incidents" are not isolated incidents at all. They betoken a very real shift of power in our society, away from the bastions of the corporate state toward what will hopefully emerge as an era of consumerism, the democracy of the marketplace.

This shift of power is part of a general crumbling of authority that was the star of stage and screen during the past two decades. Even since people were discharged from the armed forces in 1945, trust in and respect for authority—be it for the House of Representatives or the House of Dior—has been on the wane. How can one believe in a government if it's prepared to tell lies to the people it governs, as the Administration was shown to have lied by the publication of the Pentagon papers or by the disclosures of the Watergate affair?

4

And how can a student believe in the impartiality of the press when the story he reads in the newspaper and sees on television about, say, the Berkeley riots bears precious little relationship to the events he participated in? Nor is this distrust of the media just a long-haired-student phenomenon. In a survey of people in the British *Who's Who* in 1971 it emerged that less than one third felt that *any* daily newspaper was truly impartial. That newspaper, with a score of 32 percent for impartiality, was the august *Times* of London. That two thirds of the British establishment (for those are the people who reside within *Who's Who*) could regard their semiofficial newspaper as less than impartial is rather like persuading a Biblical fundamentalist that the Old Testament is a fake.

But despite the loss of impartiality, the new mass media have played a key role in the destruction of authority. (Whether as villain or hero depends upon your viewpoint.) The British politician John Profumo, for example, wasn't the only government minister to engage in sexual peccadilloes, as the recent Lambton affair demonstrated. But the media acted as a magnifying glass to enlarge, and perhaps distort, the issue into something of national proportions.

The media have also helped remove the dividing line between ordinary politicians and members of the government. Politicians have always been, in the eyes of Joe Public, a shifty band of brigands. But when a politician became part of the Administration, the mantle of authority used to be the mantle of respectability. Continual exposure to television close-ups has removed this credibility allowance, so that the government is now nothing more than a majority of two-faced politicians. Even the sacred Office of the President has proved to be less than whiter-than-white in the Watergate escapade.

Even if our rulers long ago ceased to have Divine Right, Divine Virtue was still their ancient prerogative. But that, too, has proved an illusion. One recent study by the University of Michigan, cited in the London *Evening Standard*, shows that distrust of government has almost doubled in the last five years, and that the decline is actually steepest among the silent majority of the American middle class, not the dissenting young. (Maybe their opinion of government could hardly sink any lower.)

It is not just the constitutional pillars of society that have started to shake. Take those institutions that were fixed on the map as firm as the Rock of Gibraltar, like Rolls-Royce in Britain and the Penn Central railroad in the United States. Rolls-Royce was certainly the physical embodiment of the traditional principles of British industrial supremacy. And for those principles to go bankrupt was a shattering blow to all that was left of the old order.

So, too, have been the student riots against their teachers, as at the London School of Economics or the University of California at Berkeley. The relationship of teacher to pupil has always presented the teacher as the authority. Now, however, not only are students demanding a say in choosing their teachers and their curriculum, but high school children in Britain even called in 1973 for a general strike to eliminate everything from school uniforms to censorship of the school magazine.

Pupil power, in fact, challenges the traditional concept of schooling, by which a licensed disseminator of knowledge officially opened the eyes of the blind. The blind, as we shall see, are starting to have more knowledge than the official dispensers of knowledge. And in the view of one observer (Ivan D. Illich, author of *Deschooling Society*), this phenomenon "endangers the survival of not only the economic order built on the co-production of goods and demands, but equally of the political order built on a nation state into which the students are delivered by the school."

The social order appears equally endangered. Social authorities, from Emily Post upward, are experiencing a different version of the anti-authority phenomenon. A survey among 1,000 Chicago housewives, cited in Helena Z. Lopata's *Occupation: Housewife*, showed that 54 percent of women who wanted to improve their newspaper would do away with "society news." A typical comment was that of a young woman in the Park Forest suburb of Chicago: "I don't hold the 'Four Hundred' in awe any more. The average woman accomplishes as much good in her activities."

It seems that the vicarious enjoyment which the populace gets out of reading about the bread and circuses of the rich no longer holds true. Even formalized authorities like the Army are not exempt from the crumbling of hierarchy. A few years ago *Fortune* magazine reported a Vietnam incident when a company of men, suspecting an ambush, had refused to go down a road. Mutiny

6

for disobeying the orders of authority? Not on your life. A few days later the deputy commander of the unit's brigade told CBS News that there would be no punishment: "Thank God, we've got young men who question."

What they were questioning wasn't just any particular authority, but the concept of authority itself. As Professor John Zinkin of Unilever told the 1971 Advertising Association Conference (a group of British admen desperately trying to understand what was about to hit them): "A revolt against authority itself isn't a new phenomenon. But in the past the successful rebel was a new authority. At the end of the revolution the rules were different, but the obedience of the ordinary man was the same."

It is this questioning of the *concept* of authority that marks a difference from earlier protests. The response for this is not a desire for independence. After all, who but the most ambitious recluse can be independent in our interconnected world? No, the logical response to the opposition to authority is not independence, but participation.

If authorities, of one kind or another, are a necessary part of life, then at least one should have a say in how they control you. So you find in a Brooklyn ghetto that poorly educated black parents, ignoring the sound advice of experts, demand control over their neighborhood schools. So, too, the Roman Catholic Church, the authority of authorities, finds that from Texas to Holland it is confronted by demands for more democratic government. And in France, you find that more than fourteen newspapers or magazines have seen the formation of what they call "journalists' associations," all designed to break the control of the publisher over the editorial. Even in the traditional trade unions one sees a shift of power to the factory floor as a reaction against the central union hierarchy.

The same sort of demand for a redistribution of authority shows up in the world of fashion. Who created the mini, the micro-mini, the beads, the see-through fashions, the unisex trend? Not some lisping fashion dictator of the Champs Elysées. All these fashions were started in the streets, by the same group that discovered low heels, long sweaters and the cape—not to mention triggered off the rebellion against bras.

It is not just the young who have control over their fashion.

7

Who turned down the midi, despite the blandishments of all the fashion authorities from *Women's Wear Daily* to *Vogue*? The corseted matrons of New York.

And at a national level, despite an apparent concentration of power by cabinet or presidential government, policy making now has more participants than ever before. Perhaps the most spectacular example of participatory politics has been the success of the anti–supersonic-aircraft lobby. In 1969 there was a Senate majority of 36 in favor of developing an American supersonic transport. A year later, grass-roots pressure had turned that majority for the SST to a majority of 9 against the SST. The British supersonic contender, the Concorde, may also be shot out of the skies by the same forces.

The demand for a real and active share in decision making is reflected on the factory floor too. In the past, the worker fought the boss in a way that reflected the implicit superiority of the boss. Now, instead of the concept of "superiors," the demand is for equal relationships, for participatory management instead of authoritative management.

Some companies, like Philips, Volvo and Saab, have already recognized this and dismantled the assembly line, substituting worker teams managing themselves. Others, like General Motors with its Vega plant, have merely used advanced technology to depersonalize the production process still further. However, the hostile reaction of the GM workers, who even went as far as mutilating the products they were assembling, proves that today's worker will no more accept domination by machines than domination by managers.

This new equality of relationships even shows between husband and wife. "Love, honor and obey" is a reflection of a nineteenth-century ideal rather than a twentieth-century reality. Indeed, one suggestion from sociologists is that many of the stresses of marriage, as shown by the 80 percent rise in divorces in America since 1960, are caused by the tensions of the shift toward a less unequal husband-wife relationship. Certainly, the central concept of Women's Lib is that gender determines no more than differing reproductive capacities and that in all other capacities men and women are created equal.

It is against this overall background of the home, the school

8

and the factory that the relationship of business and the consumer needs to be examined.

In fact, contrary to the trend for redistribution of power in other areas, power in business has tended to concentrate. Ten percent of the largest firms did 40 percent of all business in Britain in 1885, but three quarters of a century later they had managed to collar 85 percent. This development echoes what's happening in America, where even six years ago the nation's five hundred largest companies had 68 percent of all sales and 74 percent of all profits.

Using the automobile industry as an example, three companies make 83 percent of all cars made in America. This compares with eighty-eight independent car producers in 1921. The phenomenon which changed the automobile situation was that in 1923 General Motors put the pressure on the "weaker" companies by introducing the annual-model change. By 1935, 78 percent of these companies were out of business.

Once power is thus concentrated, it is difficult to dilute. Morton Mintz and Jerry Cohen calculate in *America, Inc.: Who Owns and Operates the United States* that it would now cost a company $779 million to enter the automobile industry. But if the industry *hadn't* been restructured by the annual-model change, the price tag for entry would be only $55 million.

Balanced against this, it should be said that both Volkswagen and the Japanese companies have entered the U.S. car market without the difficulties implied by these figures. Nevertheless, unless one is talking of a technical innovation like Xerox or a new kind of service industry like package holidays in Europe, the trend to concentrate power makes it harder for outsiders to become insiders. In fact, it is a situation in which the power of business appears to be remorselessly on the increase.

But it was not only the concentration of corporate power that was then out of phase with a society busily redistributing power to the people. Business chose also to increase its distance from the rest of the community by operating on a series of assumptions that many people were fast dismissing as ancient myths.

The first myth with which corporations deluded themselves was that if people continually bought their products, then people were satisfied with their products.

9

You can't blame the corporations too much for this belief, because nearly every economic textbook has been preaching this doctrine for years. Yet a significant number of people were disappointed in the reliability and durability of their cars. And it was often not possible to choose another make without these unsatisfactory aspects.

So, contrary to the economic textbooks, large numbers of consumers could and did repurchase those products with which they were less than satisfied. (In fact, according to a recent study by the British Consumer Association, one person in two is dissatisfied with the goods and services he buys and the way he is treated as a customer.) But to the corporations, the rising sales figures were a vote of confidence in the product. Not only that, they could also show that in proportion to units sold, complaints were often actually lower than previously. In the period 1937 to 1939, complaints received by General Motors equaled 2.7 percent of the number of cars sold during those years. In the period 1967 to 1969 (when Ralph Nader was in full cry), complaints were down to 2.5 percent of all sales.

But this sort of data, too, were a snare and a delusion for companies trying to assess how well they were pleasing their customers. For even if there was less chance of a specific product breaking down than previously, the consumer by the mid-fifties and sixties had such an inventory of possessions that each year the probability increased that something he owned would wear out or break down, and the cumulative effect was profoundly irritating.

It was irritating not just because of the increasing frequency of these product failures but also because the consumer had become enormously dependent on the product *not* failing. Before consumer goods were an integral part of the consumer's life, his suffering was always mitigated by his lack of dependence on a product that had failed. But once he was leaving behind what one writer has called "the dikes of quality control" (Dr. Joe Juran), the irritation caused by even the tiniest hole in the dike could be tremendous. Unbeknownst to most corporations, this situation was further aggravated by what one Detroit car manager has called "the phenomenon of rising expectations": "If it was good enough for my father, it doesn't mean it's good enough for me." Greater affluence (where we changed from being awe-struck by the existence of a color television set to being thunderstruck

10

if it breaks down) and promises of "good, better, best" by advertisers had interlocked to create a situation in which the consumer is led to expect a degree of product perfection that is probably unobtainable.

People's disappointment with a soap powder that merely cleans the wash and doesn't get it whiter-than-white mirrors a fundamental criticism of the adjectival barrage emanating from Madison Avenue. And for this reason if for no other, the admen themselves have triggered off the earthquake that now threatens their clients' prosperous edifices. Against these tremors, however, as against all the rumbles of discontent, most corporations remained unconcerned, protected as they were by the myth that their sales graphs proved all was well in the marketplace.

These sales graphs were, in actual fact, the basis of the second myth entrapping companies in the pre-consumerism era. This was the assumption that a corporation's only duty was to make sure that its sales kept rising; there was no audit of social responsibility in the annual accounts.

Here, too, corporations can hardly be blamed for adopting a viewpoint that had a distinguished intellectual pedigree. The conservative economists Milton Friedman and Henry Manne are just two of its more recent devotees. The doctrine declares that the notion of social responsibility for a corporation is fundamentally at odds with the concept of a shareholder's financial incentive. Fortified by this doctrine, corporations felt no guilt at the smoke that came from their chimneys or at the litter their products caused in the countryside.

The corollary of their profits-only policy was that "It sells" and became a sufficient justification for the existence of virtually any product in the marketplace—from the planes that shatter the silence of the sky to the automobiles whose effluence choke our cities, even indeed to the advertising that invades millions of living rooms every night.

But though this doctrine had no shortage of adherents in the board rooms of industry, its acceptability among large sections of the community was decreasing. In 1971, for instance, the *Wall Street Journal* reported a study by Daniel Yankelovich which revealed that the percentage of the public who felt that business achieved a good balance between securing profit and serving the public had suddenly slumped. For years this key indicator of public

11

attitudes toward business had remained stable at around 55 percent. In 1971 it nose-dived to a mere 26 percent of consumers thinking corporations achieved the right balance of profit and social responsibility.

The third assumption that separated corporations from consumers was the myth that competition between corporations provided perfectly adequate protection for consumers.

This, too, was a well-loved idea among economists. It was part of the ideology of that strange theoretical notion "perfect competition." This is a utopian situation where, with large numbers of small manufacturers to choose from, the consumer carefully casts his votes with his shopping budget. So the good manufacturers are rewarded by profit and the bad are penalized by loss. In a real world of multinational monopolies and oligopolies, the consumer may be forgiven for wondering if the protection of competition is as great as economic theory suggests. Even if it were, the nature of the products created by these corporations and the sheer volume of them would make it very hard for the consumer to behave as the perfect competition model requires. Smothered under a huge inventory of possessions, many of them too complicated to understand, the consumer becomes an amateur buyer facing a professional seller. In this situation, the conventional wisdom that buyers can look after themselves collapses. And, so to the buyers' aid came, like the U.S. cavalry to the wagon train, the forces of consumerism.

Consumerism is simply the mechanism that has developed to redress the imbalance between corporations and consumers. In the same way that trade unions in the nineteenth century used collective action against industry, consumerism developed to provide similar protection for consumers in the twentieth.

Besides being a mechanism for protection, it also created new mechanisms for correction. It established ways of putting pressure on corporations besides the pressure of the purse, which seems to be woefully inadequate. Consumerist groups, consumerist media and consumerist laws have all sprung up to challenge the corporate giants and force them to recognize the error of their ways.

The structure of consumer power that eventually developed proved, as we shall see, strong enough to chew up and spit out the largest corporations in the world. But its modest beginnings suggested no such radical shift of power.

In 1906 Upton Sinclair wrote *The Jungle* as an attack on the Chicago meat-packing industry. It was a book in the best tradition of muckraking populism and, in those best traditions, it was swiftly followed by America's first food and drug act. But this flurry of consumer concern proved to be no more than the first breezes of the storm that was to come. The issue soon faded away, and it was not until 1927 that one could see the beginnings of the sustained consumer movement, as opposed to the idealist spasm of 1906.

In 1927 an economist named Stuart Chase teamed up with a mechanical engineer from the American Standards Association, F. J. Schlink, to write a book called *Your Money's Worth*. Apart from being a best seller, it soon became the book most often stolen from the public libraries. It simply reported the results of tests made for the American government by the National Bureau of Standards. One of the discoveries was that there was very little correlation between price and quality. For example, nine makes of sheets were tested: "The make ranking eighth in quality ranked second in price. Of two makes whose quality was identical, one sold for two and a half times as much as the other. The make which ranked lowest in quality sold for 20 percent more than that ranking sixth," etc. etc.

F. J. Schlink then teamed up with Arthur Kallet to write *One Hundred Million Guinea Pigs*. This turned the spotlight onto advertisers as well as the products themselves, and out of the furor it caused grew the Consumers Union, and its publication *Consumer Reports*.

Thirty years after *Your Money's Worth* a similar event occurred in Britain. In 1957 a small group of enthusiasts, calling themselves Consumers Association and using a garage in Bethnal Green as an office, produced the first copy of *Which*. A first printing of 10,000 copies was quickly exhausted. And since then the circulation has climbed at a rate of about 1,000 extra copies a week. The fact remains, however, that neither in Britain nor in America has either of these consumerist groups increased its membership beyond 1 percent of the population. Both of them are heavily weighted toward the well-educated professional classes. They were, and are, not so much nascent power groups as a buying advisory service for the professional classes.

Backed by independent consumer research laboratories, the

group on either side of the Atlantic poured out a welter of information. What to look for when buying a TV, which dishwashing liquid contained the highest proportion of active ingredients—all could be found neatly tabulated within their pages. And equipped with this new improved information, the consumers were supposed to be safe from the blandishments and misinformation of the advertisers. In effect, this type of middle-class consumerism accepted the ethos of perfect competition. It believed that once the errors and omissions of the advertisers had been eliminated, the rationality of the housewife would assert itself and the good companies would be rewarded by profit and the evil ones by loss.

Apart from issues on product safety, there was no attempt with this type of consumerism to *protect* consumers. "We are not some type of salvation army for consumers," observed the director of the Confederation of German Consumer Associations. "Our aim is simply to ensure that they know what they're buying."

The prissy liberalism of the movement ensured that it remained a minority cult. Of course, there were sustained and lengthy assaults on the ethos of capitalism and its high priests, the admen. In the twenties, Stuart Chase had intoned that "nine-tenths or more of advertising is largely competitive rambling as to the relative merits of two indistinguishable compounds." In the fifties, Richard Hoggart in *The Uses of Literacy* had attacked the advertising practice of appealing to baser instincts of humanity, like keeping up with the Joneses, for commercial ends. And J. B. Priestley wrote *Over the Rainbow* and coined the word "admass" to describe the neon-lit, freeway-draped, ad-infested society called America. But none of this did anything to unsteady the citadel of capitalism, and its main effect was to give admen a desire to write poems and paint pictures to salve their creative consciences.

Perhaps the chief contribution of bluestocking consumerism was to lay the foundations of a consumer-information system which later consumer advocates could use to greater advantage. But as far as the readers of *Which* and *Consumer Reports* were concerned, it seems that many of them felt that the product information they received was not worth their subscription. Even in the 1970s, the average *Which* subscriber only lasted three years. And in 1972, *Consumer Reports* found that half of its new subscribers failed to renew for a second year. If this was the prevailing attitude among that small proportion of the population who subscribed to

14

consumer journals in the peak of the consumer revolution, then you can understand how in the mid-sixties businessmen tended to regard consumerism as no more than the middle classes pursuing manufacturers in the same way that the upper classes pursued foxhounds, and of no greater significance.

Why, then, should General Motors pay any attention when in November 1965 a young lawyer who was serving on a Senate inquiry into automobile safety published a book called *Unsafe at Any Speed*? Ralph Nader's attack wasn't so much on the *value* of a particular product as on its *safety* (like Rachel Carson's essays *Silent Spring* three years earlier). And Nader's charge, as shall be seen, went beyond an unsafe car called the Corvair and on to the corporate ethos behind that unsafe car.

For the first three months after the publication of *Unsafe at Any Speed*, despite the fact that there was a hearing in progress in the Senate on automobile safety, there was no real indication that the fate of Nader's attack would be substantially different from the onslaught by earlier tribunes of the people. If one compares the number of major reviews of Nader's book in the five months after publication with a number of major reviews given to *Silent Spring*, *Unsafe at Any Speed* still had only *half* the reviews of Rachel Carson's book.

Dennis W. Brezina, analyzing fifteen articles about Nader in the last two months of this five-month period, concluded that they "emphasised primarily the series of events that transpired after General Motors admitted it routinely checked Nader's back-ground." This admission was made in March 1966, as a result of charges made by Nader in the *New Republic* that he was being shadowed by private detectives. Only after General Motors owned up to this did the public furor begin. After March 1966, Nader's name was on the front page of the *New York Times* eight times, compared to once for Rachel Carson. But the furor was very definitely about "a big corporation snooping into the private affairs of a man who had almost incidentally written a crusading book" (Brezina).

The furor was the first visible evidence that consumers now felt that their relationship with business was out of line as compared to their relationship with other parts of the fabric of authority. Had Nader written the same book with the same facts in 1926 it might, like *Your Money's Worth*, have been a best

15

seller and stolen from all the public libraries. But it would not have been the first blow that started to shake the corporate giants. Indeed, it is probable that if General Motors *hadn't* behaved like a Big Brother, Nader's book would still have been limited in its impact (as Brezina's analysis of the newspaper reviews suggests). For until Nader presented the issue of the individual consumer against the corporate state instead of just the issue of the unsafety of a General Motors car, he was destined for no more than a second printing of *Unsafe at Any Speed*.

The media, of course, were the second factor that transformed Nader from a limited to a mass issue. The media did more than just supply the oxygen that kept the fire of controversy going. They magnified, distorted and simplified the issues for mass consumption. And they spread the information at electronic speed to every home from Alaska to Arkansas. By doing this, they gave chapter and verse to the inchoate, unfocused feelings about big business among many Americans.

Until this point, in fact, the word of business was by and large accepted against the word of the complaining citizen. But by taking the issue *outside* a specialist technical area (like automobile safety) and making it an issue which everyone could understand (the devious conduct of the biggest company in the land) and by providing evidence in every living room of America of this conduct (the televised cross-examination of the General Motors president at the Senate inquiry), the media changed the status of business overnight. Only since then has a company *had* to engage in corporate advertising to buttress its credibility.

General Motors' conduct in having Nader tailed by private eyes had the effect, then, of turning this from a technical into a moral dispute. In a technical dispute like *Silent Spring* or more recently the Concorde, even parties to the debate obviously biased in one direction—like the British Aircraft Corporation—can make a *technical* argument on the credible position of their *technical* expertise. When the issue becomes a moral one, they have no such natural reservoir of expertise.

Nader, like most innovators in the marketplace, soon had his imitators. Some of the more exotic were Banzhaf's Bandits. These began as an extension of the antismoking campaign run by a Washington lawyer, John Banzhaf III. Since July 1967 he has waged a battle against the tobacco companies with his group called ASH (Action for Smoking and Health). And his students, using acronyms such as SOUP (Society Opposing Unfair Practices), TUBE (Terminating Unfair Broadcasting Excesses), PUMP (Protesting Unfair Marketing Practices), SAME (Students Against Misleading Enterprises), have made brisk forays into the soft underbelly of American business (aided and abetted by sympathetic senators like Edward Kennedy).

The operating principles of second-generation consumerism as practiced by Nader and Banzhaf are very different from the pedantic fairness of the early consumer pioneers. The gentlemanly concept of recommending best buys becomes replaced by a newer one: the concept of worst buys. Nader seldom tells people what to buy; he merely tells them what not to buy, or, at best, what they could buy if companies used all the technology available to them. And his scrutiny extends well beyond electric curlers and color-television sets. Acting on the premise of vice, not virtue, he and his Raiders have probed at everything from Du Pont's grip on Delaware to land use in California, with a stab at the United States Congress along the way.

Instead of evaluating products with only the aid of white-coated technicians, they supplement this sort of data with information obtained by less orthodox means. "Ethical whistle blowing" is a term Nader uses to describe the process. It's a concept that takes us right back to the demand for more equal relationships between employer and employee, government and governed. "Ethical whistle blowing" simply means that when a consumer in the course of his role as a *worker* discovers something that is contrary to his interests in his role of *citizen*, and other citizens as well, then the demands on him as a *citizen* (to make public or inform to a consumerist body) override his duty as a *worker* (to say nothing out of loyalty to his employer). It was ethical whistle blowing that provided the information for the ITT disclosures by Jack Anderson and for the My Lai massacre prosecution, that revealed the truth about the Apollo I fire, and that made public the defect in the Ford Pinto engine which caused some of them to catch fire while the car was in use. (It is revealing of the paternalism of British industry that this particular concept has been criticized on the grounds that it is no more than an adaptation of the Com-

17

munist technique of asking children to snoop on their parents—as if the relationship of employer to employee were the same as parent to child.)

This information-gathering technique is, in fact, the basis of most exposé-style journalism. And the media have not been slow to add the topic of consumer affairs to the muckraking menu, and so cast themselves in a new role as champions of the consumer. The Washington *Post,* the Los Angeles *Times,* the *Christian Science Monitor,* the *Wall Street Journal* (with only the *New York Times* lagging) now regularly treat consumer affairs as front-page news.

In Britain, consumer information has become as much a newspaper department as foreign affairs or labor relations. In the fastest-growing working-class paper, the *Sun,* consumer affairs is behind only sex as a proven circulation builder (scotch forever the myth that this is just an educated-middle-class quirk).

This new practice on the part of the media to woo their readers by criticizing their advertisers reflects not so much a higher degree of journalistic principle as a shrewd realization of where their bread is buttered.

The news media haven't just reported consumer news. They have also gone into the business of creating the news.

The "Watch This Space" column in the St. Petersburg *Times* is a particularly vigorous exponent of this practice. Every Tuesday since the spring of 1972, it has reported on the tests it makes on the products that have been advertised. The *Times* people tried out, for instance, Procter & Gamble's disposable diapers to see if, as claimed on TV, Pampers kept babies drier than cloth diapers. They repeated P & G's TV demonstrations themselves but came up with different results, even though they had checked with P & G to make sure the exact conditions of the test were replicated. "This doesn't mean Pampers don't work," commented the column, "but it does seem curious that following P & G's own directions, the Pampers failed its own television test."

Americans have been hearing other, equally curious stories on programs such as *The Nader Report* on one Boston TV station (WGBH), a whodunit thriller from the Center for the Study of Responsive Law where the corporate robbers are copped. Even the august CBS saw fit to maul its sponsors in April 1973 when it aired "You and the Commercial" in prime time.

18

Perhaps the best amalgam of TV entertainment and consumer revelation was *The Great American Dream Machine* series, which one hundred and ninety educational stations carried in 1971. This converted *Consumer Reports* into laugh-a-line jokes. For example, Morton's lemon cream pie was shown to be made from a recipe of "good old monosodium phosphate, the same used in laxatives and cleaners . . . plenty of fresh whey solids . . . guar gum from the Texas grasslands," etc. "But you will note," says the show's star, Marshal Efron, "no lemon, no cream, no eggs, just pie."

This combination of pressure from the media and militant consumerists has led, as one would hope and expect in a democracy, to a response by government, although *The Times* of London warned in 1963 that "the consumer who relies on rules to stock his cupboard will eat a poor breakfast." Rules and regulations on both sides of the Atlantic have been increasing. And even if the rules haven't changed, they've been given a much stricter interpretation.

It was President John F. Kennedy who first gave the number-one citizen's imprimatur to consumerism. He promised that the consumer's voice would be heard at the highest level of government, a promise that was echoed in Nixon's 1965 pledge to give the consumer "a permanent voice in the White House." This, of course, doesn't mean giving license to harass business on Capitol Hill. Someone, after all, has to pay President Nixon's election expenses and it isn't the consumerists.

But in both Congress and the government regulatory agencies one can see evidence of a new attitude toward the consumer, echoing the shift of power in the marketplace that we have already spoken of. Marketplace power is, of course, also ballot-box power, and consumer affairs have become as much an ingredient of vote getting as baby kissing. Sometimes the results are spectacular. In the November 1972 elections, for instance, a twenty-five-year-old "youngster" managed to knock off the hitherto immovable Senator J. Caleb Boggs of Delaware with a vigorous consumerist platform.

The results of such pressures are twofold. First of all, in the five years 1965 to 1971, twenty consumer bills managed to get past the business lobbyists, the batteries of special-interest lawyers, and eventually onto the Statute Book of Congress. But of even more importance, in practical terms, have been the changes forced

19

on the federal regulatory bodies. In fact, there are now thirty-three U.S. government agencies engaged in approximately three hundred consumer-protection activities.

The saga of the Federal Trade Commission shows the way in which what was once just part of a national administrative machine was transformed into a vigorous consumer watchdog. The FTC was created in 1914 to be an expert on monopoly and economic concentration. For over half a century it lived in relatively peaceful obscurity, gradually choking itself to death with red tape. Over the years it became a convenient dumping ground for issues which no other government body was really equipped to deal with. As consumer protection became an issue of government, it was the cumbrously organized FTC which got much of the job. Just how cumbersome the FTC was emerged in a study made after the rehabilitation of the commission in 1970. It showed that there were forty-six distinct steps that had to be taken from the time a complaint reached the FTC until it was officially docketed for litigation. No surprise, then, that in 1969 a quarter of the deceptive trade practices being looked at by the FTC were over two years old.

This bureaucratic heaven had another failing that didn't endear it to the hearts of consumerists. It had been given considerable powers in 1914, which it persistently failed to use for the benefit of the consumer. For instance, from 1962 to 1969 the FTC fought a half-hearted battle against Geritol, an iron tonic, on the grounds of deceptive advertising. It took three years for the first cease-and-desist order to be issued, and though this order was affirmed by the Court of Appeals in 1967, in 1969 a new Geritol commercial was on the air which the FTC said represented the efficacy of Geritol no less than the commercial of 1962. But rather than ask for the fines of up to $5,000 a day, to which it were entitled, the commission just asked Geritol for a "compliance report." Not until 1973 did the FTC enforce its powers against Geritol and extract a fine of almost $1 million from the company. In fact, when the FTC's head of its Bureau of Consumer Protection claimed the right to demand from advertisers that they provide the FTC with substantiation of their claims, this demand was based on the *original* power given to the FTC by Congress in 1914.

To be fair to the FTC, however, if the commission had tried

to use its full authority prior to the growth of the consumer power, no doubt all hell would have broken loose. One has only to look at the reaction in 1962 to the proposed law giving the FTC the right to issue a temporary cease-and-desist order (without going to court), pending the completion of proceedings. According to *Printers' Ink*, this proposal made 1962 "the year advertising faced death." A distinguished lawyer (in fact, a former FTC commissioner) said of this proposal: "1962 was the first year a serious, well planned and politically powerful putsch was organized to give bureaucracy the authority to stop an advertising campaign the minute it started, and all without the formality of a trial."

One can understand the wretched FTC commissioners being so taken aback by this outburst in defense of "free enterprise" and acting more than a little cautiously in the years afterward. But this soft-pedaling made them very vulnerable to a Naderite attack (with the alliance of the American Bar Association) in 1969. As a result the FTC was purged and given new leadership, as well as being rejuvenated in a way which, while not satisfying the demands of the Naderites, must have exceeded their realistic hopes (to the extent even of having as the new FTC chairman one of the members of the American Bar Association Committee, which had attacked the ancient regime).

By June 1971 the new improved FTC was receiving 50 percent more consumer complaints than a year before and had already started—as we shall shortly see—to get its teeth well into Madison Avenue. This was almost exactly one hundred years since the first act of governmental consumerism, when in 1872 a bill was passed making it a federal crime to defraud through the use of mails.

The structure of consumer power was thus complete. It was a structure whose vigor was to surprise even some of its most ardent supporters. Instead of just the middle-class best-buys approach of the past, consumerism showed that even in the Land of the Free, where the right to make a dollar at whatever cost was practically a constitutional right, it had the strength to take on and beat even the mightiest corporations in the land.

It is to these battles, in which consumerist Davids seem forever to be slaying the corporate Goliaths, that our attention now turns.

New Improved American Dream: Now with Added Truth

●

"The consumer doesn't just want satisfaction today—
she wants vengeance!" [J. Conlan of General Motors]

It has not been long since all of the following events occurred in America.

- A bread which had presented itself to the public as a diet bread was ordered to spend 25 percent of its next year's advertising budget stating that eating this particular bread wouldn't help you lose weight.
- A promotional company was ordered to announce the odds *against* winning in its giveaway sweepstakes.
- A multimillion-dollar blue-chip company had to run advertising defending its previous advertising, which was under attack by the Federal Trade Commission.
- An iron tonic pill was ordered to include a statement in all its television commercials saying that most people didn't need it.
- A government consumer-protection agency demanded that advertisements for identical products (for instance, aspirin pain-killers) shouldn't be allowed to *imply* that one product was better than another, identical product.
- A promotional company was ordered to pay out thousands more additional prizes in a contest after a more liberal interpretation of the rules by a consumer-protection agency.

- And over a five-year period, American car manufacturers were obliged to recall the equivalent of two years' *total* production.

Events like these are becoming increasingly commonplace in the United States. Other advanced societies, taking their cue from the wealthiest nation in the world, have followed—at different speeds—along the same road. "America," declared Louis XVI's Finance Minister Turgot, "is the hope of the human race, and may well become its future." In the second half of the twentieth century Turgot's prophecy may well come true. The country that took capitalism to a new peak may be the one that shows us how capitalism is best disciplined.

According to Jean François Ravel in *Without Marx or Jesus,* "the new American revolution" will be sparked off by a new revolutionary method, originated and developed in the United States and labeled "dissent." Many of the examples in this chapter can thus be regarded as examples of dissent from the authorized version of the American dream. They make it plain that a discussion of consumerism is not just an interesting academic debate about the structure of society. The phenomenon we are talking about has already traveled like Ajax's White Tornado through the serried ranks of the *Fortune* 500 directory. Granted, it has, as we shall see, had its setbacks. But it has also had some victories which attest more to the strengths of the forces behind it than to the merits of the argument of any particular case.

The first area in which consumer power chose to flex its muscles was the area of product *safety.* This was an area where even the most ardent believer in price competition will admit the discipline of the market may operate, if it operates at all, with fatal slowness.

Nader himself began on a safety issue—the General Motors Corvair—and sales plummeted by 89 percent following his attack on the safety record of this car. And in Britain, *Which*'s constant cry about the unsafe wiring of electrical apparatuses has recently forced even the mighty British Leyland to withdraw the Marina sports coupe on safety grounds.

Certainly, as the report by the National Commission on Product Safety revealed in June 1970, in America 30,000 people are killed and 110,000 permanently disabled each year "as a result of accidents connected with consumer products." On top of this it has been estimated that 700,000 children are injured each year by the toys they play with, such as a lawn dart that can pierce a child's skull, a toy oven that gets hotter than a real oven, and a balloon squeaker that can get sucked down a child's throat.

Among adult products, the automobile has come under the strongest safety spotlight. By the end of 1969 Naderite pressure groups had forced twenty-eight safety changes in American cars. And by the mid-seventies all cars sold in America will have to be built so that the drivers can walk away from a *60 mph crash.* Moreover, if there *is* a safety-related defect in a car, under the 1966 National Traffic and Motor Vehicle Safety Act the car has to be recalled. (Not content with having two out of every five cars made in America in the last six years recalled, Nader is now gunning for a recall of *all* fifty million cars made in America between 1963 and 1971, on the basis of an alleged defective valve in their brake system.)

In singling out safety issues, consumer groups were carefully picking on a chink in the corporate armor. It is, after all, very hard to prove that any product is *totally* safe, particularly if it can be argued that the product may have some long-term effect whose consequences may only become apparent in fifty years' time. Such was the case with enzymes in detergents. The first evidence that they were a potential health hazard emerged in 1970 from medical studies of British detergent workers. The American consumer power structure then used these findings to force Procter & Gamble and Colgate to reduce their enzyme levels in detergents. Lever Brothers actually agreed to drop enzymes entirely from its American detergents (although its British products retained them).

Then, in November 1971, a Federal Drug Administration study gave enzymes a clean bill of health. If this judgment is a final one, it underscores the consequence of consumers' lack of trust in business. It means that a company of world-wide reputation like Lever Brothers has less credibility as a dispenser of scientific wisdom than the consumer power structure.

The saga of monosodium glutamate, cyclamates and saccharin confirms this new order in the scientific hierarchy. Monosodium glutamate, which intensifies the flavor of food, had to be dropped from baby foods under pressure from Nader after a study by a St. Louis psychiatrist linked the substance to brain damage in mice. (Paradoxically, the monosodium glutamate wasn't there to help baby. It was there because mothers who took a taste from the jar preferred baby food with monosodium glutamate in it, and mothers—not babies—are the ones who buy baby food.)

Cyclamates had to be dropped as a sweetener of soft drinks after it reportedly developed cancer in rats. The ban was probably as much a tribute to the ferocity of the sugar lobby as to the consumer power structure. Before long, as with the enzyme ban, further evidence began to show that cyclamates were not harmful. But whatever the outcome, the damage to the companies concerned and to their profits had already been done. Once more, huge corporations learned at their own expense that even though science might support them, the consumerists still might not. Trust, in fact, has been so far eroded that research findings by industry generally carry little credence.

It may well be true that to feed vast quantities of this or that additive to rats and deduce from the damage done that tiny quantities of the same substance are dangerous to humans makes a mockery of science. The important point is that this mockery is now more believed than science. (For example, the experiments that put a question mark against saccharin involved feeding to rats the proportional amount of saccharin that a human being would get only if he drank 875 bottles of a typical saccharin-sweetened soft drink every day.) But because American law requires that once any food additive is shown to cause tumors in animals it has to be withdrawn from public consumption, the manifest overdosing of mice has become a standard consumerist weapon. It only remains for someone to show that a continual diet of sugar is harmful to rats, and Americans will have nothing left with which to sweeten their coffee.

That ever-popular item in the American diet, the hot dog, has already come under attack. "America's deadliest guided missile" is how Ralph Nader described the apparently harmless frankfurter. The high fat levels in hot dogs, up to 51 percent, were seen as an unnecessary contribution to heart disease, cancer and strokes. And consumerists have demanded a maximum fat level of between 25 and 33 percent to be required by federal law.

Even when federal controls over a particular food already exist, consumer groups have shown that they may not be sufficiently well enforced. Take the Consumer Union's analysis of pork sausages which had been "federally inspected." They found that one eighth contained "insect fragments, insect larvae, rodent hairs, and other kinds of filth." This level of uninvited additives is rivaled only by the fecal contamination of a twelfth of all cream sold in Britain, which a study by public health inspectors revealed.

After establishing a bridgehead on safety issues, consumer power groups extended their scrutiny to other aspects of products. In foodstuffs, it was the nutritional levels that brought about the next brickbats.

A government survey in 1955 had showed that 40 percent of American families lived on poor diets. By 1965, despite the dramatic increase in wealth of the average American family, the proportion of families having a poor diet had *risen* to 50 percent. This rise coincided with an increase in the sales of soft drinks, potato chips, cookies, ice cream, candy and peanut butter. According to Dr. Paul Fine, a New York food consultant, many Americans eat as many as ten meals a day, but still do not get adequate nutrition.

Nader blamed the food companies for the downward shift in nutrition. An account executive in an advertising agency handling a cereal account put the company's point of view: "Nutrition doesn't crackle or pop." When you're selling sizzle, not sausages, that's quite a drawback.

This nonnutritional promotion of food led to what another consumerist, Robert Choate, called the prevailing level of "nutritional illiteracy." It was Choate's analysis of nutritional levels in breakfast cereals that provided the evidence for this charge. Analyzing sixty breakfast cereals sold in America, Choate found that two out of three contained little more than "empty calories that fattened but did little to prevent malnutrition." And it was the least nutritious cereals that tended to be the most advertised. "Your children's food habits are being formed by Madison Avenue cartoonists, not by nutritionists," argued Mr. Choate. "Tony the Tiger, Fred Flintstone and Captain Crunch are the food educationalists of today. Ten times per hour, using wiles that mother never thought of, they advise your children to equate sugar with health and snacks with happiness." In the beginning of 1972 the indefatigable Mr. Choate provided still more evidence of the low nutritional content of many breakfast cereals. He went before a Senate subcommittee to cite a study showing that rats which were fed a diet of ground-up cereal boxes mixed with milk, sugar and raisins were healthier than rats fed some of the cereals the boxes contained.

For food companies merely to improve the nutritional content of their products did not satisfy the consumerist attackers. They believed that whether or not nutrition is snap, crackle or pop, it was the duty of food companies to sell nutrition and not just the products themselves. As we shall see in a later chapter, even mighty companies like Kellogg's are now, with all the enthusiasm of the newly converted, treading this penitential path.

An obsessive interest in nutritional levels may be a new target for the wrath of consumerism, but that can hardly be said of the third aspect of the product—its value. Ever since *Your Money's Worth*, the backbone of any consumer association has been its reports on value for money. But these activities have now taken on a far more militant character.

First, the value-for-money tables have spilled over from the pages of the consumer journals onto the supermarket floor itself. This, going by the name of unit pricing, works by having special price tags on products indicating not just their absolute price, but their price per ounce, thus doing away with the need for slide-rule computations as to whether the jumbo size is better value than the economy pack. This transfer of what amounts to anti-advertising information from elitist journals into Main Street U.S.A. underlines the widening base of consumer power.

A second way in which traditional "best buys" were given a militant twist: the consumer boycott. Faced with a rise in supermarket prices, several housewife pressure groups started a supermarket boycott in 1966. By the end of the year the index of supermarket prices, instead of continuing to rise, was down by one percentage point. And a percentage point on this index is worth several million dollars in shaved prices.

Even more impressive was the spontaneous consumer uprising in March 1973 when, Lysistrata-like, American housewives chose to deprive their husbands of beef rather than pay rocketing beef prices. In just one week this led to five thousand meat-packing-house workers being laid off, to a 20 percent reduction in the number of cattle slaughtered, and a decline of beef sales in butcher shops and supermarkets by as much as 70 percent. In that one week the Midwest meat-packing industry, an empire of brawn and bully stretching from Iowa to Oklahoma, found itself under assault by housewives who had hitherto happily swallowed a hundredweight of prime beef per head per year.

The new structure of consumer power didn't stop there, however. Its attack on the dangers or bad value of many products was echoed by its attack on the impact of many products on society as a whole. This is an area that is conceptually different from car or food safety, because at least it doesn't involve having to drive a car or buying any particular brand of baby food. Pollution is not a voluntary matter, however. Nonmotorists suffer just as much as motorists from exhaust emissions and from lead deposited in the atmosphere every year.

Against this "silent violence," consumer power has made big demands. First, the burden of proof of no danger should be shifted from the victim to the polluter. So high are the "risk levels" and so invisible the pollutants (until it is too late) that a company should prove that its by-products are not harmful rather than merely wait, as in West Virginia, for the level of a respiratory disease among children and old people to reach four times the normal level, and then cut back their emissions.

This doctrine has not yet been established by law, but in the meantime consumer power has attacked some of the products whose quantity reduces the quality of our lives. Take the automobile. Consumer power was once again evident when in 1970 a motion was passed in the California state senate banning the internal-combustion engine after 1975. By a single vote a committee in the state assembly (lower house) failed to go along. But even to consider a law banning the car in a state which had literally been built around the automobile would have been quite unthinkable a few years ago. In September 1971 the attack was focused on big cars with large horsepower ratings. A consumer-power group persuaded a U.S. Court of Appeals to rule that television stations which carried advertisements for such cars must also broadcast information about the adverse effect of such cars on the environment—a sort of "big cars can endanger your health" along the lines of the warning on cigarette packs. It was an analogy made by the judge in his ruling: "Commercials which continue to insinuate that the human personality finds greater fulfillment in a large car do, it seems to us, ventilate a point of view which not only has become controversial but involves issues of public importance. When there is undisputed evidence, as there is here, that the hazards of health implicit in air pollution are enlarged and aggravated by such products, then the parallel with cigarette advertising is exact." And you know what has happened to cigarette advertising on television in America, Britain and Germany.

Advertising for large cars may not yet have been forced off television, but new standards are being forced on the advertisers. By 1975–1976, the exhaust gas will be so clean that the average daily emission of hydrocarbons will be no more than that emitted by a 2-ounce can of paint. And the carbon-monoxide emissions will be the same as from a three-log fire. Any backsliders who can't meet these standards won't be allowed to sell their cars, as Ford found in 1972 when one of their major engines failed its 50,000-mile emission test. Ford was also fined $7 million for illegally tampering with engines undergoing antipollution tests.

Again, like cyclamates, the anti-emission saga reveals as much about the strength of the consumer power structure as it exposes the cynicism of large corporations. Several independent experts have attacked the emission controllers. For instance, Sir Eric Ashby, chairman of the British Royal Commission on Environmental Pollution, argues that carbon-monoxide concentration throughout the world has not changed appreciably since 1945, and that the $3 billion spent to clean up America's car exhausts could be better invested in America's road safety.

Even the Environmental Protection Agency has admitted that its concern with nitrogen-dioxide levels may have been alarmist. Apparently it won't be until 1977 that even the three cities worst affected by car exhausts in America—Los Angeles, Chicago and Baltimore—will even approach the national air-quality levels.

Another major product area in which consumer power has already shown its muscle in protecting the quality of life is detergents. Consumer power in America wants them banned, arguing that their superior cleaning properties over soap powder are not worth their superior polluting properties. The first jab was to get the phosphate levels reduced. And the consumerists actually managed to get President Nixon and five U.S. government agencies to warn that phosphates in detergents were killing American rivers. One result was that Procter & Gamble's share of the detergent market tumbled as nonphosphate brands achieved in weeks two-thirds the level of sales that the industry's brand leader, Tide, had laboriously built up over the years. "Cleans your conscience, too," claimed PFD (Pollution Free Detergent), the "deep-cleaning laundry discovery with no phosphates."

In fact, the normal substite for phosphates, nitrilotriacetate, was found to lead to fetal abnormalities in rats. The Surgeon General of the United States, believing that defiling the environment was less bad than defiling the body, advised Mrs. America to return to her phosphates until a better ingredient could be found. But despite the case against the safety of nonphosphate detergents, consumer pressures were enough to force the Surgeon General to withdraw his statement.

All the examples of consumer power in action so far reported concern the product itself. But the rest of this chapter is mainly devoted to studying how consumer power has tried to affect the way this product is sold. Many of its most spectacular successes have been in this area. It is here above all that America comes into its own as a stamping ground for consumerists. That having been said, it is also true (and worth remembering) that it is quite wrong to think of consumer power as something only pushing for fairer advertising and marketing practices. "The problem of misleading advertising," said Nader himself in an interview in the London *Sunday Times*, "is nowhere near as serious as other problems in the consumer area." Some of these problems have already been discussed. But advertising as a conspicuous and blatant expression of the corporate attitude *behind* the product is nonetheless an important subject to look into. As the mirror in which business exposes itself, advertising is a fair reflection of how corporations actually see themselves; the record of the last few years shows that advertising is in fact the soft underbelly of business which has proved pathetically vulnerable to consumerist attacks.

Let us begin with the advertisement on the package, otherwise known as the label. In March 1971 one of John Banzhaf's groups, LABEL (Law Students Association for Buyers' Education and Labeling), presented a petition to Congress for a new food-labeling law requiring companies to list in order of predominance *all* the ingredients in their products (which means about seventy for things like Coca-Cola). With a 58 percent increase in the use of additives in food from 1955 to 1965, LABEL argued that people ought to know what they were getting, and for that matter, what they were not getting. Under the existing regulations, for example, a drink labeled "orange juice drink" contained as little as 50 percent orange juice. Two months later a Truth-in-Food-Labeling Bill was before Congress.

An alternative strategy for consumer power is to put pressure on one of the regulatory bodies, like the FTC, and so force them to use their regulatory powers. The case of Firestone tires is a typical example. Early in 1969 Nader criticized the FTC for not enforcing its 1967 guidelines for tire advertising. Then in June 1969 the FTC gave tire manufacturers thirty days to get rid of advertisements which emphasized the speed and safety performance of their tires, with the additional threat that any tire advertiser who persisted in these misdemeanors would be "challenged." And just six months after this, the FTC said that it intended to try to stop Firestone from using advertising which specifically said "Firestone tires stop 25 percent faster." The matter didn't end there, however, as we shall see when we look at the development of corrective advertising as a consumerist retaliatory weapon against corporate deceptions.

Consumer-power exposés of misleading advertising have concentrated on the biggest companies, such as Firestone, for the simple reason that they thus affect a greater number of consumers. One of the other big names that have come under the spotlight for misleading advertising as a result of consumer exposés was Campbell's. The bowls of soup used in press and television advertising were filled with marbles to force the appetizing solid ingredients of the soup to the top. The prosecution in 1969 against Campbell's was actually the first in four years against rigged TV demonstrations. (The most recent one had been in 1965 when the Supreme Court backed the FTC judgment against Colgate for not using real sandpaper in a TV commercial showing that Colgate Palmolive's Rapid Shave had so much softening power that you could even shave sandpaper.)

From a prosecution once every four years, the FTC rhythm seemed to change to one every four weeks (mathematicians will identify this as approximately a fiftyfold increase in activity). After Campbell's, Lever Brothers was next in line with its commercial for All detergent. In this, an actor wearing a stained garment stands in a giant washing machine and talks about the cleaning power of the product as the water rises and recedes, leaving the garment shiningly clean. The FTC point was that the clothes used in the commercial had been cleaned by a normal washing method,

31

not by the instant immersion shown on the screen. Five years earlier Lever Brothers would probably have acted like Colgate and fought the FTC judgment in the Supreme Court. But in 1969 they meekly withdrew the commercial.

Despite this toughness it must be said that in 1969 there was still little consistency of judgment between the various agencies whose job it was to control American advertising, partly because there was (and still is) a mixture of statutory and voluntary bodies trying to do the job. In 1969 one such voluntary organization, the National Association of Broadcasters, allowed on the air a commercial for Pall Mall cigarettes that had been specifically identified as being misleading by the Federal Trade Commission. "Newest U.S. government figures show Pall Mall's 100s now lower in tar than the best-selling filter king," said the commercial. To be sure, Pall Mall had a tar rating of 20 against Winston's 21, but Pall Mall also had more tar than forty-five other brands of cigarettes. Anyhow, a difference of 5 percent in tar is not thought by the experts to be of any significance. The only response by the NAB to the Federal Trade Commission's criticism was to order minor amendments to this commercial, which were described by the director of the New York office of the NAB (who resigned over this issue) as "meaningless." This example illustrates one of the basic ingredients of advertising which consumer power is attacking. Not blatant untruth, which is relatively rare, but a distortion of truth, which is common.

For example, Colgate Dental Cream (with over a third of the market) ran an advertisement for some time based on tests which essentially showed that those who brushed after every meal with Colgate Dental Cream fared better than a control group which followed their ordinary brushing habits. This is true enough, but it is probable that *any* toothpaste could have been substituted for Colgate (which was not indicated by the advertisement). A few months after a consumer-power group had argued this point before a Senate subcommittee, a panel of scientists from the National Academy of Sciences reported that eight out of ten toothpastes were worthless in preventing tooth decay. Presumably this body could have made this charge any time in the last fifty years. But science, only looking for what it expects to find, didn't see fit to reach these conclusions until *after* a consumer-power attack.

Science is often involved in adjudicating misleading advertising claims because science is often invoked by the advertiser. For example, Milk of Magnesia rides along on a claim that it is "the laxative doctors recommend most often." Possibly true, but what is less true is the implication that doctors generally recommend laxatives.

The case of Excedrin painkiller was further grist for the consumer-power mill. The advertisement that caused the furor was delivered by actor David Janssen, star of *The Fugitive*. He said: "A study of hospital patients showed two Excedrins more effective in the relief of pain than twice as many aspirin." What wasn't said was that the hospital tests were on mothers who had just given birth. And one of the doctors who did the tests said that post-partum pains bore as much relationship to headache pains as apples to oranges. At first NBC accepted the advertisement, but when it was challenged by the makers of Bayer aspirin the script was revised as follows: "Isn't the way a pain reliever performs what really matters to you? Well, the performance of pain relievers on headaches is hard to measure, so a study was made of patients with a different kind of pain that medical science does use for comparing pain relievers. One purpose was to find out how many aspirin were needed to equal pain relief of two Excedrin. The results of this particular study . . . *two Excedrin worked better for relief of the pain tested than twice as many aspirin tablets.*" This revised script satisfied two of the big three television networks, but not NBC. And it didn't satisfy Nader's Center for the Study of Responsive Law. It swiftly attacked the commercial on *The Nader Report*, its TV program in Boston, using the testimony of another doctor to say that the results Excedrin had got from its tests *did not* square with the results he'd got from similar tests. And the center filed a charge in the courts against Bristol-Myers, the makers of Excedrin, for deception in advertising.

Such an action is obviously harmful enough for the company concerned, but it becomes even more harmful when as a result of consumerist pressures, a government regulatory agency takes action in the courts as well. This was the case in October 1970 with Chevron F310 gasoline.

Chevron is owned by Standard Oil, which also produces Mobil, Esso and Amoco gas. To promote F310, Chevron's agency, Batten, Barton, Durstine & Osborn (BBDO), prepared an advertisement with a large balloon attached to the exhaust of two cars. One balloon was full of black gas (from the car without F310) and the other balloon (on the car with F310) was clear as a bell. First, a group called People's Lobby filed a $30 million suit against Chevron for this campaign. Then the FTC applied for a court order enjoining Standard Oil from advertising again for one year for Chevron *or any other gasoline* unless it "clearly and conspicuously disclose" that the FTC had found the current Chevron advertising to be false. Chevron's response, apart from fighting the FTC in the court, was to run an ad defending their previous advertising—an unusual development to say the least. (And in the advertisement, incidentally, it dropped the balloon test but printed the raw scientific data indicating a 13.9 percent reduction in unburned hydrocarbons as a result of switching to F310.)

All these examples—Firestone, Campbell's, Lever Brothers' All, Colgate, Excedrin and Pall Mall—relate to the question of what one means by "misleading advertising." But the spread of that phrase was becoming wider all the time. It was being extended from the product not living up to the performance claim to the product not living up to the *implied* superiority claim. This was a move with manifold implications, and we can see how the former grew into the latter if we look at the case of mouthwashes.

Ever since Listerine ran "Always a bridesmaid, never a bride" and Colgate invented its ring of confidence, American and British cash registers have had their own ring of confidence as the millions tried to make their breath as pure as peppermint. Then in 1969 a panel of scientists told the Food and Drug Administration that there was no proof that mouthwashes were effective germicides, and that there was no proof that they reduced mouth odor. A year later the FDA gave the mouthwash companies thirty days to eliminate their claims that these products stopped bad breath, colds, sore throats or chills, and to stick instead to claims like "a refreshing mouth rinse." So far, then, a straight factual clamp-down (albeit a little restricting for a company like Listerine, which in 1939 had said it cured dandruff, in 1944 that it cured sore throats, in 1958 that it protected you against Asian flu, and in 1969 that it killed germs by millions on contact).

After the removal of these terminological inexactitudes a second point arose, made in this case by Congressman Benjamin S. Rosenthal on *The Nader Report* in 1970: "Chemically they [mouthwashes] are all essentially the same thing." And so the doctrine grew among consumerists that it was misleading for advertisers to state or imply that their product had unique or superior properties over rival products that were, in fact, identical or substantially the same.

In February 1971 the group of Banzhaf Bandits called SAME (Students Against Misleading Enterprise) petitioned the FTC to require manufacturers of products which are chemically identical to acknowledge this in their advertisements and not to make *any* claims or comparisons which might lead the public to believe the contrary. In one sentence, the keystone of much modern advertising received a violent blow because one of the vaunted skills of modern advertising has been to give to otherwise identical products "added value" which would increase the consumer's pleasure while consuming the product. (This idea was encapsulated in Charles Revson's statement that he wasn't selling cosmetics, he was selling dreams.)

One of the product categories immediately singled out for attention was aspirin. SAME reported tests made in 1962 comparing Excedrin, Anacin, Bufferin, Bayer and St. Joseph aspirin, and reminded everyone of the findings that "there was no significant difference between any of these tablets when two tablets per day were used." It contrasted this with Bayer's advertising: "Bayer aspirin is the best aspirin you can buy." Bayer compounded the error by implying superiority as well as stating it specifically: "Bayer aspirin is *pure* aspirin."

Another superiority innuendo that was singled out was the type used in bleach advertising. All but one bleach (Purex) is said to contain 5.25 percent sodium hypochlorite and 94.75 percent inert ingredients. Yet Clorox, with the same formula as other brands, claimed: "No other bleach, liquid or dry, bleaches clothes cleaner, whiter than Clorox." Of course, Clorox is not actually *saying* that it bleaches better than other bleaches; just that no other bleach will get things cleaner or whiter, which may be true, but the way the sentence is structured carries an implication that goes well beyond this literal meaning.

These criticisms by private citizens received an official imprimatur when the FTC started action against Wonder enriched bread for its claim that it "helps build strong bodies 12 ways." FTC's first charge was against the twelve ways. But its more significant attack was on the uniqueness implication. According to the FTC:

"Wonder is a standardized enriched bread. All enriched breads are required by law to have minimum levels of certain nutrients. The amount and kinds of nutrients contained in the said Wonder bread is the same as that contained in most other enriched breads." In short, it is quite wrong for a product to imply superiority when its formula is simply based on government standards. What irritated the FTC in particular was that for all the implied superiority of Wonder bread, it fell well below the maximum level of ingredients. For instance, it had only 38 percent of the maximum calcium, 50 percent of the maximum riboflavin, 72 percent of the maximum iron, and 83 percent of the maximum thiamin.

The final twist of the knife from the FTC was this: the question as to whether a product was claiming superiority rested *not only* on the words of the commercial but also on research evidence of what consumers say about the advertisements. In the case of Wonder bread, the FTC introduced evidence showing that a significant increase had occurred in the number of consumers who rated Wonder bread excellent or very good, as compared to other breads, in terms of nutrition. And the FTC argued that advertisers have an obligation to change their advertisements if surveys of this nature show that they are, with their advertising, creating a misleading impression—an impression which hitherto advertisers have paid agencies vast sums of money to create on their behalf.

It is interesting to note the response of the Continental Baking Company (which makes Wonder bread) to this attack. Apart from calling in the legal fire power of Covington & Burling (the firm itself became the subject of a Nader investigation), the company started to run advertising defending its advertising. "An important message to every mother in America" ran the headline, and the copy argued that the company's advertising had for fifteen years been "completely honest and factual."

An advertiser having to run advertisements defending his advertising is something that we didn't see before the growth of consumer power. Equally new was the response of the consumer power structure to the evidence of misleading advertising which the group unearthed. In the past it was simply exposed in a best-selling book, but in the late sixties the response was different.

On December 11, 1969, Nader called on the FTC to adopt a rule prohibiting advertisers from making any claims regarding safety, performance or effectiveness of a product unless competent scientific information was filed with the FTC for public inspection. Article 8 of the official American advertising code might, if practiced, be regarded as an endorsement of the principle behind Nader's demand: "Advertising should avoid the use of exaggerated or unprovable claims." But the evidence presented by Nader showed that 94 percent of the advertisers whose claims he had challenged were unwilling or unable to prove them. And in 1971 two senators proposed legislation that would have made Nader's request law instead of just a regulation of the FTC.

As a result of all this, the FTC *did* start to demand claim substantiation. And even more important, it decided that the onus of proof lay with the advertiser to substantiate his claim rather than with the FTC to disprove it. Even more interesting, the commission contended that it was an unfair practice for an advertiser to make claims when he had no data to support those claims, even if those claims happened to be true. So the General Electric Company found itself being asked to show that its air conditioners reproduced the "clean freshness of clear, cool mountain air." And North American Philips was asked to show that its electric razor shaved "up to 50 percent faster."

Of course, the motor industry was not exempt from these compulsory disclosures of evidence. And when in October 1971 its answers started to come in, the consumer-power groups found further ammunition for the charge that "advertisers make their claims which give consumers no real understanding of the product's performance; invoke clinical tests with little scientific basis to substantiate claims; and otherwise deliberately mislead and deceive the consumer" (Ralph Nader quoted in 1969 in *Fortune.*)

The one hundred and nine advantages that Chevrolet claimed stopped the Chevelle from "becoming old before its time" involved such items as an outside rear-view mirror, automatic choke and padded sun visors, not to mention a number of safety and pollution measures required by law. And Ford, which had presented its cars as being more quiet than expensive European cars, emerged a little battered as well. The quietness tests of 1965 apparently matched brand-new 1966 Fords against nine older foreign cars, including sports cars and a 1963 Daimler with 33,000 miles on the clock. In all, the independent analysts employed by the FTC to evaluate the car advertisers' claims reported that the data behind roughly two out of three technical claims were not adequate.

37

The Food and Drug Administration followed in the footsteps of the FTC. In the beginning of 1972 Commissioner Charles Edwards announced a three-year study to probe the safety and effectiveness of 100,000 brands of nonprescription (proprietary) drugs. What spurred the FDA to put all headache cures, antiperspirants, laxatives and cold remedies under the federal microscope? The fact that on a sample survey of four hundred nonprescription drugs only one in four was rated "effective," and the rest were in categories ranging from "probably ineffective" to "ineffective." Already the FDA has come to the conclusion, based on its studies, that both buffered and unbuffered aspirin cause gastric mucosal damage as well as gastrointestinal blood loss. The agency has also made some interesting discoveries about the impact of over-the-counter-drug advertising on Americans. For instance, the FDA found that one third of Americans believe that it is medically necessary to go to the bathroom every day, something most doctors would scoff at. The FDA's sister body, the FTC, has joined in on this attack on over-the-counter-drug advertising by its sweeping rejection of the claims of Bayer, Excedrin, Cope and Vanquish to be any more effective than plain aspirin.

Substantiation of direct claims was not the only response of consumer power to advertising. As the case of Wonder bread showed, consumerists had also started to argue that the message of an advertisement was more than the words of the text. It is an argument that the advertising industry can hardly disagree with, for ever since the theory of the brand image became accepted, admen have argued that one picture is worth a thousand words. Yet the main control of advertising has always been on the words or at least the overt claims made by the combination of words and picture. But with the nature of the television medium it is ludicrous to base one's judgment on the fairness of a commercial entirely or even mainly on its overt claims. One of the things every cub copywriter is taught is that if his commercial doesn't work with the sound off, it doesn't work. And to go by the overt verbal claims is to go by the partial claims.

This is one of the demands of Banzhof's TUBE group: a criterion for describing deception in advertising should be "misrepresentation as to the *implication* derived from the totality of the deceptive advertisement" (my italics). Responding to this, the FTC held a series of hearings on the persuasive process of advertising. In the words of the FTC's former head of Consumer Protection, Robert Pitorfsky, in *Advertising Age*: "Those forms of advertising which are essentially noninformational in character may raise questions as to their fundamental fairness, their conformity with the traditional economic justifications for advertising as sources of information upon which a free and reasonably informed choice may be made, and the extent to which such advertising is designed to exploit such fears or anxieties as social acceptance of personal well-being without fulfilling the desires raised." Under this doctrine, an advertiser who claimed his after-shave lotion increased your attractiveness to the opposite sex, and who couldn't prove it in black and white, could look forward to prosecution.

Another area of advertising fairness to come under the consumer-power microscope was commercials aimed at children. In countries like Britain, there were already specific controls of such advertising. However, in America, not only had commercials for children been subjected to hardly more control than commercials for adults, but children had been zeroed in on by business as a market in their own right, or rather a series of markets from teeny-boppers to micro-boppers.

And so the suspicion grew that advertisers were trying to exploit the ignorance and gullibility of children. It was consumerist Robert Choate who first pointed out that of the twenty most advertised cereals, fifteen were low in nutrition, and that the National Association of Broadcasters' rules for policing toy commercials seemed to work more in the interests of the toy manufacturers than of the kids. The following example of a commercial aimed at children was one of those presented by TUBE to a Senate subcommittee. It is for a product called Johnny Lightning cars. The setting: several boys surround a race track. Dynamic music is playing in the background. Camera follows the cars and views the techniques that make the cars appear to slow down and speed up. Narrator: "Here comes the 1970 Johnny Lightning Challengers. New triple threat, three-engine dragster—the speed-hungry spoiler . . . the bug bomb . . . the powerful smuggler . . . the sand stormer . . .the explosive TNT . . . and many more new models. They are beautiful and they are fast. Race any cars against the new Johnny Lighting Challengers and see for yourself. Exciting new cars, alone or in sets, from Johnny Lightning."

One would be forgiven for thinking that one was looking at an advertisement for a supercharged Detroit speedster. TUBE commented: "The deception is caused by the impression, the speed of the soundtrack and the camera technique used. The cars seem to speed up while going around the arches and down the straightway . . . these techniques give the impression of greater size, speed and ability of the toy. The total impression derived by the viewer is inconsistent with the actual performance of the toy."

This is simply applying the FTC's doctrine of what its "claim" is, from grownups to children. For while an adult might easily recognize that the television commercial was for a simple toy, a child, it is argued, could easily be led to expect as much from his Johnny Lightning electric car as his dad does from his supercharged Mustang. "It's time," said one consumerist, "that there was some arrangement made to ensure that children are not treated as markets for exploitation by every huckster with the money to buy TV time."

For the advertiser to respond to these new onslaughts with repentance and a new code of good conduct wasn't enough for the consumerists. Being hot on the trail, they were, understandably, not to be satisfied with anything less than a good pounding. The old penalty for false advertising in America was a cease-and-desist order to prohibit future deception. But the "go and sin no more" concept was entirely unsatisfactory to a consumer group which, having exposed a company, believed that notwithstanding the cessation of the misleading advertising, the company would still benefit in its present sales from its past misdemeanors.

It was SOUP and not the FTC which first formulated a coherent expression of the doctrine demanding corrective advertising. It was called in the FTC hearing on Firestone tires the "rotten-apple concept." Very simply, if sales in year four resulted to some degree from advertising in year one, then the deceptive claims in year one became the "rotten apple" which leaves a deceptive impression contributing to sales in year four. The purpose of corrective advertising is to remove the benefit of those claims from the company by forcing disclaimers in year-four advertising of the deception in year-one advertising.

Advertising Age called such a doctrine a "death sentence," and it certainly does represent a vigorous reinterpretation of the FTC powers. It was the legal eagles of SOUP who convinced the FTC that it *had* the power to order "an affirmative disclosure" by a company that was found to have engaged in misleading advertising. (This was in the Campbell's soup case, though in this particular instance the FTC didn't feel the punishment fit the crime of filling soup bowls with marbles.)

In the case of Geritol, the punishment under the new FTC regime represented a halfway stage between the old cease-and-desist order and the new corrective advertising. After years of legal wrangling with Geritol, the FTC ordered Geritol to have the following statement in their commercials: *"The great majority of tired people do not feel that way because of iron-poor blood and Geritol won't help them."* This clearly implied the exact opposite to what most previous Geritol advertising had been working feverishly to suggest. No longer was the absence of iron permitted to be linked to "tiredness" and "loss of strength" or "that run-down feeling." Instead, "builds iron power" was the name of the game for Geritol if they wished to advertise on television. But in 1970 the FTC ruled that the word "power" had to be deleted from this, leaving "Geritol builds iron" with a disclaimer that most people don't need an iron build-up.

In 1972 the FTC finally decided that Geritol was not complying with its earlier rulings and, in January 1973, after prosecution in a New York court, the manufacturers, J. B. Williams Company, was fined $812,000. The penalty, in fact, could have been $1 million, so, considering the levels of sales achieved by Geritol (two billion doses sold between 1950 and 1962 alone), the company perhaps got off reasonably lightly. Certainly, it might have cost J. B. Williams more if it had had to engage in the full application of the corrective concept: the public admission in 25 percent of your advertising over a twelve-month period that your previous advertising was misleading. This was first demanded in the Firestone case, when it was shown that Firestone had been making unjustified safety claims for some of their tires.

The most interesting part of this case wasn't so much SOUP's attack as Firestone's defense, supported by the Association of National Advertisers (representing about 90 percent of all advertising budgets). *The defense was simply that there was no significant residual carry-over of advertising from one year to another,* that there was no "substantially persisting" communication of the advertisements' claims. This put SOUP in the extraordinary posi-

41

tion of having to present an argument normally made by agencies to their clients about the long-term effects of advertising. It was the attorney from the Association of National Advertisers who argued that "taking into account the thousands of advertisements and thousands of advertising claims, the general rule regarding advertisements is rapidly forgetting rather than memory." It was the SOUP attorney who called Dr. Darell Lucas of New York University to talk about the "sleeper effect," an impression that one receives which can become the basis for action at a later date when one has forgotten the source of the message. In addition, Dr. Douglas Greer was called to argue for the capital value of past advertising campaigns. He actually calculated, against *opposition* from the Association of National Advertisers, that the value of Firestone's 1968 campaign in 1970 would represent about 35 percent of its 1968 expenditure..

This extraordinary role reversal by the advertising establishment was a measure of their blind desperation—the feeling that their only defense was to deny the power of their magical arts. Notwithstanding this extraordinary defense, however, the corrective doctrine became established, and the FTC has sought to apply it to, among others, Wonder bread, Ocean Spray, Chevron, Hi-C Fruit Drink, Profile bread and the Sugar Association. And so far, they have been successful in half these cases.

It was in July 1971 that what had been called "this doomsday weapon" (in an *Advertising Age* editorial) received its first trial workout. Profile "diet bread," from the same stable as Wonder bread, agreed to spend 25 percent of the next year's budget on a disclaimer commercial. "I'd like to clear up any misunderstandings you may have about Profile bread from its advertising or even its name," said a trim young lady. "Does Profile have fewer calories than other breads? No, Profile has about the same per ounce as other breads. To be exact, Profile has seven fewer calories per slice. That's because it's sliced thinner. But even eating Profile will not cause you to lose weight. A reduction of seven calories is insignificant." Profile was followed into the confessional by Ocean Spray Cranberry Cocktail, admitting that "when we said Ocean Spray Cranberry Cocktail has more fruit energy than orange juice or tomato juice . . . we didn't mean vitamins and minerals. Fruit energy means calories. Nothing more."

In June 1973 an even tougher version of corrective advertising was wheeled into action by the FTC: retractive advertising. A Boise, Idaho, tire dealer, accused of misrepresenting the performance of a Uniroyal Zeta steel radial tire, was ordered to run ads that not only totally retracted previous claims but carried in large type as the focal point in the advertisement the statement that "this advertisement is published pursuant to an order of the Federal Trade Commission."

The corrective doctrine doesn't just apply to advertising. For instance, a version of it has already been applied to consumer contests. In one particular case the FTC argued that Coca-Cola had not disclosed a key rule in its nationwide contest, and that *two* correct answers might be required on some of the questions instead of the usual one. The FTC decided that the only way this unfair practice could be corrected would be for Coca-Cola to pay $100 to every contestant who had misunderstood the rules and would have won except for this "undisclosed rule." (This new interest by consumerists in contests and sweepstakes followed their disclosures to a congressional subcommittee that usually only about 10 percent of the prizes offered in the advertising for "preselected winners" sweepstakes were actually awarded.)

Following corrective advertising came counter-advertising. This was an extension of the so-called Fairness Doctrine, whereby a TV station was obliged to give adequate coverage to both sides of important public issues. The Federal Communications Commission allowed this doctrine to be applied to TV advertising in the case of cigarettes, declaring that one antismoking advertisement should be run for every five cigarette commercials.

The Stern Concern is the particular consumer group which pioneered the wider application of this doctrine with counter-ads to encourage, for example, the recall of Chevrolet cars and the discouragement of the use of aspirin brand products. In the case of aspirin, Burt Lancaster, surrounded by bottles of all the big budget headache remedies, opines: "The American Medical Association has found remedies like these to be either irrational, not recommended or unsound . . . Next time you buy something for your head, use your head. Buy the least expensive plain aspirin that you can find." At one stage the FTC even carried this doctrine further and suggested that counter-advertising by consumer groups would be appropriate against a particular point of view in an advertisement which, while not being positively untruthful, might not tell the whole story—for example, advertising relying on scientific claims that were themselves still the subject of controversy in the scientific world, or advertising which did not reveal some negative aspect of the product. The FTC cited the example of cars: "In response to advertising for small cars and deciding the factor of low cost and economy, the public could be informed of the view of some people that such cars are considered less safe than large cars. On the other hand, ads for bigger cars, emphasizing the factors of safety and comfort, could be answered by counter-ads concerning the greater pollution arguably generated by such cars" (quoted in *Time*).

Not a little of this onslaught on the admen has crossed the border into Canada. In some ways, indeed, Canada seems to be even further along the road toward consumer power than America itself. At one time it looked as if an advertising agency north of the border might have to face a situation that looked something like this: first, the agency lawyer would have to OK the copy, then the company lawyer would have to OK the copy. If either had any doubts, he could ask the advice of the people at the Ministry of Consumer Affairs. The advice would come with the proviso that in the event of litigation, the fact that the Ministry of Consumer affairs had advised him was no defense. The advertisement would then appear in the press. Following that, one of the government inspectors in one of Canada's five provinces, having seen the advertisement, might decide to prosecute it, possibly on a hair-splitting technical offense (for in Canada, the test of the *credulous man* was the test to be used). If the prosecution succeeded, both the client *and* the agency *could be sent to prison* (the offense would be a criminal, *not* a civil one), even if they took all reasonable and due care to avoid creating a misleading advertisement.

It now seems unlikely that all this will be implemented. Nevertheless, there are already moves to take all advertising aimed at children off TV. Under pressure from Tory MP James McGrath, private broadcasters in Canada have already banned not only Tony the Tiger from commercials, but even Santa Claus is not allowed to deliver well-wrapped sales spiels from his sledge.

Although controls such as these have been achieved by consumer groups, it would be quite wrong to imagine that Nader & Co. is heading for a runaway victory. By no means all the battles fought by the consumer-power advocates have ended in victory. Once Madison Avenue realized it was fighting for survival, it made its counterattacks and was by no means without success. The FTC, for instance, lost its battle against Hi-C Fruit Drink advertisements, which were ruled not to be misleading. It dropped a major part of its charges against Chevron. And in the case of Zerex antifreeze, they backed down completely in the face of a very tough counterattack by the head of Zerex's advertising agency, BBDO.

An even more devastating defeat was the outcome of the previously mentioned Wonder bread case. This had been built by the FTC into a test case for such practices as corrective advertising, advertising aimed at children, nutritional claims and the pre-emptive claim (i.e., a product makes a claim for itself which virtually every product in that field can also make, but because this particular product makes it first, it "pre-empts" the other products and is able to imply uniqueness for these product attributes to itself). Characteristically, the FTC attributed this defeat to the judge erring thirty-one times in his assessment of the case. But though the FTC lost this battle, it would be quite wrong to assume that consumer militants are losing the war. The very nature of the judicial process, where decisions are very much based upon past legal precedents, automatically favors the status quo. Social changes, be they female emancipation or marijuana usage, very often precede an adaptation of the law of the land to these changes. Until this adaptation occurs, as the case of consumer-power groups demonstrates, the courts are more likely to rule in favor of the established doctrines than the new heresies. In this context, perhaps one of the most important legal breakthroughs which favored the FTC was that of the United States Court of Appeals for the District of Columbia. This reversed a previous court ruling, and gave the FTC the right to make blanket rules defining various business practices as illegal, unfair or deceptive.

However, even when the law eventually catches up with society, the law may not always be enforced. The horse-trading of politics dictates that while the consumer lobby can be assuaged by, say, the passing of the Truth-in-Packaging Bill, the business lobby can then be pacified by allotting only three federal employees to administer this complicated law (a type of defensive manuever that will be outflanked by the development of "class actions," whereby ordinary citizens can bring liability suits on behalf of millions of consumers with a single legal action).

When one sees how President Nixon, with former employees of J. Walter Thompson at his side, contrived the butchery of the Consumer Protection Bill in the Senate in 1971 (*Et tu Brute?*), the despair of the consumer-power leaders is understandable. But in the long run, and in the context of the new consumer attitudes we will talk about in a later chapter, these rear-guard actions will be increasingly seen for what they are: emergency action by groups with vested interests in the inequalities of the status quo struggling to preserve their commercial psyches.

The significance of consumer power is not so much that it has suffered some defeats but—remembering how easily Madison Avenue shrugged off earlier attacks—that it has won so many victories. Its true strength shows up not where its case was patently just, but in cases like enzymes or nitrous-oxygen emissions, where the evidence favors the other side. Not only does consumer power pack this sort of punch, but its status is such that even manifestly being proved wrong is not sufficient to dent its credibility and the willingness of millions of consumers to take its work as gospel.

Take the case of mercury in tuna fish. You will doubtless remember the scare when word went around that the mercury levels in tuna fish, because of man's pollution of the oceans by mercury products, had led to an alarming rise of mercury in tuna—which for some reasons attracted more of this mineral to its body than other fishes. This story was all over the newspapers, and it was used as one more stick to beat business with by the consumer lobbyists. Then some American naval scientists in 1971 bored into the permanent ice floes of Greenland and measured the mercury content of the frozen sea water going back for several millennia. They concluded that the slight increase in mercury levels that this revealed was no reason to knock tuna off your menu.

The interesting point is that not one of the papers that had carried the "mercury-danger story" carried the "no-mercury-danger story" with anything like the same weight. No news may be good news. but good news is certainly no news. *The Times* of London, for instance, ran the story under the heading "Pollution: No Danger from Mercury" at the bottom of the Court page, appropriately buried beneath the obituaries. So even when there is a prima facie case for the loss of credibility of consumerists

46

as an information source on any particular issue, the media, perhaps sensing that their readers would not thank them for the attempted destruction of their new gods, let the opportunity slip.

Apart from this instant forgiveness for their sins, the way huge corporations have been forced to kowtow to consumer power underlines its very real strength. Those who would dismiss consumerism as no more than a ritual cleansing of the capitalist process must explain the volte-face of company after company that first tried to beat and then had to join this new cause.

But before we probe the confused and frightened response of business to consumer power, it is worth seeing just how widespread the phenomena is which we are analyzing. In the same way that Coca-Cola civilized nations in the image of the society that first discovered this mystic concoction, militant consumerism also turns out to be a major U.S. export. For having colonized half the globe with one set of values, America has now seen fit to develop an antidote to these values which, though not classed by Congress as Foreign Aid, may prove as helpful to over-developed nations as the Midwest surplus grain is to the starving millions.

The American Invention That Swept the World

●

"The great advantage of being on the same planet as the
United States is that it reveals to other countries the pleasures
and horrors that will afflict them only a few years hence."
[J. K. Galbraith, the London *Observer*]

In 1965 Europeans watched Nader's destruction of General Motors
with the same sort of fascination that they watched Watergate's
destruction of President Nixon in 1973. Unlike Watergate, Europeans felt it could never happen there. For a start, America was
three thousand miles away, and since a mere twenty-one-mile-
wide channel had kept Hitler off British soil, a far wider stretch
of water would keep Nader out of Europe. Even if some wicked
person smuggled in the consumerist heresies, far from their native
lands and planted in a hostile clime, they would surely wither and
perish.

Militant consumerism, so the feeling ran, was as American as
pumpkin pie and likely to be just as localized in its popularity.
After all, had not America ever since the Boston Tea Party developed into a very different sort of society from that of Europe?
Did not Americans have to do everything to excess, be it an
excess of virtue like Prohibition in the twenties or an excess of
vice like segregation, presidential assassinations, organized crime,
or even indeed the incredibly wasteful biggest-and-best syndrome
seen in everything from American cars to American advertising?

Europeans felt that such excesses were not part of their character. A well-developed sense of hypocrisy (elevated to a position just behind cricket as a national sport in Britain) protected them against overdoses of virtue. And a stiff-upper-lipped decency that made their word their bond saved them against vice. Thus it was that with their eyes on America, they persuaded themselves that the whirlwind would pass them by and go on to punish less fortunate lands.

There was, indeed, a measure of reality in such hopes. Business values were more likely to be out of phase with the rest of society in overdeveloped America than in, say, a country like Britain with two and a half times less per capita GNP (gross national product). Nevertheless, consumerism has not remained a peculiarly American concept, even if Nader is still a uniquely American phenomena. Although it is less than a decade since Ralph Nader declared the consumer revolution open, consumerism is alive and well and living in every advanced society from Sweden to Japan, and, indeed, in some European countries it has gone even further than in America itself. This growth was partly a home-grown phenomenon, and partly an export from the Land of the Free. The chief instrument that transported consumerism across the oceans, often unwittingly, were the multinational corporations.

Take the case of automobiles. By 1975 European and Japanese companies exporting cars to America will be selling cars that are considerably safer and less polluting than the cars they sell to their own countrymen. Nader has already attacked the European car manufacturers for a discrepancy between the safety standards of domestic and exported 1972 models. But by 1975 the difference will be so great as to make it increasingly difficult for European automobile companies to defend their position of selling one standard of safety at home and another abroad.

Increasingly, multinational corporations find it necessary to bring their business practices into line in all the countries they operate in. Shell, for instance, found that pressure to change their Plat-formate advertising in America led to pressures to change their advertising in England, for once it became known in America that the black car in Shell's TV commercial was running on a type of gasoline only available to black cars appearing in Shell TV commercials, then all similar commercials Shell were using in Britain had to be modified.

49

The international baby-food companies dropped monosodium glutamate from their products in Europe after the attack on this additive in America, even though they hadn't been subjected to any criticism outside America.

Almost as important as the multinational companies in spreading the consumerist gospel were the media. The media have done more than report the activities of consumer militants in America; they have consciously aped the exposure techniques used by these militants. The attack on the secret coding of food by the London *Sunday Times* was a direct copy of a similar attack mounted by newspapers in California. Nevertheless, despite these pressures encouraging the spread of American-style consumerism, the consumer movement outside America has been marked more by its national than its international characteristics.

Take the area of product safety. While Nader achieved a recall of two out of five American cars sold, the British consumer movement has achieved a recall of no more than one in eight cars sold, and often only 35 percent of these cars are actually pulled back into the dealership for modifications. On the other hand, Britain will probably adopt rules making seat-belt wearing compulsory before America does. Evidence from Australia shows that compulsory wearing of seat belts cuts road casualties by 16 percent. But the Nader philosophy rejects this sort of legislative proposal, believing that it lets the car manufacturers off the hook too easily. Safety, according to his doctrine, is the responsibility of the car designer, not the car driver. In Europe, however, the trend is still toward cars with advanced road holding (i.e., the ability to stay on the road at high speed on twisty roads), good braking—or accident-preventive features. In America, Nader's pressure may lead to what European car designers regard as prehistoric tanks charging at one another on the freeways with the crunch of the bodywork drowned only by the explosion of air bags. The end results of these differences may well be that it would be easier to avoid an accident in a European car but less dangerous to have one in an American car.

The enzymes issue also shows the variance in the consumer power structure on either side of the Atlantic. The evidence that enzymes in detergents were a potential health hazard emerged from medical studies on *British* detergent-industry workers. But it was American consumerists who first used this to attack the detergent companies.

After product safety, it was on product value that American consumerists focused their new militancy. Japan, too, though she has given birth to no inscrutable Ralph Nader, has developed new techniques of business harassment in this area. The American beef boycott, for instance, was a successor to the series of national boycotts which Shufuren, a Japanese housewives' association with six million members, had organized. Everyone from rice growers charging excessive prices to canned-food manufacturers using labels that conceal the truth has taken a pummeling. Going even further than the boycott, a local women's association, Chifuren, has started to put pressure on manufacturers by bringing out its own rival products. In 1968 they started to manufacture Yen 100 cosmetics (compared to prices of up to Yen 1,000 charged per item by the big brands). By the end of 1971, it was selling at a rate of $10 million a year, a small market share in value terms, but because of Yen 100's low price, a good deal more significant in volume terms.

In Britain, no such anti-brands have appeared on the market. There was, however, a minor beef boycott, largely the result of sustained newspaper incitement of the readers. But it was a far more modest affair than its American counterpart and caused hardly a ruffle in the beef-auction rooms.

Although the cattle markets may not yet have tasted the consumer revolution, the advertising emporiums of Europe have had it in plenty. Not only are the rules controlling advertising stricter the farther one goes from Madison Avenue, but consumer groups have been stimulated by the success of the onslaught against advertising in America to both tighten the rules and make sure they are enforced.

Some of these rules would bring a warm glow to Ralph Nader's cheeks. In Italy you would not be allowed to say, for example, "Ford recommends Shell oil" if Ford also recommends other brands of oil (which, of course, they do). In America, and indeed in some other Europen countries, this sort of testimonial can be made with impunity. In Germany, the Unfair Competition Law has led to some rules that would strike terror on Madison Avenue. It is prohibited to present something which is a matter of course

51

as though it were something of special merit. "Twice-distilled schnaps," for instance, is not allowed as an advertising claim if the double distillation of schnaps is prescribed by law. You may recall that one of the planks in the FTC's case against Wonder bread was exactly the same as this: that the nutrition levels in Wonder bread were commonplace within the baking industry and therefore not a fair topic for advertising. Under German law, the FTC would have won the case.

German law also prohibits anyone from designing an advertisement in such a way that someone reading it hastily might draw the wrong conclusions. If you put "price reductions up to 30 percent" with "up to" in tiny type, you would be infringing this rule. A rule banning small print is something that even the eager beavers of the FTC have not yet got around to drafting. Perhaps toughest of all is the rule that you can't describe something as an extra feature if it is not a genuine advantage. "Margarine packed by hand" gives you one example of a phrase that was banned under this rule in Germany. The decision as to whether a deceptive claim has actually been made doesn't just rest with a German court; a public-opinion research institute usually polls members of the public to discover their reaction to the claims. In one way, this protects advertisers against arbitrary and hairsplitting interpretations of the rules. But in another, it makes advertisers vulnerable to any sudden growth of hostility by consumers toward advertising, for this hostility would lead to opinion-poll verdicts that would be even tougher on the admen.

Neither is France no kinder to the hidden persuaders. Admittedly, at first consumerism made little headway. The French equivalent of *Consumer Reports* is called *50 Million Consommateurs*, a name which reflects the French approach for individual action rather than group pressure. If you add to this an inbred French suspicion of any politico-cultural force emanating from America, then you can see why consumerism was a late developer in France.

In 1972, consumerism suddenly became a mass issue and not something to be discussed solely at Left Bank cafés. It was a combination of a victim-hunting trip to Paris by Ralph Nader and a sudden realization by French politicians on election eve that there were votes in consumerism which triggered everything off. Suddenly newspapers started scrutinizing advertisements in a way that would have done credit to Banzhaf's Bandits. One typical case concerned a campaign run by an egg co-operative in Brittany. The factory manager was told by his agency that what people wanted from eggs was not brownness or cleanliness or even size. What people wanted was naturally fed hens laying eggs that were sold fresh in the shops. The factory manager then started packing his eggs in rustic little boxes instead of plastic packs. Huge posters showed old farmers looking after the hens that laid the eggs. Then a consumerist probe revealed that these apparently free-range eggs were laid by the millions in henhouse coops.

The result of such exposés was that the Minister of Finance, Valéry Giscard d'Estaing, asked the French parliament to introduce stringent laws controlling advertising. The resulting bill showed that Nader's visit to Paris wasn't wasted. Not only does it make the advertisers prove the veracity of their claims (instead of requiring the consumer to disprove them), it also provides for an immediate withdrawal of suspect advertisements. More than that, the bill provides for corrective advertising if the advertiser is unable to prove his claims at a court hearing. Laws like this are, of course, simply paper tigers unless they are enforced (as consumerists have discovered to their cost in America). The situation in Britain demonstrates that controls that seem tough in theory are still open to abuse in practice.

Britain, characteristically, has her own unique way of controlling advertising, a system which the chairman of the British Advertising Association described as "the envy of virtually every other country." This enviable technique is to have a loose mesh of laws that would be entirely inadequate save for a voluntary adoption of a code of good conduct by the advertising industry, anxious lest the mesh become any finer. About a quarter of all British advertising is an exception to this principle in that it appears on ITV (the Independent Television network; BBC-1 and BBC-2 are noncommercial), where it comes under the Television Act of 1954 and, by extension, under the Independent Television Companies Association (henceforth ITCA) rules and regulations. But the other three quarters of British advertising is controlled by the voluntary adoption through the Advertising Association of a code of practice that in principle differs little from the codes of practice of the American Association of Advertising Agencies (though its enforcement procedures are different).

The British advertising controls are composed of a hodgepodge of sixty-one statutes covering relatively important things, from the buyer's right in a transaction (the 1893 Sale of Goods Act) to prohibitions against the advertising of cures for pernicious anemia or barber's itch. A television advertisement must be approved by the ITCA before it is allowed on the air, but a press advertisement has to be approved by the Code of Advertising Practice (CAP) committee only if someone, either a media owner, rival advertiser or member of the public has complained about it. The committee does not act of its own accord.

There is no particular rationale for differing standards and differing enforcement procedures for press and television advertising. It is merely that while it may be possible to check the six thousand or so new commercials every year prior to transmission, it is a lot harder to run a similar previewing system for the twenty-five million different advertisements that are published every year. (Since America, with its more developed television system, has vastly more than just six thousand new commercials every year, it is doubtful that this system would be appropriate on that side of the Atlantic.) Of the six thousand or so scripts that are submitted for clearance in Britain, 88 percent receive approval without any alteration being requested. (The figure for over-the-counter-drug commercials is much lower, with only 66 percent getting first-time approval.)

It would be wrong to deduce from this that the British advertising censors are acting in a way which would satisfy the consumer lobby. For a start, of the scripts they turn down, three times as many are rejected on the grounds of taste as on the grounds of misleading claims. Some of these rejections are downright absurd. For instance, a magazine wishing to run a series of one-minute commercials in which a comedian told a joke before delivering his sales spiel ran into difficulties with the ITCA. In order to obtain clearance of the twelve jokes for the twelve commercials, the advertising agency had to submit one hundred and twenty different jokes for the ITCA to consider. Nearly all of them had already been used on television during comedy shows, but despite this the television censors banned most of them from this series of television advertisements.

Not only are jokes thoroughly checked, but the props used in commercials receive equal scrutiny. Nothing is allowed which in any way encourages any sort of permissiveness. Ladies can be seen wearing bras in TV programs, but in TV commercials it is virtually forbidden. Indeed, the ITCA has taken upon itself the job of protecting the sanctity of marriage. As the man responsible for controlling commercial television told the Townswomen's Guild, "The girl who sets up house in a television commercial is never without her wedding ring. Have a close look and see!"

Alas, this pedantic literalness has in the past been applied in a remarkably one-sided way when the ITCA looked at advertising claims. For instance, an advertiser was allowed to say "Nothing acts faster than Anadin" (Anadin is the British version of Anacin), provided no other analgesic actually acts faster. The basic implication of the claim, however, is that Anadin is the fastest-acting analgesic, and this remains unchecked.

But when it comes to reviewing claims for which rebuttal could lead to a major loss of revenue for the television companies, then the ITCA has tended to act in a way which makes them look like guardians not so much of the public interest as of the profits of the television companies. Take the case of advertising small cigars on television (an issue which has also arisen on American television). In 1965, cigarette advertising was banned on British television. More than that, under Clause 15 of the ITCA code, anything to do with cigarettes was also banned. Clause 15 states: "An advertiser who markets more than one product may not use advertising devoted to an acceptable product for purposes of publicising the brand name or other identification of an unacceptable product."

Despite this clause, the ITCA has allowed the advertising of small cigars that not only share the brand name of certain cigarettes but, in one case, also share its slogan. Up to 1965, these were the brand names that the tobacco companies thought were most appropriate for their small cigars: Manikin, Hamlet, Tom Thumb, Doncella and Castella. After 1965, the cigar names were all linked in some way to cigarette names:

Benson & Hedges Special Panatellas (launched in 1967)

Embassy Slim Panatellas (launched in 1968—Embassy is Britain's biggest-selling cigarette)

Embassy Miniature Cigars (launched in 1970)

Rothmans Slim Panatellas (launched in 1970—Rothmans is the biggest-selling king-size cigarette)

Rothmans Mild Whiffs (launched in 1970)

Rothmans Grand Panatellas (launched in 1970)

Between them, these cigar brands spend several million pounds a year on television advertising that is openly flouting the law. Yet the law remains flouted.

The Public Interest Research Centre (a British version of Ralph Nader's Center for the Study of Responsive Law) has pointed out an even graver abuse of the ITCA code. In Britain, under the 1954 Television Act, "The total amount in time given to advertising may not exceed six minutes an hour average over a day's programmes."

Using the official logs of television commercial broadcasts, the Public Interest Research Centre was able to show that the Independent Broadcasting Authority had been allowing this rule to be broken, and 30 percent illegal advertising was appearing on television screens in certain parts of Britain. The problem, in fact, with respect to the control of television advertising in Britain is not that the watchdog has no teeth, but that he has forgotten whom he should be biting.

The control of printed advertising is weakened by a different type of loophole. The advertising industry has established a body called the Advertising Standards Authority to self-regulate the industry. In 1972, out of the twenty-five million different advertisements that appeared in print, this body investigated and checked out just one hundred and ninety of them. That the advertising industry should appear to be making so little effort to keep an eye on itself only encourages the scrutiny of less amicable elements. For instance, in just one week in 1973, the Public Interest Research Centre found over three hundred examples of what they believed were flagrant breaches of the Code of Advertising Practice.

To see just how vulnerable the British advertising industry would be to a consumerist probe, I myself have repeated the procedure used by Ralph Nader in 1969 in America. I wrote to a random selection of twenty-three major advertisers asking them to substantiate their claims. Some of the claims I challenged were simply "trade puffs," a type of adjectival boast that is specifically allowed under British law because no one is meant to be taken in by it. Others were hard factual claims.

The table on pages 58-59 summarizes the results. (Anadin,

as previously stated, is the British version of Anacin. Fairy Liquid is the British version of Ivory. Elida Gibbs is a Unilever toothpaste brand. Omo and Radiant are Unilever detergent brands. Tyne Brand pie fillings is a product of one of Britain's largest food conglomerates, Spillers. In short, you have in this table a cross section of Britain's major advertisers.)

The first interesting point that this table shows is the very wide range of time these companies took to give an answer. Quickest was Beecham's with three days (but their answer really only amounted to no more than a polite raspberry). Slowest were Omo and Colgate with almost a third of a year to reply to my questions. And Radiant didn't even send me an answer—only an acknowledgment. If fourteen days is a reasonable response period to this sort of question (as I believe it is), then only half the companies replied within a reasonable period of time. And for two of the companies, it took three special-delivery letters to squeeze any attempt at substantiation out of them.

The extent to which the companies were able to substantiate their claims is of course a matter of subjective judgment. They would doubtless argue that they had either substantiated their claims or provided as much substantiation as the law or common sense required. My view of the extent to which their claim was substantiated by the evidence that they supplied is given in column 4. And column 5 is the amount of effort I felt, from the correspondence, that the company put into making their substantiation.

Assuming, for the moment, that my assessment is fair, this means that not one of the trade puffs were substantiated; it means that only two of the specific claims were fully substantiated; and it means that another four specific claims were partially—though not completely—substantiated. Finally, it means that five companies were either unwilling or unable to provide full substantiation for their claims, *even though these claims were not trade puffs* and should have been covered by the existing regulations.

One of the most entertaining substantiations was supplied by Courvoisier to explain why the cognac is called "the Brandy of Napoleon." Apparently, when Napoleon was about to flee from France after meeting his Waterloo, two ships were made ready for his escape from the Bordeaux area. M. Emanuel Courvoisier, as a tribute to his former emperor, placed a consignment of his

57

COMPANY	CLAIM	REPLY TIME (DAYS)	SUBSTAN- TIATION CON- FIRMED?	SUBSTAN- TIATION EFFORT
Anadin	"Nothing acts faster than Anadin"	15	No	Slight
Bass Char- rington	"The most welcoming pub in the world"	10	No	Slight
Colgate	Gardol and "the ring of confidence"	123	Partially	Reasonable
Courvoisier	"The Brandy of Napoleon"	5	Partially	Reasonable
Elida Gibbs	Signal: "the mouth- wash in the stripes"	5	No	Slight
Fairy Liquid	"Hands that do dishes can feel soft as your face"	33	No	Slight
Flour Ad- visory Bureau	"Six slices a day is the well-balanced way"	6	Yes	Good
Heinz	"More tomato in Heinz spaghetti hoops"	4	Yes	Adequate
Heinz	"The happiest sounds come from babies fed with Heinz"	8	No	Reasonable
Iron Jelloids	"Puts back the iron you're missing"	3	No	None
Haig Dimple (Pinch)	"Rarest Scotch whis- key" and "best- known bottle in the world"	13	No	Slight
Harvey's Bristol Cream	"The best sherry in the world"	5	No	Reasonable
Kellogg's Cornflakes	"The best to you each morning"	20	Partially	Slight
McKewan's Export Ale	"The best buy in beer"	11	No	Reasonable
Nabisco Shredded Wheat	"And I give them both the best with natural Shredded Wheat"	23	No	Reasonable
Omo	"The understains"	105	Partially	Reasonable
Player's Special Virginia	"The best Virginia cigarette in the world"	19	No	Slight

COMPANY	CLAIM	REPLY TIME (DAYS)	SUBSTAN-TIATION CON-FIRMED?	SUBSTAN-TIATION EFFORT
Radiant	"The whiter white"	No reply		
Rothmans King Size	"The best tobacco that money can buy"	7	No	Slight
Sanatogen Tonic wine	"Glowing goodness" for tiredness	28	No	Slight
Rank	"Litton's speaker sounds better than a live orchestra in your living room"	20	Partially	Good
Triumph cars	"Chosen by Concorde men"	14	No	Slight
Tynebrand pie fillings	"The fork test"	7	No	Good

brandy aboard these boats to console the fleeing ruler. Then the plan changed. Napoleon chose to surrender to the British, and the two ships that had been prepared for his escape were used by the British to convey Napoleon to his place of confinement. British officers traveling with Napoleon as escorts soon discovered the consignment of cognac, and as they drank it they referred to it as "the brandy of Napoleon" (perhaps in the same sense as one talks of "*la plume de ma tante*" or "those are Charles's socks").

Since the term "Napoleon Brandy" is the highest praise granted to cognac, it is understandable that the shrewd men at Courvoisier should exploit this historical coincidence to increase their sales. But no evidence was supplied to me to show that Napoleon either asked for this particular brand of cognac to be waiting for him, or that it was in any sense his favorite tipple amongst cognacs, both of which facts are surely implied by this phrase.

But this substantiation was certainly a lot more satisfactory than that proffered by Rothmans to prove that their king-size cigarettes contain "the best tobacco that money can buy." This apparently is so because "expert buyers in important world growing areas are under instructions by the company to buy the best tobaccos available with our special blend in mind." The idea that Rothmans can afford to have the tobacco auctions scoured, with no regard to cost, to buy tobacco destined for a cigarette retailing at by no means the highest price on the market seems an unlikely act of charity from a hard-nosed tobacco company.

Maybe Player's was being a little more honest in its reply to a similar question about the claim that John Player's Special is "the best Virginia cigarette in the world." They frankly admitted that their "advertising slogan comes within the realm of advertising puffery and such slogans are common to all consumer advertising." Of course, companies are entitled to a subjective opinion as to the merits of their product. One would have thought, however, that a large number of "blind tests" (when consumers don't know which brand is which) conducted by Player's before putting the brand on the market could have resolved this question.

Certainly, a declaration like "our reputation is a guarantee that we would not make any claim that we did not believe to be true" supplied by Harvey's of Bristol is no substitute for a few hard facts. The Harvey's superlative, "the best sherry in the world" has two things to support it: Harvey's Bristol Cream is the best-selling sherry in the world, as well as the most expensive. For these two things to be true it must also, in the view of Harvey's, be the best (otherwise the company would never manage to charge so much and sell such a quantity). There are several chinks in this defense, not the least being a sherry-tasting report in *The Times of London* (February 1972). The tasting was done by both amateurs and professionals. After a tasting of fourteen cream sherries which "included all the big names" and therefore presumably Harvey's Bristol Cream, Harvey's was not placed in the top three by either group. Harvey's specifically refused to comment on this sherry tasting, and a director of the company wrote to tell me that they had decided to terminate the correspondence.

Haig & Haig was no more convincing in its defense of the claim that its Dimple (Pinch) Scotch is "the rarest Scotch whiskey in the best-known bottle in the world." Haig's advertising agents wrote to inform me that "they [the claims] emanate from a company whose integrity and quality of products are beyond question and the superlative is used to convey a sincere belief." Sincere it may be, but that is all. Single-blend malts are clearly rarer than a nationally advertised brand of whiskey. And how an allegedly rarer whiskey can have "the best-known bottle in the world" defies both common sense and veracity.

A slightly different defense than the Haig/Harvey's—"Our word is our bond"—came from Kellogg's and Anadin. Their defense rested on a hairsplitting interpretation of their words. "Nothing acts faster than Anadin" was defended by arguing "that the slogan does not claim Anadin tablets act faster than any other painkiller; we do not say 'Anadin is the fastest painkiller" or "nothing acts as fast as Anadin': the message is just that you won't find a faster-acting painkiller than Anadin and it is so simply expressed, we don't believe anyone can be misled by it."

No evidence, even of the parity position of Anadin with other headache remedies, was provided. And some reports that I have heard (for example, a major drug company suggests that Alka-Seltzer—even though not promoted as a headache remedy in Britain—is in fact the fastest-acting headache remedy) make me doubt that Anadin would even be able to substantiate a parity claim.

Kellogg's also engaged in special pleading to defend its claim "The best to you each morning": "We maintain that Kellogg's Cornflakes offer 'the best to you each morning' because they lead all other *cornflakes* [my italics] in texture and flavour and because they are the only ones which are vitamin fortified." The fact is that they are the only brand of cornflakes in Britain. There are certainly some retailers' own brands, but Kellogg's real competition isn't these so much as *other cereals*, and it is against them that this claim needs to be measured.

While Kellogg's uses the fact that its cornflakes *are* vitamin-fortified, Nabisco, by contrast, boasts that its cereal *is not*. Substantiating the claim that "I give them both the best with natural Shredded Wheat," Nabisco spoke glowingly of the product's "natural goodness," and critically of their rivals, which are "synthetic or boosted with additives." Despite such enthusiasm for its product, the nutrition table that Nabisco supplied showed that even with all its "natural goodness" it was still short of thiamin, riboflavin and niacin, compared to Kellogg's.

Perhaps the most extraordinary way of attempting to substantiate a claim was Fairy Liquid, which simply denied that it was even making a claim. "Fairy Liquid," the company stated, "is a very mild product, and we believe that we are entitled to draw attention to that fact. The phrase quoted above ("hands that do dishes can feel soft as your face with mild, green Fairy Liquid")

61

is a vivid figurative way of doing this and *not a claim as such* [my italics], and our experience is that this is readily understood by most housewives." Knowing Procter & Gamble a little, I suspect that its arsenal of research must be full of evidence that this phrase *is* seen as a claim, and an effective claim at that. I do not believe that they would have spent millions of pounds over the last twelve years publicizing a phrase, however figurative, if it was not seen as a good solid claim for the product.

Colgate-Palmolive had a stronger defense for its claim for Colgate toothpaste with Gardol. Gardol was "not a mouthwash but a detergent with anti-enzyme properties." Most bad breath arose from the "oral cavity" (mouth?), and brushing with an efficient dental cream (namely Colgate with Gardol) was "necessary in order to remove the debris which forms the incubating medium for the flora responsible for creating malodour." A dental consultant confirmed to me that these statements were accurate. What wasn't confirmed was the statement in the Colgate promotion that "only Colgate can be relied on to do all this." Colgate has already been singled out in America for making claims which, though true, are not as unique to Colgate as Colgate implies. There seems no reason why the same sort of attack couldn't be made against Colgate in Britain.

Of the twenty-three advertisers, only the Flour Advisory Bureau provided the detailed chapter-and-verse substantiation that would satisfy a militant consumerist. They sent the exact information requested in the letter to substantiate the claim that "six slices a day is the well-balanced way" (which truth, I must admit, came as something of a surprise to me).

The evidence from Britain, and it could well be true of other European countries with apparently strict advertising controls, is that there is a large pile of dirty washing just waiting to be exposed by a little bit of ethical whistle blowing.

The media, as mentioned in the previous chapter, are already taking it upon themselves to challenge the claims of advertisers. And new consumer groups, like the Public Interest Research Centre under Charles Medawar, have sprung up to both enforce the laws and press for tougher ones.

Parliament, too, has not remained immune from all this. A bill making invalid the small print in guarantees has already become law. A Fair Trading Bill which would set up a Director of Fair

Trading is currently before Parliament. But though this bill creates no new consumer rights, the Director will have the power to request legislation to deal with any unfair trading practice. This means that his (or her) powers will greatly exceed those of the now defunct Consumer Council, which was axed by Tory Prime Minister Edward Heath in 1970 during a fit of ideological indignation at something that interfered with the notion of perfect competition. That this same gentleman, merely three years later, could set up a far tougher consumer watchdog demonstrates the power of the consumer revolution to make unwary politicians eat their words.

It is not just British politicians who are having to bow to this new wind of change. In 1964 the British Food Standards Committee recommended against compulsory open dating of fresh foods. Eight years later they reversed their recommendation, and one of their main reasons, according to the committee chairman, was the change of public attitudes in recent years.

This change also shows up in the bombshell recommendations of a House of Commons select committee investigating the Independent Broadcasting Authority. One of their recommendations went as follows: "The Authority should institute discussion programmes, for the service as a whole, to examine the claims of advertisers' products and to report the results of tests and to consider whether it might enable consumer associations which test products to be given time on the air to answer the claims of advertisers."

If this recommendation is carried out, Britain would only be a step away from the corrective advertising situation facing Madison Avenue, or, indeed, the situation that faced the two Japanese automobile companies Toyota and Nissan in June 1969. A story in the *New York Times* revealed that thousands of the cars sold in America and Japan were being secretly recalled. The Japanese press picked up this story (one more example of consumerism being exported from America) and expanded it by showing actual accidents that had been brought about by defects in these cars. The net result was a virtual order from the Japanese Diet to Toyota and Nissan to run advertisements admitting that they had sold the Japanese public defective cars. So Toyota had to admit in print that it had to recall 617,247 defective cars, and Nissan made a similar confession—over 395,300 cars.

A form of corrective advertising also exists in Sweden under the truth-and-nothing-but-the-truth Marketing Practices Act. Some Swedes actually believe that like suicide and free love, consumerism is a Swedish invention. Certainly the growth of state consumerism in Sweden rivals even the most vigorous phase of FTC and FDA activities.

The Swedish government has officially declared the 1970s to be "the decade of the consumer," and in the last ten years there have been no fewer than fourteen different royal commissions dealing with consumer policy. The last of these, in 1971, developed the doctrine of paternalistic consumerism that goes beyond anything Ralph Nader has proposed: "When appraising the household needs one cannot rely to any conclusive degree on the consumer's pretensions, expressed through the demand for products or in another manner. It is a well-known fact that in many significant respects—in matters of diet, for example—these preferences can be altogether too modest. As in other public sectors, the needs here must be formulated in terms of norms, based on the community's ambitions regarding the well-being of the individual."

Although this quotation loses something in the translation, it is still a radical exposition of a novel, almost Marxist, twist to consumerism. The crucial question is: How would the real needs of the consumer be discovered, if not by the exercise of his purchasing power in the marketplace (complete with the panoply of advertising)? The answer is that a benevolent Big Brother would look after the consumer's well-being: "Through household economy studies, and in other ways, one acquires in the consumer-policy work a good knowledge of the essential household problems, and then the investigation leads from that to the consideration and conducting of suitable measures."

Instead of letting the marketplace dictate to the business, the Swedish government believes the marketplace needs help—and so dictates to business itself, on behalf of the consumer. And, naturally, this means a close scrutiny of the admen. Indeed, there was even a half-serious forecast that a certain oil company would be asked to produce the tiger in the tank of the cars containing its particular gasoline. And woe betide them if they couldn't.

Consumerism, then, can be seen to be flourishing not only in America but in most of the world's advanced societies. And the greater the affluence, the more it flourishes. But there is one extra element in its growth which was touched upon in the first chapter and now needs expanding. It is the way in which business, by fighting consumerism, has unwittingly encouraged its growth.

Just why the initial response of business to consumer pressure should have been to behave like a cross between an ostrich and King Canute is the task of the next chapter to reveal.

The Businessmen Who Forgot They Were Consumers

●

"A day without advertising is like a day without sunshine." [John Hobson, chairman of the British Advertising Association]

"Only Shell gasoline in all the world is spelled 'S-H-E-L-L.' " "Only Bayer aspirin comes in the Bayer aspirin package." These caustic suggestions, from the creative director of a Texas advertising agency, are a common response to the new rules of making consumers part with their pay checks, a response which says that these new rules are an undeserved strait jacket worthy of either a hammer-and-sickle society or one of *Alice in Wonderland*'s absurdities. And certainly not appropriate for the United States, where not only what is good for General Motors is good for America but, to quote the head of J. Walter Thompson, "good business is good for the world, for the true business of the world is business." The implication here is that the good sense of Americans will prevent them from biting the hand that so graciously feeds them, and that when irritating ladies like consumer specialists Esther Peterson and Virginia Knauer are well and truly chased from the White House, all will be well.

It was in this spirit that a former chairman of General Foods urged the American Business Council in 1967 to fight "the rising tide of consumerism." Tides, of course, recede, and the businessmen relaxed their vigilance. At the end of 1971, after all the corporate harassment already described, Dr. Joe Juran (no friend of militant consumerism) went on record that American businessmen "think consumerism is going to walk by and not attack them." In 1972 an American Management Association study showed that one in two marketing executives *was not* concerned about the question of truth in advertising, and one in three expected no real change in his company's approach to advertising. All this, please note, after the furor described in Chapter Two.

One reason for business resistance to consumerism is that a substantial part of it is still sustained by the sort of argument advanced by the publisher of the now defunct *Look* magazine, Thomas Shepherd. In an address to the 44th annual meeting of the Soap and Detergent Association in January 1971, he used the phrase "disaster lobby" to describe the consumerists, calling them "the most dangerous men and women in America today." Not Black Panthers, not Weathermen, not the Southern Segregationalists, but the Naders, Knauers, Ribicoffs and Mosses of this world that imperil "the consumer freedom to live the way he wants and buy the things he wants without some Big Brother in Washington telling him he can't." The attentive audience was further informed by Mr. Shepherd that air and water pollution was less of a problem, and that the youth rebellion was just "a very small gaggle of young troublemakers who are sorely in need of an education, a spanking, and a bath." It may be that some of Mr. Shepherd's ferocity in attacking the foes of business was motivated by his need for business's support to save his ailing magazine. But, alas, no white knight on a charger arrived.

However, other patriots have taken up this same chant. Barton A. Cummings, chairman of the American Advertising Federation, told its 1973 conference that the critics of business were simply "controllists" out to muzzle the spirit of free enterprise. In almost the same words the chairman of Pepsi-Cola told an FTC inquiry into advertising, "I believe very honestly that advertising offers the highest silhouette, the most convenient aiming point for these people. But I think their ultimate target is free enterprise itself." After all, if you say "consumerism" fast enough and slur the middle syllables it *does* sound a bit like "communism."

In the first round of the confrontation between business and consumerism, such views were fairly widespread. For example, this is what happened when E. B. B. Weiss, executive vice-president of Doyle, Dane, Bernbach, wrote in 1968 to *Fortune*'s top 500 companies asking them: "Would you be willing to furnish me with an outline of just one project recently developed by your organization that represents a new step in implementing a broader policy of social responsibility?" Of these, 200 didn't even reply; 100 admitted they couldn't cite a recent project representing such a step; 100 cited projects that weren't recent; and 50 cited their minimum responsibility projects. Only 50 out of the 500 reported projects that could be said to represent any form of advanced concept of social responsibility. And even when a similar letter was sent out by Weiss to 300 companies in 1972, it hardly got a better response: still no more than one in ten had a significant social responsibility program to report.

This narrow sense of corporate responsibility (which makes a company vulnerable to consumerist pressures) showed up when the biggest of the *Fortune* 500, General Motors, was cross-examined by Federal Trade Commissioner Phillip Elman in 1969 (quoted in *Advertising Age*). H. Bridenstine of General Motors was asked, "What do you think of the limitations you have in your warranty?" Bridenstine replied, "Well, I think with the type of product we're talking about, Mr. Chairman, the limitations are reasonable." "Reasonable?" parried Elman. "That is correct, there must be an understanding" or an attempt to "eliminate argument with consumers." (Elman had earlier observed that what General Motors referred to as an "occasional mistake" represented 160,000 complaints from buyers of General Motors cars in 1968).

"Does any General Motors customer have a choice?" asked Elman, fastening on to the key issue. "Is it a take-it-or-leave-it basis?" After all, he continued, the consumer must buy a car "with the warranties they are given, and, contrary to what a lot of people believe, these warranties take away from the car-buyer's rights. They give him less than he would have without his warranty . . . the consumer has nothing to say about this understanding." But this was not true, insisted the man from General Motors: "He doesn't have to buy the car."

An equally telling example which shows the blinker type of obligation companies feel toward their consumers emerged when in December 1970 Ralph Nader asked 58 advertisers to substantiate to him as a private citizen their advertising claims; 55 of these 58 were either unwilling or unable to do so. The kinds of reasons they gave are illuminating (quoted in *Advertising Age*):

From Bristol-Meyers, those wonderful people who brought you Excedrin, bafflement: "We can recall no other inquiries like yours. In the past, consumers seemed not to have felt it necessary to obtain advertising clarification or substantiation from us."

From Whitehall Laboratories, which makes Anacin, the reassurance that the "product has been sold for many years to millions of satisfied users."

From Beecham's, which claims that "a major dental clinic's studies show that Macleans gets teeth whiter," the brush-off: "No company can afford the time and expense to detail its operations for every inquiring consumer."

This is a point of view which receives a lot of support among the men of Madison Avenue who turn out these questionable claims. That aging creative whiz kid Jerry Della Femina told the London Creative Circle in November 1971 that just as Hitler had chosen to persecute the gypsies, so the American government—in looking for something to persecute—had chosen advertising.

One could continue to relate the views of the not so silent majority of American advertisers and admen who have found their own Spiro Agnews. But even the more moderate admen greet the impact of consumerism with a good deal less than enthusiasm. Andrew Kershaw, president of Ogilvy & Mather, New York, has argued that the tighter controls will lead to *less* informative advertising. Since the tighter controls are a direct result of a lack of informative advertising, this seems a paradoxical outcome. But in Mr. Kershaw's view, the tighter the controls the greater the business uncertainty about what they can say; consequently we get more of the empty advertising, the sort of emotional stuff that says "We're very good" and "Gee, aren't we nice people" and "Look at this pretty package," and so on. As we shall see, this development is certainly a real danger. But one should also remember that the tighter controls which are being objected to are precisely the kind that will stop things like the Shell Platformate commercial from getting on the air, a commercial that was made by Mr. Kershaw's own advertising agency.

Apart from outright hostility to the very concept of consumerism, there are still a number of admen who believe that this particular plague hasn't yet spread farther than the East Coast Ivy League ghettos, and that it is still a minority cult blown up by the media. For instance, John Crichton, president of the American Association of Advertising Agencies, gleefully pointed out at a conference of British admen that out of over 200 million Americans, only 168 went to see the much-vaunted substantiation data on automobile claims that had been made public at all FTC offices. Whether this just proves that most consumers are happier to read about these data in newspaper reports than trudge along to FTC offices or whether it suggests that no one is really interested in the advertising substantiation issue is a matter to be discussed in a later chapter. Suffice it to say at this stage that the American advertising establishment has tended to support the latter interpretation of these facts.

Outside America, consumerism has had a similar initial reception from business. Most businessmen have simply echoed the antipathy shown by their American brethren and treated consumerism as something that is a menace to their business. "It undermines consumer confidence," said veteran businessman Sir Miles Thomas about *Which* in 1964, "and is a very bad factor in the present economic system." The response of the twenty-three British advertisers to the questions asked in my small study, reported in the previous chapter, doesn't suggest that this sort of attitude has disappeared: only a third of the companies gave any indication that a consumerist-style letter would be taken seriously.

One explanation for this curt dismissal of my questions comes from Arthur Shenfield, director of the International Institute for Economic Research. He represents a fair body of British businessmen in his view that consumerism is a short-term unpleasantness that must be suffered and will then wither away. "The roots of the consumerist movement," says Mr. Shenfield, "are ignorance and discontent. There will always be ignorance and there will always be discontent." Ergo, there will always be a consumerist movement? Not at all: "We shall not hear much of Mr. Nader in a few years' time" (and that remark was made a few years ago).

Equally revealing was the retort made by the head of the London office of Leo Burnett when a Canadian marketing professor had the temerity to call the agency's slogan for a cigarette a "lie." "There is nothing less useful than the ill-informed personal judgments of an overseas academic on individual British advertisement," snapped the managing director—a reply which would have carried more weight had not the advertiser (John Player) himself admitted that this claim for Player's Special cigarettes ("The best Virginia cigarette in the world") was to be regarded as no more than advertising puffery.

Others, however, have taken a rather more subtle approach to consumerism. While the American business establishment wants to counter consumerism by fighting back, the British business establishment is anxious to quickly institutionalize this new phenomenon—to part ranks, to let the wilder elements through (as they exhaust themselves in extremist follies), and then to so smother the more reasonable elements with respectability that they quite lose their nasty cutting edge. (If Ralph Nader were British, he would already have been offered a peerage of the realm.) Hence the plethora of bodies in Britain anxious to turn consumerism into as much a department of government as sanitation or sewage, so that by institutionalizing these new forces, they may be harmlessly neutralized. But this response to consumerism, though perhaps shrewder than the course of outright confrontation, still falls far short of welcoming consumerism with a red carpet.

Before one berates businessmen too soundly for their attitude, it is worth recollecting a point made in the first chapter, namely, that one factor behind the development of consumerism was that business was quite out of touch with consumers, and that one reason for being out of touch was that business had been supplied with a set of ideologies, like "perfect competition" and "profit is the only responsibility of a corporation," which were totally inappropriate for the second half of the twentieth century. In this sense, it is perhaps redundant to say that businessmen failed to respond to consumerism. If they hadn't been so removed from the forces that were gathering pace in the marketplace, the very phenomenon to which they were failing to respond would not have existed in the particular militant form it did.

Although it is instructive to watch the slow response to consumer pressure gathering momentum (now some companies are behaving as though consumerism were something they had themselves invented to serve the greater glory of mankind), the response was, however, far more hesitant in the beginning. Under a deluge of consumerist-style mudslinging, the instinct of business was to

71

engage in some P.R.-style campaign to scrape some of this mud off. This is an exercise in changing the image rather than the reality, perhaps because after fifteen years of brand-image advertising, businessmen find it difficult to tell the image from reality. Or if the reality is changed, it is certainly not enough to justify the image which is built upon it. This shows up clearly enough in the case of industrial pollution. The pressure here from consumerists has been that industry should replace the social capital it uses, like clean air, clean water and clean soil, when it makes its products. The public relations response is to spend money *not* on trying to accomplish this, but telling people that you're doing it, and to pat yourself on the back for being a front-line fighter against the pollution you've been churning out for years.

As a result, you have a situation where the American glossies show advertisements telling how Company X's selfless concern for its fellowmen is the only thing that makes being in business worthwhile; how Company Y is benefiting workers by the thousand by cleaning up the mess it made yesterday; how Company Z demonstrates that, in so many little but important ways, the products they produce help make your life worth living. Such wisdoms all receive crisp encapsulation in phrases like "men helping man," "progress through chemistry," "the discovery company," etc. However, Senator Henry Jackson recently estimated that if business is to clear up the air and water pollution it makes, it will have to spend $8 billion a year for the next five years. It is currently only spending a fifth of this rate. The missing four fifths is the gap between image and reality.

Despite this glaring credibility gap, corporate advertising is perhaps the fastest-growing type of advertising in America. After all, it may not be as effective as actually doing something about the problems created by business, but—by golly—it's a lot cheaper. So you find, for instance, all can people—American Can, Continental Can, National Can and Heekin Can—engaged in social-responsibility advertising programs, as well as steel companies like Bethlehem Steel and U.S. Steel, and oil companies like Mobil, Shell and Exxon.

In many cases these responses don't represent a substantial shift from the "what can we get away with" morality. It's just that one can get away with less. The animals are getting craftier, so we must hunt them more cunningly. And it is not so much that a change of heart occurs as that a new layer of make-up is applied to the old face. If finally that cracks, you still have one card left to play. The "it's not possible" syndrome.

"A degradable soft-drink container sounds like a fine idea," said Coca-Cola, "but it doesn't exist. And the chances are that one can't be made." Nonpolluting car engines are a fine idea, too. But according to the president of General Motors, "The technology does not exist—inside or outside the automobile industry—to meet the stringent emission levels in the specified time." Ford has even run television commercials criticizing the airbag—another fine idea that no one knows how to make safe enough for the public. (However, it is perhaps significant that Ford has changed its slogan from "Ford has a better idea" to "We listen better.")

The advertising industry, apart from coating us clients with a new layer of glossy paint (the varnished truth), has tried to do a similar restoration job on itself. Dan Seymour of J. Walter Thompson told an International Advertising Association conference that the blame for the rising hostility toward business lay with a "generation of faculty members" who taught the young that no business is good business. And this, according to Mr. Seymour, is a myth which has only been accepted because business hasn't fought back; hence the need for a mighty counterattack to reburnish the image of commerce. For the truth is that "we [in business and advertising] are among the few people who can go home every night knowing that we have done something to make the world better."

The accuracy of this viewpoint is not as important as whether or not it is credible in an environment where consumers, as we shall see, are becoming more and more hostile to advertising and less and less enthusiastic about the products it brings. In any event, Time Inc. has given away $600,000 worth of free space to let advertising agencies polish up their professional image. No doubt that was intended to answer Mr. Seymour's suggestion that "perhaps it's time we did for ourselves what we did for Smokey the Bear." But Smokey the Bear, advertising's most successful public-service campaign, is alas a blind alley. The late Nicholas Sanstag, who was a prominent member of the West Coast advertising anti-Establishment in the sixties, was once provoked to observe: "To explain to the advertising industry that public responsibility goes beyond Smokey the Bear is like trying to convince a ten-year-old that making love is more fun than a cone of chocolate ice cream."

To believe that a Smokey the Bear approach is the solution is to reveal not only a diminished sense of responsibility but also an overdeveloped belief in the power of commercial persuasion. Maybe the advertising men feel that if they don't show their belief in advertising, who will? That certainly helps to explain the statement published by the British Advertising Association about "the social contribution of advertising" (which was singularly ill received by the people it was designed to promote understanding with, namely, the various consumer organizations).

The French advertising industry has taken to the big spaces with even more vigor. A campaign of $1.7 million worth of media space was run to demonstrate the need for advertising. Underneath a photograph of various unidentified products in plain, unlabeled packages the copy says: "Choose! But what is it? What's it for? How much does it cost? Where can I buy it? Advertising tells you." It is, of course, the label on the package that tells you most of this, but the French approach does at least make a little more sense than the advertisement for the U.S. Freedom Foundation with the headline "Think of freedom as 11 kinds of chicken soup."

The pity of all this virtuous mouthing is that, as we shall see later, it is not so much the principle of "advertising in a free society" that is attracting the brickbats as the practice of it in a media-saturated one.

One more annoying advertisement to prove that advertisements aren't annoying is hardly a solution, for, as will become clearer when we look at the techniques of the advertising industry, it's these techniques that annoy. There is no evidence to date of any widespread attempt by the advertising industry on either side of the Atlantic to try to develop techniques that can raise sales without raising blood pressures. It is no more than a surface solution to tell the world all about the useful ways in which advertising people have applied their talents to solve the ills that beset our society if the next moment the commercials are back on the air and spoiling the evening's viewing.

Of course, it is good that a campaign by Campbell-Ewald tripled the number of applicants for police jobs in Detroit (unless, of course, you happened to be on the receiving end of a riot stick). Of course, it is good that seventy-five American P.R. and advertising agencies should band together to help a summer youth-opportunity project. Of course, it is good that the Women's Advertising Club in Chicago runs a campaign designed to help Spanish people to shop wisely for food. But probably some of the energies behind such projects are fueled by a guilty conscience. (One reason, for example, why more policemen are needed in Detroit is that the number of drug users has increased. And one reason for this increase, according to the commissioner of the Food and Drug Administration, is the "tremendous wave of advertising over the media, especially TV, in which the consumer feels that in reaching for a pill, she is getting a panacea for all ills".)

Apart from desperate efforts to prove how virtuous they were, some agencies tried to purge themselves of vice by eliminating anything from their advertisements that might provoke a consumerist challenge. In January 1972 the *Wall Street Journal* reported that "A number of copywriters say that they are under orders to keep virtually all specific claims out of their work, no matter how strong the supporting evidence appears." One advertising trade paper even reported: "Latest ad gimmick—no-claim advertising" (which takes us back to Shell's exclusive way of spelling its name). But in fact, occupying newspaper space and television time with empty, useless, pap-filled ads may generate as much consumer hostility as the misleading informational advertisements they replace. If people want reliable, believable information from advertisements, then to provide them with an avalanche of adjectival puffery is no way to win forgiveness.

The next stage on the route from responding to consumerism with rhetoric and feeble gestures, and responding to it with serious reform, is the halfway house of conspicuously making an effort. In the period January 1970 to June 1971, for instance, more than a dozen major companies appointed top-level officers to new positions solely concerned with consumer affairs. Mostly they were dubbed "vice-president" (as at Pan Am and RCA). But at Swift & Company the even more imposing title of "Director of Public Responsibility" was screwed onto the office door.

Chrysler, Ford and General Motors all announced that each of their customers had access to a special "Man in Detroit" who could deal with the complaints that the Big Three's dealers had not dealt with. For the Chicago area alone, General Motors had a staff of twenty specially trained girls to answer the phones and to try and get an answer back to the complainant within twenty-four hours. Ford had its "We listen better" monitoring system.

One interesting analysis of the first eight thousand letters Ford received was that only 34 percent contained complaints. When Ford tried a similar approach using a telephone bar at the Chicago Car Show, where people could record their complaints, they got fourteen hours of solid obscenities on their tape.

A similar feedback technique was tried by the Travellers Insurance Companies after it found out that 47 percent of people thought insurance companies wouldn't talk straight to people. You can now call, toll-free, the Travellers Office of Consumer Information to get any sort of information you like about insurance, without any selling. And Avis has run advertisements inviting the public to "yell if Avis does something wrong. You'll get it out of your system. And we'll get it out of ours," with an invitation to call the Avis Hot Line, again toll-free. (Maybe the whole thing is something cooked up by old Ma Bell.)

In one sense, of course, these are no more than what Nader might call "Band-Aid solutions." Shouldn't car companies cut down on the things that cause complaints and not just hire pretty little voices to pour oil on troubled waters? Shouldn't insurance companies give better value for money, and less small print, and simplify claims procedures rather than make token gestures of free telephone calls?

Perhaps sensing these questions, corporations began to adopt a more self-critical tone in their corporate advertisements. (After all, everyone who knows the parable of the prodigal son will remember that heaven is always open to sinners who repent.) So instead of claiming perfection, advertisers started to admit imperfection, attributing it to human error. In the fall of 1972 the General Motors corporate campaign (instead of just trumpeting about GM: Mark of Excellence) coyly admitted: "We spend millions of dollars a year on inspection, quality control and reliability . . . but it's a real world we work in and there can be mistakes." More than that, General Motors actually distributed 2.5 million books to schoolchildren explaining how and why the automobile pollutes. Here, in twenty lavishly produced pages, Professor Clean tells the story of Harry Hydrocarbon, Pete Particulate Matter, Ollie Oxide of Nitrogen and other dirty villains against which the mighty resources of General Motors were now deployed.

Ford, too, has been among those who have bared their breast in public. "On September 13th, Ford Motor Company and 6,035

Ford and Lincoln Mercury dealers announced a new goal: no unhappy owners," said the new-look corporate ads in 1972. And carried away with the apparently novel idea of removing consumer dissatisfaction from its products, Henry Ford II formed a Committee for Constructive Consumerism made up of nineteen prominent industrialists.

Self-criticism even began to be heard along Madison Avenue. In the September 25 issue of *Advertising Age* in 1972, for instance, of the thirteen major stories on the front cover, six featured criticisms of advertising. Four of these six criticisms came from people within the industry.

Again, one can compare the statement in 1970 by the president of Ogilvy & Mather arguing *against* tighter ad controls (page 69) with the 1972 statement by the chairman of the same agency arguing *for* stricter controls of television advertising: "Today, the overcommercialization of television has become an abomination, an affront to us all." Even the National Association of Broadcasters, who as we saw in Chapter Two were hardly in the vanguard of consumerism, decided it was right to reduce by 25 percent the time allowed on weekend programs to advertise to children.

If the companies who engaged in these gestures believe that this "tokenism" will propitiate the consumer gods, they are mistaken. Once a company starts to offer these responses for the consumer at a modest level, sooner or later the consumer will demand the response at a much higher level. And all these attempts, including the multifold claims of social responsibility, to show a response to consumer pressure merely create a greater consumer pressure for further response.

Perhaps it's only when you give the impression in black and white that you don't pollute, that you're responsible toward the environment, that you're sensitive to consumer needs, that consumers really demand higher performance from you. It was, after all, only *after* the Potlach Timber Company ran an advertisement saying it spent a small fortune keeping the Clearwater River clear, but actually used in that advertisement a photograph of the river several miles *upstream* from the Potlach factory, that this timber company found itself under great environmental pressure. (In this sense, the exaggerations of the advertisers can be said to have done the consumerists and pollution cause a good turn.)

The spur that finally gets businessmen and advertisers to do something is usually fear. "Let's face the facts," said the president of Norman, Craig & Kummel, "we are scared. Make no mistake, we are." In the words of the chairman of the Missouri Air Pollution Control Commission, "They moan and gripe, but in the end they comply"—and not just because of tougher laws; it's actually starting to get through to the big corporations that if you can't beat them, you'd better join them.

Some companies have already learned that to ignore the things consumerists are paying attention to can cost more money than the expense of paying attention to them. But they have learned it the hard way. In 1970 the giant Unilever combine's fourth-quarter results in Britain were "adversely affected" by the ban on cyclamates. In 1966, after Ralph Nader had finished with Corvair, General Motors found that sales of the Corvair were reduced by 89 percent of the 1965 level.

Pressure from the shareholders has had an influence, too, for seeing companies torn apart in public has changed a lot of shareholders' views about what "responsibility" means. In 1973 a poll by the Opinion Research Corporation showed that 65 percent of American stockholders thought that business should play an active role in the war on poverty. This means, in the short term, smaller dividends.

Perhaps the most vivid demonstration of the way in which shareholder power can force a major rethink on a corporation was not Campaign GM, but the case of the Distillers Corporation and thalidomide children. Distillers, which had marketed thalidomide in Britain, was forced by the pressure on the directors by major shareholders to increase by *six times* the amount of compensation offered to thalidomide children. The London *Sunday Times* described this as "the most remarkable instance ever recorded of shareholders' influence on the affairs of a major company."

It is not only among their owners that large corporations are finding a change of heart. Their retail outlets, which are far closer to the marketplace, are sending some fairly frightening shock waves into head offices. Retailers have started to apply the techniques of the media—namely, attacking manufacturers in the consumer cause to win public support. In New York, for instance, one supermarket chain stopped stocking Lady Scott tissues when Scott Paper Company began placing 175 tissues in a box which previously contained 200. And in the wilds of West Texas, a car dealer told Chrysler (and released the news to the nation's news-papers) that he wouldn't sell the Chrysler Colt and Cricket sub-compacts because he felt that they weren't safe. The dealer, Dewey Ray, actually equipped his salesmen with copies of Ralph Nader's book *What To Do With Your Bad Car* in an approach to selling cars that might flabbergast Dale Carnegie but seems to work with today's consumer. And it is to these consumers, last but not least, that corporations are now giving baffled, almost wounded glances. For at last their crude measuring sensors are starting to pick up some of the key grumbles among their customers. General Foods now conducts more than thirty thousand consumer interviews a year. The Hoover Company has tripled its market-research budget in three years. Even Detroit has started to listen better. "There are a growing number of people," observed the marketing director of Chevrolet, almost regretfully, "who look on a car as they would a well-engineered lawn mower."

Some businessmen are beginning to realize that their deafness to consumerism was the phenomenon that created the environment in which consumerism could flourish. Only now have they started to accept the philosophy of some of the flower children which businessmen scorned and derided: "American businessmen must accept that humane and ethical values are going to have to be corporate products just as much as what we manufacture." The speaker wasn't Charles Reich or J. K. Galbraith but the president of Hunt-Wesson Foods. Hunt-Wesson's support for Forest Service tree planting in three national "children's forests" is an example of the new approach.

To be sure, the lion hasn't lain down with the lamb in a hurry. (By and large, the greatest response of a company to consumerism is only when the company is carried screaming into the second half of the twentieth century.) As in the case of Union Carbide, which kicked and struggled for almost ten years before they agreed to cut their emission of sulfur-dioxide gas by 70 percent in West Virginia, and this was only after a determined grass-roots campaign by the people who had to breathe all this in (one stack down there used to spew out a third as much particulate matter as all of New York in a year). Following this example, the Alyeska Pipeline Service Company, which wanted to build a 789-mile pipeline in Alaska, felt it necessary to present twenty-nine volumes of pro-posals of how it was going to minimize the mess it would create.

79

Boulders which aid fish runs would not be displaced. Construction timetables would avoid lambing and high-salt-lick seasons for sheep. Simulated pipelines would test the response of caribou and reindeer. But even all this hasn't been enough to win approval from the environmentalists.

Another industry which has responded only after coming under the consumerist lash has been the cereal industry. And the response is interesting because the companies seem to have realized a little more quickly than the automobile manufacturers which way the wind was blowing.

In March 1971 *Marketing Communications* reported: "To a company the major ready-to-eat cereals marketing men told M/C that impact from the [Robert] Choate contentions had been modest at most." But according to *Advertising Age,* "In the wake of Mr. Choate's attack on breakfast cereals, sales of the cereals that he had rated high in nutritional value had soared, while some of the cereals at the bottom of his list had fallen." Apparently sales of the top five cereals Choate had singled out had gone up by 85 percent compared to a similar period before the attack. For the marketing men to admit that nutritional values *were* useful selling points would be to admit their failure to detect this prior to Mr. Choate's attack. But in their new advertising they quickly started to put their money where the consumer's mouth now was.

Kellogg's Cornflakes (no. 38 out of the 60 cereals on the Choate index) ran ads after Choate's attack showing a bowl of cereal with milk and fruit with a caption saying that everything from niacin to riboflavin was inside those golden flakes. And Rice Krispies (no. 39) informed its readers that rice is "one of the world's most nourishing grains." In fact, of the 40 dry cereals which Choate described in July 1970 as being overadvertised and undernutritious, 26 had been dramatically reformulated by November 1971. Not content with upgrading the products, some of these companies then undertook a nutritional penance. Kellogg's, for instance, paid for television spots which merely explained the importance of nutrition to children with the sotto voce payoff, "presented in the interests of good nutrition by Kellogg's."

Nutrition has become as much an accepted thing as motherhood. Miles Laboratories, for instance, became another advertiser to run public-service spots about the importance of vitamins. And Del Monte even relabeled their canned fruit to give total nutritional disclosure. It revealed that a one-cup portion of cling peaches, for instance, contained 190 calories, 1 gram of protein, no fat and 50 grams of carbohydrate. After displaying the various daily requirements of the nutritional elements in the can, it went on to issue a nutritional disclaimer of the apparently healthful things that cling peaches didn't contain.

Whole industries that once would have fought the federal regulatory bodies tooth and nail began to submit meekly to scrutiny. For instance, the Cosmetic Toiletries and Fragrance Association initiated a move whereby industry members would *volunteer* formula information to the FDA. They did this not out of a sudden love of the FDA, but because they had observed what had happened to other industries under the consumerist lash.

A parallel example of a sensible response only after a hefty kick in the backside is that of Schweppes and its nonreturnable bottles in Britain. Nonreturnable bottles aren't exactly the pinup products of the ecologists. In America, Coca-Cola has switched back to returnables, and Canada Dry has set up centers to recycle not only its own glass, but any other glass the public brings to it. The first response of Schweppes' chairman to a campaign by the Friends of the Earth trying to get Schweppes to follow these examples was: "It's a bit of nonsense. We're not proposing to do any more than we have done." But after six weeks, after thousands of Schweppes bottles had been dumped on its doorsteps by the Friends of the Earth, and their shareholders had been lobbied (all this well covered on television and in the press), only then did Schweppes make a sensible response. They met with the head of the Friends of the Earth, and together they agreed to ask the government to look into the environmental effects of packaging.

The question that arises from all this is why it takes the members of the advertising and business community so long to reach positions where they are able to regard consumerism not as a new formulation of the Red menace, but—at the very least—as an important new ingredient in the marketing mix. Why this charade of denial, discrediting of critics, blaming it on other, P.R. phony response, and then, only as a last resort when all else had failed, a full and sensible response.

Is consumerism really a threat to the profits of a company? In the nineteenth century that's what industry thought of trade unionism. But little by little, out of the dialectical clash a new

81

synthesis emerged. And by and large, the most successful companies in the long term have been those which most reorientated their thinking toward the workers.

This reorientation will probably happen much more quickly in the case of consumerism, because while there are very few employers who also have a role as employees, all businessmen have a role in life as consumers. And as consumers they are changing in the sort of ways that the following chapter will describe. It is only the conditioned reflexes of how businessmen "should" behave that is holding them back. And the evidence I have seen is that it is atrophying the younger managers less and less.

But even if business *didn't* have this dual role, it would still find that it was more profitable to put on the butter generously rather than skimp with margarine. A British study of fifteen large companies and their responsibilities to shareholders, employees and the community concluded that in the long run, rather than a battle which leads to a conflict of interests, there was a balance that led to an eventual sharing of interests (*Company Boards: Their Responsibilities to Shareholders, Employees and the Community*, by Shenfield, P.E.P. [Political and Economic Planning] pamphlet). Socially responsible corporate behavior and long-run profit maximization can be more or less equivalent, *provided* social institutions and the pressures of the market are sufficiently strong.

There is, moreover, quite a lot of supporting evidence for this point of view. In a seminar given in London in 1969, Ralph Nader cited a study in New York State which showed that the lowest-polluting companies were also the most profitable. So, far from being the smell of progress, pollution may well be the stench of decay. And Whirlpool, which has stuck its neck out to respond to consumerism, finds that its reward is not only in heaven. In the last three years, Whirlpool's rate-of-sale increase has tripled that of the industry average.

In Britain one finds that those companies which are best at dealing with consumer complaints and have the most "generous" policies of accepting returned merchandise are also the ones which are the most profitable, for example Marks & Spencers, Mothercare, Selfridges, Tesco, Sainsburys. But the ones who are less generous, such as British Leyland Motor Corporation, have less impressive profits.

Maybe the best example of how consumerism can actually provide companies with new marketing opportunities that make everybody happy comes from the food industry and concerns the issues of open dating and unit pricing. The life cycle of this issue has been quite normal. First, newspapers exposed the practice of hiding the freshness of packaged foods behind secret codes and so making consumers buy items whose shelf life had expired. This was met by a manufacturers' response that it wasn't their fault, but the fault of the retailers. The retailers said that if consumers knew the relative freshness of the various food items on their shelves, the less fresh ones (though still perfectly fresh) would never sell. And open dating, like anything from less pollution in the air to safer cars, would—of course—push prices up. But the media replied that if open dating worked for fresh food, like vegetables and meat, which have nature's own version of date stamping (called mold), why shouldn't it work for packaged food? Why should the supermarket escape a discipline that the greengrocer and the butcher and the fishmonger had to submit to?

The argument was irresistible to supermarkets trying to win new customers. Only nine months after the original charges in Congress about secret dating had sparked off such a furor, *Business Week* could report that "food chains had discovered a hot new marketing tool." They were talking not about plastic daffodils or trading stamps but about open dating. By the end of 1971, unit pricing was available in virtually every urban area of America.

The same is already happening with unit pricing. Even individual companies are trying to use it as a way of showing consumers they're really on their side. Purex ran an advertisement in New York with the headline "Why you should shop an ounce at a time," with the copy offering all purchasers of "Sweetheart line washing-up liquid" a handy little pocket calculator to tell the housewife at a glance the cost per ounce of an item.

The evidence is that these new consumerist approaches to marketing really do pay. One food chain in America using both open dating and unit pricing is Pathmark. Its per-store average of $7 million in annual sales volume is double that of its competitors. One reason why was revealed by an executive of Jewel Supermarkets, another food chain using these same techniques: "We have found that making the dates available eliminated the customers' feeling that they had to check the dates . . . as with unit pricing, we are simply enhancing the reputation of the store."

But what happens when a similar exposé of secret dating is made in England? The head of Lyons Groceries (one of the companies which didn't use open dating) gets on television to trot out the standard—and unconvincing—arguments about it being impossible and that it is up to the shops to control their stock properly. It won't, however, come as a surprise to those who invest in shares to learn which was the first food store to go over to open dating: Marks & Spencers, a company with a return on its capital that makes most British managers turn green.

Some critics regard all such responses by companies with cynicism. Michael Harrington, author of *The Other America,* observed that businessmen "have acquired a conscience at the precise moment when . . . there is money to be made in doing good." But in a capitalist society, is that such a bad reason? The real charge against businessmen is not that their motives are commercial, but that they took so long to realize that "doing good" and profitability were not natural enemies.

Why businessmen had to prolong the period of conflict with consumers, why indeed they had to engage in conflict at all, is a question that goes right to the heart of the impasse that business and advertising now face. Guided by advertising men who have very often no more idea of the consumer than what they read in tabulated columns in their market-research reports, the blind have entrusted themselves to the blind. And the revolutionary changes among consumers in the last decade, changes that ensure that Mrs. 1974 resembles her predecessor of ten years ago in name only, have been ignored, overlooked or forgotten.

It is to this changing consumer that our attention now turns.

Birth of the New Consumer: The Child Is Father of the Man

●

"Plus ça change, plus c'est la même chose."

Propelled by such brave sentiments, the advertising industry has leapt boldly into the second half of the twentieth century. As they say in the advertisements, "unbelievable but true."

Who would have thought that a profession which claimed to be equipped with the tools to see into the souls of men would not be able to foresee the crumbling of the concept of authority and predict the development of consumerism as a result? And that having failed in this respect, it would also fail to predict that consumerism would be a real force in the marketplace and not just a matter of housewives wanting 10 cents off instead of a premium of plastic roses? And finally, who would have thought that once consumerism did turn out to be a man-eating shark and not just a shoal of intellectual angel fish, admen would also fail to help their clients market their products in this new situation?

But as the previous chapter endeavored to show, there was no intelligent response from the majority of businessmen or advertising agencies to consumerism until it became a threat to the survival of their business (as opposed to a simple opportunity to make more profits). Then, having been forced to change, they tended to talk about "consumerism" as though it were their own private invention.

Businessmen were perhaps less guilty for their conduct in all this than the admen for theirs. The agencies, after all, were meant to be the advisers to business, keeping in touch with changes in the marketplace. But this, as the evidence shows, they lamentably failed to do.

The basic reason behind admen's wearying challenge and non-response to consumerism is distressingly simple. Okay, they say, Mrs. 1970 isn't Mrs. 1950. But in your heart you know she's still white, willing and able to buy your goodies. In short, the same as ever, just wearing a new wrapping. Okay, they say, Mrs. 1970 has a different shell than Mrs. 1950. But probe beneath that oh-so-shallow surface and you'll find a heart that beats with the same old rhythm. But there's a fly in the martini. The sociologists have noticed it. The economists have noticed it. Even the politicians have noted it. It's the wealth and information explosions of the last twenty years. And it's such a taken-for-granted phenomenon that one tends to forget the enormous implications packed within that rather humdrum term.

First, a few statistics. Advanced societies are now doubling their output of goods and services about every ten to fifteen years. Even in a so-called depressed economy like Britain, the GNP grew 87 percent between 1960 and 1970, and 127 percent in the United States. So perhaps the most truthful political slogan for some time was Harold Macmillan's "You've never had it so good."

In the thirteen years from 1947 to 1960 the real income of the average employee both in Europe and the United States rose by almost as much as it had in the entire preceding half-century. In dollars of 1970 purchasing power, in 1929 only one in six American households earned over $7,500. By 1970 more than one household in two had this income.

This explosion of wealth, then, is one that differs not only in degree but in direction from previous sudden increases in wealth (like the Spanish discovery of gold in the New World). Previous increases of wealth had been characterized by much for the few. This one was characterized by more for the many. We are in fact talking about the first mass affluent society.

Never before have so many people lived so far above the subsistence level. Of course there is poverty, but the poor are now a minority, not a majority. Of course there are old-age pensioners, people with large families and small family allowances, unskilled immigrants, and so on and so forth, but the plain fact is that the average worker has a wealth today which only fifteen years ago was a well-to-do middle-class ideal.

It is perhaps unfair to use America, the world's most affluent society, as an example of current affluence. So let us use instead what *Time* magazine dubbed "the oldest newly submerging nation," Britain.

Fifteen years ago the most widely owned domestic appliance was the vacuum cleaner. Five out of ten homes had one. Now nine out of ten homes have one.

Fifteen years ago only four out of ten homes had a television set. Now over nine out of ten homes have one.

Then, only one home in six had a car. Now almost four homes in six have a car.

Then, only one home in five had a washing machine. Now four out of five homes have a washing machine.

Then, only one home in fourteen had a refrigerator. Now eleven homes in fourteen have a refrigerator.

Then, only one home in twenty had central heating; now over eight homes in twenty have central heating.

Then, only one home in ten had a hairdryer; now six homes in ten have a hairdryer.

And in those fifteen years, while the total population increased by 8 percent, the number of people taking a holiday abroad increased by 87 percent. In fact, now at the end of this fifteen-year period, the majority of all homes in Britain has a car, a TV set, a vacuum cleaner, a refrigerator, an electric iron, a washing machine, a sewing machine and an electric hairdryer.

All this has happened in backward Britain, the country which had the lowest GNP increase of any European country for the last decade and also the lowest increase in consumer goods. But despite the comparatively slow growth of affluence, the absolute change has been tremendous.

How this increase of wealth has altered people's attitudes to wealth itself is a story for a later chapter. Suffice it to say, at this point, that companies have got so used to seeing their sales graphs rising that they have forgotten to look beyond the graph, to the full meaning of that ever-skyward-pointing thin red line.

Another change which is not fully appreciated is the information explosion. This has two dimensions: formal and informal. Looking at the formal level of information, otherwise known as education, what is true for wealth is also true for this. Ours is the first mass-educated society. And this means both a larger proportion at school and a larger proportion going on to higher education.

In the 1920s there were twenty thousand people in Britain in higher education; in 1970 there were almost half a million. In 1963, only one third of the 21–29 age group had a higher education. But by 1971, half as many children again—or 55 percent—were staying on in school beyond graduation age to get a higher education.

If you make the assumption that one year in a British school equals one year in an American school, it becomes obvious that higher education is even more widespread in the United States. According to Professor George Katona (*Aspirations and Affluence*), almost every second American youngster aged eighteen, boy or girl, is in college, while in Europe only every tenth youngster of that age goes to school full time. Fifty years ago this tremendous gap didn't exist. Then, in America, only 2 percent of the college-age population actually went to college. But the gap came about because America has recently treated education as her biggest growth industry (particularly after being edged out by Sputnik).

It has been estimated that by the middle of this decade, one third of all American homes will contain a graduate. But even in Britain the average girl leaving school has spent 25 percent more time at school than her mother, as well as having been educated by superior education techniques. There is no simpler measure of educational efficiency, of course, but school is obviously not what it was in *Tom Brown's Schooldays*: "A grey tedium relieved by moments of brutality." Pestalozzi, Froebel, Herbart, Freud, Adler, Dewey, Montessori and even Dr. Arnold have seen to that. From the marketing and advertising standpoint, all this means that every year the proportion of well-educated consumers in the marketplace is rising, and the proportion of spending power at their disposal is rising too.

But as every schoolboy knows, his schoolteacher isn't his greatest teacher: it's television that really wears the mortarboard. According to Dr. Gerald Looney of the University of Arizona, the average American pre-kindergarten child spends 64 percent of his waking hours watching television. And the French journalist Jean Jacques Servan-Schreiber has calculated that a child in Europe sees about 2,000 hours of television before he goes to school. Then when he gets to school he pays almost as much attention to the television set as to the teacher. The British Bureau of Television Advertising estimates that the average viewer watches television for more than 18 hours a week—over 2.5 hours every day.

With homework, and so on, you might think this would be lower for schoolchildren. But according to Gilbert Youth Research, the figures for high school students in America is on the average 2 hours 13 minutes of television a day, plus 1 hour 45 minutes of radio (plus 36 minutes of reading a newspaper). By the time a child leaves school, aged sixteen, he has probably spent 2,000 more hours in front of the small screen than in front of the teacher. And he'll go on watching. By the age of forty-five he will have seen about 50,000 hours of television (which, if taken at one sitting would mean over 6 years of solid watching).

What the new consumer sees on the screen in all that time does something to him that never happened to the pre-television consumer. Tiny tots of two and three learn things from *Sesame Street* that years ago they would not have learned until they went to kindergarten. It's part of a phenomenon that may eventually replace the school system as we know it today. In the words of Ivan D. Illich (*Deschooling Society*): "A major illusion on which the school system rests is that most learning is the result of teaching. Teaching, it is true, may contribute to certain kinds of learning under certain circumstances. But most people acquired most of their knowledge outside school, and in school only in so far as school . . . has become their place of confinement during an increasing part of their lives." Television is a new kind of knowledge outside school. World series, Cup finals, moon landings, cowboys and Indians, the news from Biafra by satellite . . . all the clichés come true and the classroom has become the world. Dr. Richard Feinbloom of Harvard University has argued that parents are now "turning their children over to the television set." And the set in this sense becomes the father of the child.

Alvin Toffler in *Future Shock* calculates that "at the rate at which knowledge is growing, by the time a child born today graduates from college, the amount of knowledge in the world will be four times as great. And by the time that same child is fifty years old it will be thirty times as great, and 97 percent of everything known in the world will have been learned since the time he was born."

Marshall McLuhan has argued that it is not the content of the electronic medium which is the most shattering thing about it, but the way that content is delivered: instantly, with a low-definition, high-involvement picture. By thus extending the viewer's senses, by letting him be part of the program, by being present ten thousand miles away at the battle front in Vietnam, or on the baseball mound at Shea Stadium, or on the lawn of the White House, or on the surface of the moon, he is educated, aroused, stimulated—McLuhan uses the word "massaged"—in a way that the pre-television consumer never was.

The media-developed sophistication is, of course, in a different dimension from IQ tests. In Britain, for example, it is not so much that it makes more people understand what the term "sterling area" means (which only 9 percent of the lower-income group does). Even people in this group have their senses exercised in a way that makes them able (and eager) to cope with more sets of stimuli than their predecessors. According to experiments done by the U.S. Navy, for example, a child of four-and-a-half today (i.e., who hasn't yet been to school) has the awareness of a seven-year-old of twenty years ago.

Expressing the equation of change in a mathematical sense, it is simply that $W \times I = ?$, where Wealth represents the wealth explosion and I the information explosion. The unpredictability of the interaction between W and I tend to make the consequences not only unexpected but also so profound that many people in business and advertising find them unacceptable. It is this, perhaps, as well as sheer short-sighted orneriness, which explains their non-response to the new consumer—for what is inconceivable is by definition unacceptable. If you take many of the consequences of $W \times I$ separately, they appear harmless and of the nothing-but-good-can-come-out-of-it variety, yet when multiplied together, these changes pull the rug from under many of the assumptions of marketing and advertising.

The first consequence of $W \times I$ which has both this effect and this reaction is its impact on what used to be called the "generation gap." If you talk to a businessman about the "younger generation," the typical response is that it differs only in degree and not in principle from earlier younger generations. The "I-was-young-once" syndrome."

There are still many who dispute the principle of the generation gap being anything more than a kind of intellectual acne, curable by moderate doses of hygiene and common sense. To return to Mr. Thomas Shepherd, formerly of *Look* magazine: "The big difference between 1970 and 1940 is that today's youngsters are being listened to seriously by adults. When we were children, the adults were too smart to pay attention to us." But according to anthropologists like Margaret Mead, we are witnessing the start of a totally new cultural pattern. The particular events that trigger off revolts among students in China, England, Pakistan, Japan, Holland, the United States and New Guinea are not enough, she argues, to explain the revolts themselves. Mead attributes them to two new things: the emergence of a world community, which is really the product of the information explosion, and the fact that this community has emerged during the lifetime of one generation (which is really Alvin Toffler's point about the speeded-up rate of change).

The result is that the generation gap becomes a great divide that may be unbridgeable. For the parental generation, life has to be lived in an environment where the eternal verities, such as Rolls-Royce or the British Empire, are crumbling left, right and center. One is obliged to quote from Miss Mead once more to find the very words which describe their state of mind: "Today, everyone born and bred before World War II is an immigrant in time—as his forebears were in space—struggling to grapple with the unfamiliar conditions of life in a new era." The immigrant in space, *par excellence*, were those who emigrated to America. "As the children of the pioneers had no access to the memories which could still move their parents to tears, the young today cannot share their parents' response to events which deeply moved them in the past."

And in this so important sense, the generation gap of 1970 is very different from the one that split the oh-so-darling flappers from their Harris-tweeded parents in the 1930s. "Today, nowhere in the world are there elders who know what their children know . . . in the past there were always some elders who knew more than any children in terms of experience of having grown up within a cultural system. Today there are none. In this sense, we must recognize that we have no descendants as our children have no forebears." This final quotation from Margaret Mead should be engraved in the foyer of every advertising agency in the affluent society of the world. For in just a few words it shows up the futility of trying to get your message across the generation gap by yelling louder or frugging faster. And it implies a development of an entirely new sort of consumer.

The end of the myth that elders are wiser will have consequences that will be restructuring the marketplace, as well as life itself, for many years to come. For when the ancestral wisdom goes into the ashcan, it takes with it many of the component parts of the society that worshiped at the temple of its forefathers. A society without traditions is a totally new sort of phenomenon, and the mass media fill the vacuum to become the new arbiters. By communicating globally any new development by the avant garde, the media diffuse and outdate innovation at electronic speed. The result of this is that the avant garde—be they pop musicians or shirt designers—have to search more relentlessly for another innovation (thus ensuring that the rate of change increases in direct proportion to the rate at which change itself increases).

Alvin Toffler uses the term "future shock" to describe the disease that is brought about by this accelerating rate of change on those who are unable to deal with it. Adaption to it requires developing an approach of temporariness, for by living too firmly in the present one becomes embedded in the past. In terms of physical distance most people have managed to make the mental adaption. We have adjusted to the fact that New York is closer to people in London than York itself was to Victorian Londoners. What we have yet to recognize in its entirety is that next year is closer to us than next month was to the Victorians. We have yet to develop in our lives, let alone in our marketing, a full recognition of how a process of continual change leads to the development of what Toffler calls "a system of temporary encounters" (think about what that means for brand loyalty). He quotes a coed at Fort Lauderdale who was taking part in the annual Easter migration to the Florida beaches for what amounts to an orgy in the sand, giving as one reason for permissiveness: "Frankly, you'll never see these people again." This is just a nonacademic way of saying what Dr. Richard Farson, dean of the California Institute of the Arts, said in an article in *Saturday Review*: "The only people who can live successfully in tomorrow's world are those who accept and enjoy temporary systems."

A philosophy which states that it is better to build on sand than on rock because rock anchors you too firmly turns upside down both the old values of small-town American and the ethos of the Protestant work ethic implicit in the liberal concept of the capital state.

In *The Greening of America*, Charles Reich analyzes the development of these new values—one may almost call them *counter-values* because they are in almost every degree the antithesis of the ancien regime's beliefs. Using the term "Consciousness III" to describe the new world view that has developed out of the wealth and information explosions outlined earlier, Reich observes: "In the world that now exists, a life of surfing *is* possible, not as an escape from work, a recreation or a phase, but as a *life* if one chooses. The fact that this choice is actually available is a truth that the younger generation knows and the older generation cannot know."

To what extent can one say that the Consciousness III syndrome is accepted by a significant part of either British or American society? First of all, the section on which it has the strongest hold is without doubt the under-twenty-fives—46 percent of American society and 38 percent of British society. The majority of the under-twenty-fives are students. Taking the American population as a whole, one person in four is a student, and one student in six is in college. The normal assumption is that the attitudes of Consciousness III are only accepted by the college population, and by a tiny minority at that. But this, in fact, is just one of those pieces of conventional wisdom that trip off the tongues of the Spiro Agnews of his world. As for the college population itself, Daniel Yankelovich reported in *Fortune* that in 1970, 40 percent of them—2.5 million Americans—had already adopted a Consciousness III point of view.

And the adoption of Consciousness III attitudes can be shown to be not just a campus phenomenon. The strikes at the General Motors factory at Lordstown, Ohio, is a practical demonstration that you don't have to have majored in philosophy to reject the work style that your father and grandfather so meekly accepted.

The Lordstown rebellion has an extra significance in that these young workers were not only well educated, they were also well off. "My take-home pay is one hundred and forty dollars a week and sometimes two hundred and sixty a week, and that makes GM a gold mine," said one young worker there.

To some critics of youth the fact that these prosperous workers are the ones who are dropping out demonstrates "modern youth's" ingratitude and selfishness. And when this criticism is applied specifically to the upper classes it is to suggest, always with an undertone of venom, that this "dropping out" is no more than a fashionable activity akin to scuba diving off Nassau or making the Grand Tour of Europe. What these critics overlook is that those who are saying "No" are the very people who have been born with a silver spoon in their mouth, who have been fattened and cherished by all that money can buy, whose career patterns—be they on the factory floor or in the executive suite—stretch glowingly and enticingly ahead. Previous dropouts, going back as far as the Protestant fundamentalists in seventeenth-century England, were not those who had everything and decided it wasn't for them. They were generally those who did not have everything and in that position decided to try to build their own utopias. It is this that gives the real significance to the development of Consciousness III in America, for the fact that the typical dropout is an Ivy League WASP carries with it the suggestion that the more educated (in every sense) the young generation becomes and the greater the amount of wealth and abundance that is showered on it, the higher will be the proportion of those who reject all this and instead decide to explore the possibilities of life outside the framework of their parents' lives.

But it is not only on the other side of the generation gap that a new consumer is emerging. The forty-year-old mother may not look as revolutionary as her freaked-out teen-age son, but she is part of a revolution whose short-term effects may be even greater than her son's remodeling of our society. Mrs. 1974 may not have been reared by television, but she has still seen 40,000 hours of it. She may not be as transformed as her son by the wealth explosion, but she is still fundamentally changed. And so she is starting to question her role in society in a deeper, more serious way than bra-burning with Women's Lib. She is finding that she can no longer fit into her mother's shoes. But what can she put on instead?

That the question is even being asked is a serious development for any company trying to persuade housewives to loosen their purse strings. If the supermarket shoppers were to be in any degree infected by the new heresies, if they started to reject in any significant number the role that society asks them to perform, then those companies whose fortunes are linked to that role need to change gear very fast indeed.

For a short term, at least, the advertising and marketing industries can breathe a sigh of relief that a significant number of housewives seem, on the surface at least, to be following in their mother's footsteps with satisfactory diligence. The adoption of this traditional role may not, however, be an entirely voluntary matter. There is a whole web of cultural assumptions that leaves Mrs. 1974 trapped like a fly on a sticky filament. These assumptions state two things: first, that a woman's place is in the home, and second, that this home is a place for routine, unimaginative, not mentally stimulating activities by a creature who understands neither her husband's career nor her children's future (as soon as they are old enough to escape from the apron strings).

This is not just an assumption of Western culture. In Japan, though the housewives' consumer groups are more active than in any advanced society, they do not challenge the traditional role of women. For them her place is still in the home. And probably, if a public-opinion poll had asked Japanese housewives to complete the sentence "My family most appreciate me when . . ." 90 percent would have given an answer that had to do with cooking, just as their American soul partners did in 1971. These ladies revealed, in a poll for Virginia Slim cigarettes, that baby hadn't come such a long way, after all. It showed that most American women saw themselves as "home bodies" and considered housekeeping and child raising "more rewarding than having a job." This confirmed a report (*Sociological Review*, 1965) "Buying and Selling: A Study in the Sociology of Distribution," that 56 percent of housewives in Britain thought their task of providing food and looking after the home "compared reasonably" with the interest and satisfaction of their husbands' jobs.

But both these studies, which do something to confirm the sales manager's belief that Women's Lib is just a lot of nonsense confined to overeducated and undersexed Amazons residing within six miles of Times Square, contain the seeds of doubt. In the British survey, almost a third of the housewives thought they got a worse deal than their husbands, and in the American survey, over 40 percent said they would welcome a broader role in society. Both these figures point to tension even within the traditional role. What keeps it, for the most part, under control, is the tremendous effect of all the years of having been told that the woman's place is in the home. Who, after all, learns domestic science at school (when in the end 41 percent of the boys will be involved in cooking when

95

they become husbands)? Who gets strange looks from her school-mates and often her parents if she is "interested in books" (isn't that just for plain, fat girls who aren't popular?), and so on and so forth.

Paradoxically, Women's Libbers probably reinforce the dominance of the traditional role when they write as though work for money is the only worthy alternative. Work is certainly a popular escape route from being chained to the sink, but for the very reason that nearly all the militant ladies are also career women, they can hardly help but write in a way which justifies their desertion of the hearth for the office. In short, by going out of the home to fulfill themselves, these ladies are endorsing the cultural assumption that there is nothing really worthwhile a woman can do by staying at home.

Once a young girl has left school and started to act as her traditional role commands, she is subjected to a bombardment of reinforcing propaganda to ensure that she doesn't stray from the path that others have chosen for her. Chief among them are the well-phrased words of the advertisers. It is probably naïve to blame businessmen for trying to profit from a situation which they had no direct hand in creating, as, for example, Betty Friedan does when she says, "Somehow, somewhere, someone must have figured out that women would buy more things if they were kept in the under-used, nameless-yearning-to-get-rid-of state of being housewives."

Ms. Friedan is driven to this conclusion by the absurd reports of the motivation researchers of how to sell to women (whereas, in fact, all that was being sold was the motivation researchers themselves). In *The Feminine Mystique* she described a survey reporting in the mid-fifties that today's woman "finds in housework a medium of expression for her femininity and her individuality." To support this, the job of advertising, apart from stamping out that growing evil influence, the graduate career woman, is to justify her menial task by building up her role as "the protector of the family—the killer of millions of microbes and germs . . . emphasize her kingpin role in the family, help her be an expert rather than a menial worker . . ." The results of all this would be that "losing herself in her work—surrounded by all the implements, creams, powders, soaps—she forgets for a time how soon she will have to re-do the task . . . she seizes the moment of completion of a task as a moment of pleasure as if she had just finished a masterpiece of art to stand as a monument to her credit forever."

For a woman stuck in the rut of her traditional role, feeling incompetent without having a satisfying concept of competence to move toward, this is highly provocative. She knows that shining the furniture with lemon-scented polish does no more than get the furniture clean. But worse than that, there is in the corner of her living room a small screen which tells her that all the cleaning, polishing, sweeping, mending that she does is trivial and peripheral compared to what goes on in the big wide outside world. And that small screen is, of course, the television set.

It is bad enough that aging poets and blind visionaries can write such absurdities (the filing cabinets of the biggest agencies are crammed with thousands more examples of such statements). The tragedy is that businessmen have taken their soothsayers seriously. The effect of this propaganda on some traditional housewives must have been to restrict them to their traditional role, but on others it may have helped to push them over the threshold toward what Helena Z. Lopata's *Occupation: Housewife* has dubbed the "uncrystallized housewife." For the "traditional housewife"—relatively uneducated, homebound in a noncreative sense, often deprived of anyone to be close to, not very successful with her children, and feeling, as a result of all this, rather inadequate—it is reality itself which provides the core of tension. But for the uncrystallized housewife it is the gap between reality and the ideal that is more disturbing. Marriage, with the arrival of children, means a considerable tension between the horizons she scanned in her youth and the limited vistas that the cultural norms now allow her. Two changes within the home itself have particularly contributed to the frustration that this uncrystallized woman feels.

First, as Philippe Ariès observed in *Centuries of Childhood*, the location of the home in relation to society has changed. Before the eighteenth century the home was indeed an open house, a center of social life. It was only in the eighteenth century that homes became closed-off, private places of family residence and not places of public meeting as well. It may be, as Marshall McLuhan has suggested, that it was the invention of printing which introduced the concept of reading to oneself, and with it the concept of privacy in the home. Prior to this invention, "reading" meant listening to

97

manuscript books being read aloud, a public activity. In this context it is worth noting that television has had an influence on developing group activity (not private like a book or public like a manuscript) which is reflected in the rise of open-plan apartments.

Besides the withdrawal of the home (and hence the housewife) from society, the other change in the home's function concerns not leisure but work. Prior to industrialization, the home was also the workplace for almost all adults, and it still is in agricultural societies. But industry removed the workplace from the home and transferred it to the factory. The result is that ever since then, woman has lost an empire without finding a suitable substitute role. It is this loss of a sense of usefulness which strikes particularly hard at our uncrystallized woman, for not only is she out of a job but industry is forever finding new ways to put her out of work at home. Canned, frozen and dehydrated foods that can be prepared in twenty painless minutes, ready-to-wear clothes that need no handsewing, stockings that need no darning, shirts that need no ironing, floors that need no polishing, detergents that obviate scrubbing, not to mention a battery of polishers, whisks, mixers and blenders to complete the life of ease. And the pill even takes away the unwanted extra children that added on ten years to the childrearing phase of her life (where she at least had a role which she could understand and appreciate).

It would be foolish to argue that the uncrystallized woman wishes to revert to the domestic bondage that these mechanical servants save her from. But their presence underscores the emptiness that waits for the woman who uses them. The industrial society can only provide the housewife with freedom from; it does not provide her with freedom to. It is a simple case of "cultural lag," the sociologist's term for a condition in which the reality of a social situation outdistances the cultural norm that structures that society.

Possibly the rise of sexual permissiveness is an attempt by the uncrystallized woman to prove her usefulness to man, confronted by the redundancy of her traditional role. The eighteenth-century woman had no need to wiggle her fanny as a reason for her existence; she not only had a large family to rear, she had a home to run and her husband's work to help with. But if you rob a woman of all her traditional roles, what is left to her but a nonreproductive use of her reproductive organs? In this, as in several of the partial responses to her problem, she may only be digging herself deeper into the rut because the probable net result is that the last bastion of her role, the institution of marriage, begins to shake. In some ways this may not be a bad thing, but within the current assumptions, that probably still leaves our uncrystallized lady no closer to crystallization. And it certainly leaves her with the worst deal. For example, Desmond Morris reported in *The Naked Ape* that while by the age of forty 26 percent of married women will have engaged in extramarital copulation, 50 percent of married men will have done so.

If sex isn't the best way an uncrystallized woman can fill the vacuum within herself, what is left to her? The main way, of course, is to go to work.

The sad irony of a housewife becoming a meaningful person only by leaving her home is something that probably escape the working mothers who clock in beside their men every day. And one third of all wives are now clocking in (compared to one tenth a decade ago). By 1979 there will be 50 percent more women working than there were in 1959 (even though the overall size of the work force will only have increased by 16 percent), and two thirds of these women will be married (average age: around forty). Being through with bringing up children, they are vigorously reacting against the prospect of being thrown onto the scrap heap.

Perhaps even more interesting than the high percentage of married women who work is the percentage of married women who don't work but would like to. Viola Klein in *Britain's Married Women Workers* found that 46 percent of the housewives she interviewed who didn't work either full or part time wished they did. What keeps many of these women at home against their wishes are their husband's wishes and their worry about the effect on the children of leaving home. This is more a worry for Europeans than for Americans, twice as many of whom approve of a mother of children at school going out to work. Certainly, the evidence is that the woman who takes on a passive, homebound role "because of the children" is misguided. The Swedish sociologist P. Teller concludes that "the decisive factor is probably the quality of the contact between parents and the children rather than the quantity." One half of the crystallized woman knows this. But the other half is still vulnerable to the sort of remark made to a career woman: "I sup-

pose you won't mind when your baby doesn't recognize you"
(quoted in the Political and Economic Planning publication *Sex,
Career and the Family*).

The kind of woman who makes this remark may refuse to separate herself from her child by sending herself to work. But strangely
enough, she is generally far less unhappy to send the child away
to boarding school for an equal, and some might argue, more harmful separation. Separating parent and child for educational reasons
is accepted within the British cultural norm, but parental and child
separation for work reasons is less accepted. And the argument
about the effect on the child is really an alibi for a confused,
unfocused feeling that she is not fully able to express.

The confusion about her role shows through clearly if you probe
and find out why a woman works. Very often she will talk first
about the financial advantages, but the evidence is that money is as
much an alibi for working as children are an alibi for staying at
home. Viola Klein found that about the same proportion of upper-
class as lower-class married women did full-time work. If money
were really the main reason, one would expect the figure for the
lower-class housewives to be higher than the figure for the upper-
class housewives (after all, the latter has about double the household income of the former). And this point was confirmed by
Professor Katona's study from America showing that the higher her
education, the more a married woman plans to go on working,
even though the husband's higher-than-average income makes it
increasingly unnecessary.

If it is not money that lures housewives from the hearth, it is also
certainly not the sort of job they'll be going to. Only 13 percent in
Viola Klein's survey mentioned "enjoy work/doing a useful job"
as their reason, which is hardly surprising if you look at the jobs
that are available for married women: they tend to be the least
well paid and the least attractive. Added to which is the fact that
women generally get a raw deal in employment compared to men.
For instance, half of all male workers in Britain are in a pension
program, as compared to a quarter of all women workers.

In fact, by going out to work, our uncrystallized housewife will
be exposing herself to a set of cross tensions as unsatisfying as if
she had stayed at home. As the jobs she will accept indicate, she's
desperate. She is caught like a nut in a nutcracker between a whole
series of cultural norms, and whatever solution she adopts she will

not find peace of mind. She feels that to go out to work is to some extent an indication that as a woman she is failing as a housewife, but if she stays at home she feels that she still can't be a success as a housewife.

It is only among what Helena Lopata calls "the multidimensional woman" that any successful reduction of these tensions is found. What the multidimensional woman is endeavoring to do is sort out the confusion that results from a situation in which the traditional role becomes clearly impossible and in which there is no alternative role available. She tries an exploratory and experimental role. It is not, incidentally, what any of the militant Women's Libbers would regard as "liberated," for liberation in a multidimensional sense begins at home. Free contraception, abortion on demand and twenty-four-hour nurseries—the key planks in the Women's Lib platform—may be worthwhile demands, but they are demands in a different dimension, for unless the housewife has a role to expand into, answering these demands only removes inconveniences in her life, and thus makes her more aware than ever of its true emptiness.

One of the earlier breeding grounds of multidimensional woman was the suburbs of America in the late fifties and early sixties. Young marrieds migrated away from the traditional controls on their behavior and started to look for like-minded neighbors to solve the problems that left their uncrystallized sisters so baffled. Mrs. Lopata's statistics on the reduced influence of the mother in this new suburban situation is revealing. Whereas half the working housewives and two fifths of urban housewives referred to their mothers as a source of knowledge after entrance into the home-making world, only one quarter of suburban housewives saw their mothers as such a helpful influence. "Their grandmother had tradition," observes Lopata of runaway marrieds; "these revolutionaries only have each other."

In a structural sense, the multidimensional role that these women created for themselves resembled both their lives before marriage and also the lives lived by upper-class women in European society. Many of the current ways of multidimensional middle-class society are adapted from the upper-class European cultural norm. Their dinner parties, their afternoons of sports, the evenings of conversation and music where husbands and wives both have a role, contrast with the sex-segregated leisure life in lower-class cultures. Men going out to the bars and leaving the wives behind is a very common but simple example. (In this sense, for all its low-brow connotations, an evening spent with the whole family watching television is a real descendant of the upper-class Victorian family sitting around the piano while the eldest daughter sang Schubert.)

From this shift to women being merely home-based instead of being totally homebound come some fairly profound consequences. The first of these is a changed position vis-à-vis the husband within the family unit. The multidimensional woman drops the traditional role, i.e., she was primarily the one who prepared the bread paid for by the breadwinner. One of the implicit assumptions that held this belief in place was that in a money-based economy, an occupation that doesn't result in earning money has neither value nor status. Since housewifery is an occupation for which no pecuniary reward is made (until, ironically, divorce breaks up the household), it was kept in the traditional role in a defensive and cringing posture. The multidimensional woman has gone past this stage. Even taking Mrs. Lopata's sample as a whole (consisting of all three types of housewives—the traditional, the uncrystallized, the multidimensional), two thirds of the men assisted in making the purchases needed to run the house. And this figure will increase as the traditional role of the housewife who purchases all the household goods withers away.

The consequence of this development means that housewifery, instead of being the housewife's raison d'être, becomes no more than a chore which is to be jointly shared by all members of the family. And once housewifery has been put in its proper place, the things that interest the housewife will no longer come in little plastic boxes with plastic roses attached. So the advertising and marketing processes, unless they change tack, will be thrust into a peripheral position, offering the consumer things which are no longer of importance to her. But it does introduce a practical consequence of the existence of the multidimensional woman: a change of relationship not only with the breadwinner but also with the bread shop.

Shopping, for a traditional woman, was a very different exercise than it is either for the multidimensional or uncrystallized woman. Personal contacts with the shopkeeper and elaborate examination of the merchandise were ways of both fulfilling the roles of, and showing expertise in, being a housewife. But in looking at the supermarket explosion, the changes in housewives that make the very concept of supermarket shopping acceptable are forgotten.

Supermarkets turn the bulk of routine shopping into as rapid an exercise of household management as possible. Its attraction is less time spent shopping and not just a smaller shopping bill; though item for item she saves, the open-shelf structure of the supermarket encourages her to buy things she would otherwise not have thought of, so the total bill is probably larger. Incidentally, the growth of the supermarket would have been impossible without the growth of a feeling of competence by Mrs. 1974, for in going to a traditional shop she could easily ask the shopkeeper for advice, but in going to a supermarket she has to make the decision herself: something that would not have been possible until education and the media provided her with a feeling of self-confidence.

These consequences of developments away from the traditional role as a housewife are clearly of some importance to marketing companies. But a phenomenon of even wider significance emerges when one considers how the multidimensional wife will regard the one-dimensional life of her husband. By "one-dimensional" one is talking of the career-orientated pre-Consciousness III man (to revert to Reich's phraseology). The findings of Drs. R. and J. Pahl in *Managers and Their Wives* is that the multidimensional wife could be the Trojan Horse that starts to move her husband away from the rat race and toward Consciousness III. While their husbands are churning away ("They have internalized an ideology of self-coercion," say the Pahls), the wives are not under the same pressure to accept the logic that seems so natural and automatic to their husbands. The Pahls found, for a start, that the majority of wives did not wish their children to follow in father's footsteps. The "professional life," where there is time free for wife and children, and no need to rock around the clock in Ulcer Gulch, is what these mothers want for their children. If the husbands don't have this feeling, it is because they are so trapped by the rhythm of their lives that they are unable to ask themselves the question as to whether the long hours of toil are really worth it. But the Pahls' conclusion for those who earn their living by trying to persuade the rats to scramble up one more rung of their ladder is a little chilling. "Basically, we consider that what we may be detecting is the beginning of a middle-class reaction against competition."

The Pahls' study was concentrated on the middle classes, but their conclusions show that the stirrings of Consciousness III are not restricted to those who wear flower headbands. It may well be that this group has acted as a catalyst, and that though the majority of housewives don't want to go all the way to living in a commune of free love, they regard the solution of the hippies as being no more than an extremist version of the point of view they are beginning to hold themselves.

The fact that there are different degrees and speeds of development by consumers in this direction should not allow one to miss the central point—that there *is* development and that most of the development is in this one direction.

As consumers, the under-twenty-fives and the younger housewives are not the children of their parents. "As consumers" is, of course, shorthand for saying "in their role of consuming the goods and using services created by society." And if the consumer changes, so will her consumption. It is this changed attitude to consumption that forms the next step in our study.

When the Standard of Living Stops Being the Standard of Life

●

Uncertainty + Greed = Growth. It may not be quite as neat as $e = mc^2$, but strip the affluent society of its jargon and this is the magic formula which gives it its energy. An apparently limitless appetite for more goods and services leads to an endlessly upward spiral of consumption, where even a stop-go economy is more go than stop. But though the spiral is ever upward, there is always the specter that the golden times will end. Economists have worked out all sorts of basic rhythms for the economy, sophisticating the seven-fat-year, seven-lean-year econometric model that sufficed for the Israelites.

Thus, despite the continual sunshine, there's always the prospect of a rainy day. So, besides increasing consumption, there is also a need for savings. Savings return to the economic system as investment and stoke once more the factory furnaces, which will spew out yet more products for the ever-open mouths.

This is more than a theory. This is how the economies of all advanced Western societies have functioned since World War II. The question which has to be faced by any businessman planning his marketing effort over the next decade is whether this equation of growth can still operate. Or will the new breed of consumers that is emerging with new attitudes toward business call a halt to the golden years when the GNP grew like Topsy?

Part of the answer to this question lies in the key assumptions about the theory of limitless growth. The first of these was well expressed by Robert G. Merton in *Social Theory and Social Structure*: "In the American Dream there is no final stopping point. At each income level, Americans want just about 25 percent more (but, of course, this 'just a bit more' continues to operate once it is obtained). The family, school, and work place . . . join to provide the discipline required if an individual is to retain intact a goal that remains illusively beyond reach." But for this, prosperity would be its own gravedigger. However, as long as satisfaction of existing wants stimulates the arrival of new ones rather than sates them, consumers will become hungrier through feeding.

Ensuring the continuance of this apparently unnatural situation is the job, according to the theory, of the marketing industry. "Demand management" is the phrase used by J. K. Galbraith to describe this function: "In the absence of massive and artful persuasion," he writes in *The New Industrial State*, "increasing abundance might well have reduced the interest of people in acquiring more goods." And so "advertising and its related arts helps to develop the kind of man the logic of the industrial state requires—one that reliably spends his income and works reliably because he's always in need of more." One reason why this is possible, according to Galbraith, is that the further a man is removed from the basic physical needs—like hunger and shelter—the more he's open to persuasion as to what he should buy. Status, for instance, means little to the starving African anxious to get some dried milk, but it may mean a lot more to the film starlet buying a fabulous mink stole. Conspicuous consumption, in fact, is the result of all these pressures. And America, as the most advanced—or degenerate—consumer society, is the one where consumption is the most conspicuous. Conspicuous consumption, after all, has been practiced by many societies to enable one member of that society to indicate to another their relative relationships. In some parts of Africa and India, women still wear all their wealth as jewelry, and so enable strangers to assess their importance very quickly.

The role of products in establishing the relative position of people in society is far more necessary in a migrant, rootless society like America than in a static European society. Income in itself can't be a status symbol, because earnings are secret, so people, in the limitless-growth theory, inform each other of their income (and hence their importance) by their purchase of goods and services.

It is possible to argue from this that the increased interclass movements in European society, and the increased physical mobility of individuals, will make this sort of "signaling" as important in Europe in the next decade as it is in America, and so make its consumption equally conspicuous. This is the unqualified conclusion (albeit one based on quite different reasoning) made by *Advertising in the Twenty-first Century* (a book which, incidentally, doesn't use the word "consumer" once). "Over the next fifty years," say the British authors, "the upward spiral of 'keeping up with the Joneses' is bound to increase in intensity as it has in the United States. When the position is reached where almost everyone has a car, washing machine, refrigerator, etc., the ownership of the latest model will become supreme." And one reason for this, according to another exponent of the limitless-growth theory, Ronald Brech of Unilever (*Britain 1984*), is that "basically a man is uncertain of himself, and to bolster up his own esteem he must win the esteem of others." And this, according to the model, conspicuous consumption provides.

Brech's model of the theory has two interesting variations. First it recognizes that "temporary satiation" may develop. People may suddenly get fed up with keeping up with the Joneses; a "maladjustment" occurs and they decide to stay where they are. But after a couple of years the basic urges return and the economy starts growing. According to Brech, "temporary satiation" occurred in Britain in the latter half of the nineteenth century. One of the pressures that sets the economy moving again, according to this analysis, is that the product graduates from satisfying mere material needs to satisfying psychological ones, and by answering the needs of the psyche the GNP once more rolls healthily forward.

These are the assumptions on which our economy is founded. And they are, as I shall argue, founded on sand, for they are part of a theory of economic growth which did not include a prediction of the consequences of its own success. The first of the consequences that it failed to foresee was that the economic boom would not only put cars in our hands, it would put exhaust fumes in our throats and send suds foaming out of our taps. And with our affluence it would give us so much effluent than even rivers could spontaneously ignite. Even when identified, the problem

107

might be insurmountable. For instance, if we are to avoid gassing ourselves with exhaust fumes, we might have to resort to car engines that use so much fuel that we render ourselves powerless with an energy crisis.

America, of course, the society that is first with everything, leads the way in per capita output of pollution. But because of the sheer size of the country, it can absorb more, before the effect shows, than can the more densely peopled countries like Britain, Germany and Japan. For example, though the amount of lead discharged by exhausts from American cars is thirty-two times greater than the amount discharged by British cars, as the American land mass is thirty-eight times the size of the British one, the lead levels in Britain per square mile are 18 percent higher than in America. It's for this kind of reason that the first country to have brought in low-lead gas by law was car-saturated West Germany, not open-space America.

Something which one tends to regard as being an exclusively American phenomenon is photochemical smog, caused by the action of sunlight on exhaust fumes and sulfur dioxide. But it is already developing in Europe. A team of scientists from the Atomic Energy Research Establishment at Harwell found in the depths of the English countryside a level of photochemical smog that was as much as the daily average for smog-choked Southern California.

A great transport innovation of the affluent society is the airplane, yet before one even reaches the age of the sonic boom with the Concorde, it's clear that there's more to air travel than bustling hostesses pouring out the duty-free. Dr. J. B. Large of the Institute of Sound and Vibration Research has shown that nearly 30 percent of the population in Britain suffers from what the scientists call "aircraft-noise nuisance." The exact meaning of this neutral-sounding phrase was put into context by the professor of theoretical aeronautics at London University. He calculated that a Boeing 707 jet makes as much noise on takeoff *as if every person in the world shouted simultaneously as loudly as they could.* It will come as no surprise, then, that the study by Bauer and Greyser (to which reference will be made in Chapter Seven) found "noise" the most annoying everyday event faced by Americans.

The position has probably now been reached, on both sides of the Atlantic, that if the affluent society were offered to its beneficiaries with the type of "full disclosure" that Naderites demand for advertising (no holding back of information about possible harmful side effects, etc.) it is doubtful that it would find many customers.

The impact of the new environment on the new consumer has been manifold. At one level is a distortion of humans themselves. "You cannot defile the air and the environment," wrote Phillipa Pullar in the London *Times*, "without defiling the people as well, without frustrating them, lowering their performance, their literacy, their humour, their means of communication." This viewpoint is confirmed by a Swedish government study carried out by Dr. Hans Lohman on mental health. He found that between 25 to 40 percent of Swedes needed psychiatric treatment as a direct result of the kind of life the affluent society obliged them to lead.

The reaction of humans to this desecration of themselves and their environment is revealing. Because if people *are* being raped, they're certainly not taking it lying down. Where once schoolboys collected sticklebacks in empty jars and that was an end of the matter, the children of today's environment think differently. A change in the *level* of sticklebacks could be due to that big factory up river. The London *Sunday Times* certainly found a massive interest by young children in their environment. A total of 10,000 children took part in an experiment arranged by this newspaper to discover the pollution level in British waterways. One of the conclusions which stood out, according to the director of the environmental agency which analyzed the replies, was that "children care about pollution."

A TV program on pollution, arranged by the German Study Group for System Research which used a new participatory technique, found that 70 percent of the three thousand adult viewers who took part would be prepared to pay 10 percent more in taxes to deal with pollution.

In America, in 1965, only 22 percent of city residents thought pollution a serious problem. In 1971 they had increased to 49 percent, and 76 percent of these blamed industry for it. (That doesn't just mean the power station with its belching stack, it also means the factory which churns out products with power from that belching stack.)

This backlash—biting the hand that has fed you with chromium-plated goodies—has one more side to it. It is the realization that affluent societies are using up more than their fair share of the world's resources, the so-called spaceship earth concept. With 6 percent of the world's population, America currently uses 40 percent of the world's minerals and spews out half the world's industrial pollution. If we really *are* knocking at the limits of the world's natural resources, then one man's growth becomes another man's starvation.

And so a mixture of the discomforts of affluence, plus a guilty conscience about having too large a slice of the cake, is starting to change attitudes to economic growth in a way that the theory of limitless growth never predicted.

First, contrary to the theory and for the first time in the history of capitalism, economic growth is no longer an end in itself, and not just because of the arguments reviewed earlier, for now, when vintage Cambridge dons like F. R. Leavis write to *The Times* deploring the fact that nothing matters that "can't be weighed, statistically handled, and if necessary priced," *now* people listen. (The learned doctor's central argument, interestingly enough, was that the mere fact that the economic growth of the European Economic Community surpassed that of Britain was, by itself, no reason for joining the EEC.) Even President Nixon has started to climb aboard the bandwagon (proof positive that it really is a bandwagon). Commenting on the 50 percent forecast growth in America's GNP by 1980, he queried (in the State of the Union message): "Does this mean we will be 50 percent richer in a real sense, 50 percent better off, 50 percent happier?"

In fact, the march of economic progress was fired not so much by a vision of plenty as by a fear of poverty. The world at the end of the eighteenth century, when life was mean, brutish and short, inspired men to build engines and develop new sciences to lift man from the mire of desolation and the scourge of disease. In such a situation growth *did* mean a better life. Hence the GNP worship which declares that except ye have an expanding economy, ye have nothing. Now, however, the very notion of GNP as a measurement of the health of a nation is increasingly under suspicion. After all, if you look at the automobile industry, you find a parasitic subeconomy adding $5 billion to the GNP every year (thus equaling almost the entire GNP of Brazil) made up of things like accident repairs, spare parts, traffic-accident lawyers— in short, from the malfunctions of the main motor industry. Yet

110

all this appears on the national balance sheet as profit, not loss. Again, if air pollution makes it necessary to repaint a house, calling in a painter and buying paint boosts the GNP.

But even if the GNP could be recast as a measure of real growth, several voices are now asking what's so advantageous about being on a growth escalator that's always moving upward. As J. K. Galbraith has observed: "In a rational life style, some people could find contentment working modestly and then sitting by the street—and talking, thinking, drawing, painting, scribbling or making love a suitably discreet way. None of these requires an expanding economy." And, so the argument goes, if this sounds like life in the despised mañanadoms of the Middle or Far East, maybe they know something that the Puritan ethic doesn't. It's an argument that doesn't have dropouts as its supporters. The Dreyfus Third Century Fund, for instance, has announced that it is prepared to sacrifice some degree of growth in its investment policy in order to support companies that have done work "to improve the quality of life in the United States."

Of course, all those who would like to see the end of the belching smokestacks don't accept as fully as Dreyfus and Galbraith the ultimate extension of their arguments. No doubt there are still many on whom the full realization has not yet dawned that you can't have your cake and still eat it. Whatever the inconsistencies, the essential *feeling* about the new consumer which separates him from his predecessors remains: that more no longer equals better.

"Industrial nations," declared Henry Ford II to the Harvard Business School in December 1969, "have come far enough down the road to affluence to recognize that more goods do not necessarily mean more happiness. They recognize that more goods also mean more junk." This from the son of the man who really invented the affluent society back in 1914, when he introduced an eight-hour day in his factory and at the same time doubled wages, giving the worker *leisure* (hitherto an upper-class luxury) and a new sort of consumer choice.

All these fifty or so years, the mere act of production has been a virtue. Now the mere act of production starts to look like a vice. Perhaps it won't be long before Presidents boast that the GNP went *down* 2 percent last year (to tumultuous applause). Extraordinary though it seems, this has already started to happen in some states in America. Delaware, for instance, has enacted into law a measure that will ban new industry along the state's entire hundred-mile coastline. This means going without $758 million of investment and several thousand jobs; in effect, a lower standard of living (measured by traditional criteria) than if the development occurred. But if we are to fully grasp the full extent of the change of heart by consumers, the argument needs to be taken still further, for it is not just that we have got tummy ache from eating too many strawberries, or that we are conscience-stricken about being the only family on the street to live on a diet of strawberries. The comforts of affluence—strawberries every day—also have the effect of sating the appetite.

The theory of limitless growth doesn't, of course, allow for the achievement of affluence to reduce the demand for further affluence. But consider the case of a fifteen-year-old boy given by Alvin Toffler in *Future Shock*. If, as in most advanced societies, the GNP has doubled since he was a baby, this means he is *literally* surrounded by twice as many things man-made at the age of fifteen than when he was a baby. This fifteen-year-old cannot be expected to share his parents' appetite for what is to him no more than part of his basic environment. Nor can one sensibly expect his parents to get the same pleasure from the satisfaction of material needs at the end of the fifteen-year period as at the beginning. The law of diminishing returns is likely to apply. When you already have one car, does the second car mean as much? And when you have two cars, how much does a third car mean to you?

Professor Katona and his partners (*Aspirations and Affluence*) found that in advanced societies only about half the population indicated that they had any outstanding "unsatisfied wishes." The other half of the population had all the wishes that they could conceive of already satisfied. And the unsatisfied ones weren't so much yearning for refrigerators and floor polishers either. The still-to-be-granted satisfactions increasingly came from things which can't be packaged and put on a supermarket shelf (like peace and quiet).

It is now ten years since David Riesman wrote his essay "Abundance for What?" and the question has now traveled beyond the groves of academe. "We appear to be in a trap," wrote Riesman, "in which we may become weary of the goods we have learned to miss not having, without having learned—other then inchoately—what we are missing when we do have them." Hence the new litany of Consciousness III. But this particular aspect of Consciousness III affects many who don't wear flowers in their hair (or have acid in their veins), but who increasingly feel that consumption has no status and find that possession buys few pleasures. It is these people who start the move to a stage of development that few of the prophets of abundance foresaw. W. W. Rostow called it "beyond high mass consumption."

Here are some of the apparent characteristics of this stage of development that one may expect in a society where at least three quarters of the population lives *well* above subsistence level.

First, the desire for things *for their own sake* declines. Second, the value of consumption *for its own sake* declines. This is the antithesis of the mythology of Thorstein Veblen, who believed that the more an individual consumes, the more that person thinks others will think of him. "Beyond high mass consumption" it comes as no surprise that the newer (i.e., younger) members of society are increasingly turned off by today's consumer products. Total sales figures pumped up by inflation disguise reductions or slowing down in per capita consumption in several key areas (in, for example, the semi-fashion market, where durables like blue jeans are retained for longer than pure fashion clothes, or, in Britain, among the 18–34-year-old group where patent medicines are not booming, their sales depending on an older generation). After all, if conspicuous consumption has no status, all you need is the basics without all the extras. Health foods are a basic. So are compact cars. So are craft goods. (They also represent a deliberate decision not to support the mass-production economy.)

The third characteristic of a "beyond mass consumption" stage of economic growth is a trend to life simplification, described by Daniel Yankelovich. This happens when the consumer, instead of being surrounded by choice, feels that she is surrounded by muddle, when she feels she has become a tool of her tools, and so lost control of her own personal environment. To get away from this overwhelming swarm of goods and services, she may simplify. This doesn't necessarily mean that the dishwasher is fed down the waste disposal unit. But it does represent a substantial difference from the consumer into whose house one more domestic appliance was forever welcome.

Some measure of the extent to which consumers welcome additions to their material environment is the degree to which they welcome new products, and eight out of ten get the thumbs down. Of course, very often a major reason for these failures was the way the product was marketed or inadequacies in the product itself. But even the sheer increase in the number of new products means that the majority can't succeed, or the consumer would never stop buying. The scale of this rejection of the products of the marketing industry must surely give its executives a twinge of the ulcers. Can they really be turning out something for which there is a demand when there is an 80 percent rejection rate? Is industry in fact merely turning out the kinds of products that were right in the days of glossy materialism? Below you can see a list of new products introduced in America in November 1971, a month taken at random from the pages of *Advertising Age*. You can thus see the kinds of new products that are being rejected.

NEW PRODUCTS LAUNCHED IN AMERICA, NOVEMBER 1971

"Slight variations, or 'me too' changes in some toiletries and cosmetics products, are not included."

AEROSEAL CORP.—Hot Melt self-heating de-icer spray.

AIRWICK INDUSTRIES—testing ABT (Airwick bathroom tablets) in Atlanta.

AMERICAN CYANAMID CO.—testing Breck Dri-Odorant aerosol extra-strength deodorant.

AMERICAN TOBACCO CO.—Pall Mall filter kings national. Testing Mermaid and Lucky Ten brands.

ARMOUR & CO.—testing Toaster Things, six varieties of frozen toaster products in four markets, including Columbus and Boston.

BEECHAM INC.—re-staging Macleans toothpaste by going national with Macleans freshmint.

BORDEN CO.—testing chocolate-covered candies in Texas markets. Eight varieties.

BRAZIL COFFEE CORP.—introducing Brazilia ground coffee, New York, Boston.

BROWN & WILLIAMSON TOBACCO CO.—testing Lyme lime-menthol 85 mm. filter cigarette, Fort Wayne.

CHIPURNOI IMPORTS—to introduce Chips, Italian-made hard licorice candy.

CLAIROL INC.—testing Final Net hair control spray, Indianapolis. Sunday supplements. To introduce permanent hair coloring. True Brunette. Marketing the Skin Machine, automatic face cleaner, and Air Brush styling dryer. Plans to introduce the Steam Comb.

CLOROX CO.—Clorox disinfectant cleaner testing in undisclosed markets.

COOPERVISION INC.—Marketing a new self-contained home-entertainment rear projector.

DOW CHEMICAL CO.—reformulated Dow oven cleaner with a lemon scent.

FLEISCHMANN DISTILLING CORP.—nears national distribution with Zhivago vodka.

GENERAL FOOD CORP.—introducing cheese-flavored Gainesburgers in Eastern states. Semi-moist dog food available in Blue and Cheddar cheese flavors. Jell-O division introducing semi-sweet chocolate chip and walnut cookie combination. Newspapers, Grey. Birds Eye division adds to International Recipe line with Hawaiian and Parisian-style items. Spot TV, magazines, newspapers. Adding Chinese Italian-style vegetables to International Recipe line, Eastern markets.

GILLETTE CO.—toiletries division, Foamy Face Saver, aerosol lubricating shaving lather. Personal Care division tests You're a Woman antiperspirant and feminine hygiene deodorant, Denver.

GISMAN ENTERPRISES—Jiffy Spreader, device to spread butter, margarine, catsup and mustard on bread, introduced in Florida, Indiana, Michigan.

HUNT-WESSON—testing Pizzands, refrigerated French roll with pizza-like topping. Also Reddi-Bacon, refrigerated, foil-wrapped bacon that cooks in a toaster, Phoenix.

HABITANT SOUP CO.—introducing three soups in New England and upstate New York.

JENO'S INC.—rolling national with Break 'n Bake pizza, cheese and sausage varieties.

JESUS WATCH CO.—marketing multicolored watch depicting a smiling Jesus.

S. C. JOHNSON & SON—introducing Regard cleaner/preserver for wood paneling.

KITCHENS OF SARA LEE—Sara Lee Snack Loaves in three flavors introduced nationally.

KRAFTCO CORP.—Kraft Foods division, introducing five chocolate-covered candies in fifteen major markets. Marketing five natural cheeses under the Casino label, Los Angeles.

LIBBY, MCNEILL & LIBBY—going national with Libbyland Adventure frozen dinners for children. Expanding tests of Le Kitchen line of frozen fish entrees.

LIGGETT & MYERS—Austin Nichols & Co. subsidiary, 86.8-proof version of Wild Turkey 101-proof bourbon. Adam cigarettes for men.

LIPTON PET FOODS—testing Tender Dinners for cats.

LOEW'S CORP.—Lorillard division, testing Maverick, "the taste cigarette," Houston, San Francisco, Atlanta. Expands distribution of Stag tipped cigars to Chicago from Indiana.

MENNEN CO.—introducing Protein 21 conditioner nationally after Jan. 1. Introducing Trouble men's cologne nationally.

PHILIP MORRIS INC.—testing Marlboro Lights 14 mg. low-tar cigarettes.

NOXELL CORP.—testing Free Choice men's hair conditioner.

OVALTINE FOOD PRODUCTS—testing Ovaltine in individual packs, Boston, Chicago.

115

PALE CORP.—introducing Colibri Electro-Flame butane fuel lighters.

PROCTER & GAMBLE—testing Epic freeze process coffee, Louisville, Lexington, Ky.

QUAKER OATS CO.—going national with Aunt Jemima frozen French toast. Introducing chocolate-flavor oatmeal.

RALSTON PURINA CO.—going national with Piccadilly Circles ("the English muffin with the meal on top"). Tender Vittles cat food makes gains.

R. J. REYNOLDS TOBACCO CO.—Camel Talls continues test in Kansas City, Atlanta.

ROBINSON LLOYDS LTD.—Strawberry Duck fruit-flavored wine, Apple Dapple apple wine, Cold Bird red-grape wine, metropolitan markets.

SCHICK ELECTRIC—testing Lady Schick Warm & Creamy heated cleansing and moisturizing cream dispenser.

SPECIAL-T HOSIERY CO.—Lady Bubbles hosiery line.

STERLING DRUG—Lehn & Fink division, Mop & Glo floor cleaner-wax going national.

TERINEX LTD.—testing Look roasting wrap, New England markets.

WARNER-LAMBERT CO.—American Chicle division, testing Trident brand sugarless candy mints.

SCHICK SAFETY RAZOR DIVISION introduces Easy Rider protective razor. TV.

WESTINGHOUSE CORP.—introducing "cooltop" cooking range next year.

A different slant on the same phenomenon occurs when workers cease to be satisfied with offers of more pay (more pay, in this context, being the equivalent of new products).

In an article in the *New York Times*, Sylvia Fox wrote that New York City policemen had rejected an excellent wage settlement because they wanted something more. In the words of one police official: "They're turning their backs on material things and going after other things—ego things." If this sounds strange, consider how often workers appear to act *against* their best interests. But if you look at a strike as a collective ego trip, it makes a lot more sense.

New attitudes to work are, in fact, the other side of the coin of new attitudes to consumption. At first sight this may seem rather unlikely. For all the predictions in the past of the new leisure society, the average weekly hours worked in an affluent society like Britain in 1966 were only 45 minutes a week less than in 1948. As the official week was reduced, either the overtime increased (from an average of 2 hours per week then to 6 hours per week now) or the worker took up a second job. About one sixth of American and British workers now have a second job. Modern urban man, in fact, is working about 240 days a year, compared

116

with the 190 days of work a year that medieval man worked (judging by the vast numbers of saint days and festivals).

Politicians have naturally forecast that work will soon be a thing of the past (if only you'll vote for them). Against the politicians' view, the chief executive of Electric & Musical Industries, one of Britain's main leisure companies, told an industry conference that by 1978 the average working day was likely to be only thirty minutes shorter than in 1970. And going by a study published by the Survey Research Center, 49 percent of Americans under thirty-five want to work more and only 7 percent want to work less.

Can one really take all these statistics at their face value? Or are consumers simply mouthing the platitudes of a Protestant ethic in which they decreasingly believe?

As attitudes toward work affect attitudes toward consumption so greatly, it seems sensible to follow this question in a little more detail. First, what is it that sends millions of people to clock in every day? Karl Marx's view was simple: "Work is *external* to the worker . . . it is not part of his nature . . . consequently, he does not fulfill himself in his work but denies himself, has a feeling of misery rather than well-being, does not develop freely his mental and physical energies, but is physically exhausted and mentally debased. The worker, therefore, feels himself at home only during his leisure time; when he is at work he feels homesick. His work is not voluntary, but *forced labor*. It is not the satisfaction of a need, but only a *means* for satisfying other ends."

In this analysis, affluence becomes the opium of the people. In a 1969 study of automobile workers by John Goldthorpe, 70 percent of the assemblers referred to the level of pay as a reason for staying in their present job, and in the case of 31 percent it was the only reason offered. In a production-line economy the satisfaction of the job, which a craft economy provides, is missing. Even in Japan, the world's most go-go economy, almost half of the workers have a negative attitude of one kind or another to their jobs.

The situation at the strife-torn Lordstown Vega plant shows clearly that the new consumers are increasingly rejecting the mass-production techniques which were, in fact, the foundation of their affluence. Lordstown is probably the most automated consumer-goods factory in the world. It has robot welding machines called

"Unimates," a computer which works out the automatic production flow; it can produce one hundred cars an hour, and each of the workers has to spend only 35 seconds on each assigned task. This is where the problem lies, for the workers at Lordstown, who are typical of the new breed that will be coming into factories in all affluent societies, are striking for more interesting and responsible work, work that doesn't treat them as a machine.

These young workers are not motivated by the Puritan work ethic one tiny bit. This shows clearly in the form their protest action has taken; they did not just refuse to work, but actually engaged in Luddite-like sabotage on the cars they were meant to be making. Seats were slashed, paintwork was deliberately scratched, gear levers bent out of shape, etc. This total alienation from their work even goes so far as telling people not to buy Vega because it's a "lousy car."

If you think this reaction is just the result of GM's poor handling of its personnel, look at this recent report of the National Industries Conference Board: "Today's younger, better educated worker is unenthused by dull, repetitive and dirty work in factories. Today's worker puts his personal life ahead of his work. A good percentage of the work force has seen nothing but affluence since earliest childhood, he is younger and far less hungry than his depression scarred parents and is willing to skip a day or two to convert a weekend into a four day holiday." Charles Reich could hardly have said it better.

Nor is this attitude peculiar to American workers. When Fiat in Turin introduced eighteen of these Unimate robots, industrial trouble followed shortly. It was precisely this section of the factory where, in 1969, the major strike began, a strike which cost Fiat over 250,000 cars. Even when these strikes were settled, absenteeism in the Turin factory stayed at an 18 percent level. Those workers who do keep their noses to the grindstone work not just for the money, they also work for the lack of an alternative way of satisfactorily spending the day. It was this reason, in fact, that was given by 80 percent of industrial workers in a study quoted in Riesman's essay "Leisure and Work in a Post-Industrial Society."

Both the consumption urge and the lack of alternatives are likely to be very different for the new consumer as the Lordstown rebellion showed. Professor Katona found that almost one third of

118

American households were aware of better jobs; yet, despite the competitive spirit meant to be driving them on, they did not act on this information by moving. No wonder that on Labor Day 1971 President Nixon felt it necessary to call for a return to the "work ethic." However, the "leisure ethic" won't be blown away by such puffs of oratory. Leisure, according to Max Weber's analysis of the Protestant ethic, is necessary for a man in order to work better. But for Aristotle, and increasingly the new consumer, work is only necessary to have leisure (rather than consumption).

It is significant that the automobile industry in Europe is depending to an increasing degree on a new type of cheap labor: 50 percent of the assembly labor force at Volvo and Saab are non-Swedes; the German car industry employs three million foreigners, many of them Turks and Yugoslavs; and the French automobile industry owes much to the semiskilled Algerians doing many of the worst jobs (63 percent of the workers at Citroën's Paris factory are, in fact, foreigners).

These workers have yet to develop into new consumers, so they are still prepared to repeat 240 identical motions every day, five days a week, fifty weeks a year. But apart from these exploited workers, in the new consumer society the chances of a "better job," i.e., greater pay for more stress, is no longer the lure it was.

All this, of course, is based on the assumption that the good times will continue. For a generation not living in the shadow of the 1930s, until the crises of 1973 the arrival of a rainy day seemed remote indeed. And anyhow, was it so bad not to be able to have a job? Americans, particularly, were confident that the good times would go on and that the continuing progress wouldn't fizzle into a depression or slump. According to Professor Katona, in 1967, one American in three felt better off five years ago and *also* anticipated being better off five years hence. This compared with one Briton in four and only one German in eight. The greater the degree of uncertainty about the future, one would expect the higher proportion of disposable income that is saved and not spent. And in the ten years up to 1965, British and Americans saved on an average about 6 percent of their disposable income and Germans about 13 percent (and the insecure Japanese saved 16 percent). Then, from 1970, the American savings rate increased by a quarter, to 8 percent, as America in a mini-depression (what most countries in the world would call a boom) felt a bit less sure about the future. This "uncertainty" is of course measured by the criteria of personal well-being in a material sense, aggregated on a national level as the GNP.

As GNP worship and a minimal consumption society with a welfare-state safety net keeping you above the breadline gather momentum, the impact of "uncertainty" causing people to go out to work, and work harder, will be less. In the short term, the savings rate may well rise (as people decide not to buy things they don't really want). But a nonconsuming consumer will increasingly see less point in working to save for future nonconsumption. Savings *rates* may stay at about 6 percent, but the actual *amount* saved could, within a decade or two, show a substantial decrease.

There are those who give a nod to some of the broad trends about this new philosophy of consumption, but say that, for the foreseeable future, these people will remain a tiny minority, of sociological rather than business interest. But Arnold Mitchell of the Stanford Research Institute in California has estimated that the number of Americans holding this viewpoint (he uses the word "unfolders" to describe it) will rise to about one fifth or one sixth of the American population. Thirty-five million "unfolded" Americans is an awesome prospect, and it may well prove to be a serious underestimate.

For those in the marketing business, equally interesting is the fact that in Europe the working classes are steadily refusing to become middle-class. They're not adopting the consumer ethic in the way everybody expected them to. This phenomenon has less impact, perhaps, on American society, where roughly 60 percent of the population are graded as middle-class. But in Britain that proportion of the population can be considered working-class. Contrary to the expectations of many eminent sociologists, the process of embourgeoisment is not occurring. It was the work of John Goldthorpe and his fellow researchers looking at British manual workers which finally laid that ghost to rest: "It appears to us," they concluded, "that the idea of appreciable numbers of manual workers and their wives "turning middle-class" in a way that has been frequently suggested is shown by our research to be highly questionable."

Affluence simply didn't result in an integration of the manual worker into the middle classes. For instance, manual workers who had been enriched by affluence still kept the same kind of social structure in their lives as before affluence. That is, they still treated their home as a place reserved for kin and very close friends. Socializing was done *outside* the home (e.g., in the pub). This compares with the characteristics of the middle-class, white-collar workers who invited much less close friends into their homes. Clearly then, the manual workers may acquire the apparatus of the mass-consumption society, but they don't necessarily acquire its attitudes, included among which, of course, is a desire for consumption for the sake of being conspicuous.

This reluctance of the higher-income European manual workers to acquire the middle-class symbols of consumption was also noted by Professor Katona. He and his fellow researchers felt it "testified to the persistence of a ceiling to their goals and horizons." Others might argue that it testified to their common sense in not worshiping the new golden calves.

There is certainly a different philosophy of consumption operating in Britain, America and Germany. Of the three, America has developed farthest beyond high mass consumption and so has farther to bounce back. Britain hasn't had as much growth, and hence less of an explosion of consumption, so the British appetites are probably less sated. On the other hand, there is the theory of Professor Galbraith that Britain may be deliberately sluggish in the GNP race due to the collective, albeit intuitive, realization that "enjoyment does not come from working more and more and yet more to consume more and yet more." This would argue that though the British are not yet as saturated with consumption as the Americans, their reaction against it may be equal to the Americans'. The Pahls' study foresaw an "acceptance in Britain of a less affluent and less materialistic way of life."

Germany is a vivid contrast to all this. The Germans are driven not by the desire half of the equation that began this chapter but by the uncertainty element. Professor Katona found that whereas only 26 percent of Americans in 1968 expected a major recession in the next twenty years, over twice that proportion of Germans are expecting one. So where Americans are happy to buy on credit, two thirds of the Germans express unqualified opposition to it (*Schuld*, the German word for "credit" is also the word for "guilt"). German advertising has to spend twice as much per dollar of consumer expenditure as advertising in Britain, such is the reluctance of the *Herrenvolk* to part with their marks.

This is a different reason for a low consumption society and it is, of course, in no way the same as Consciousness III's rejection of the consumer ethic. But it is significant nonetheless: the Germans have failed so far to adapt to a doubling of goods and services every ten years in the way that the mass-consumer model of society demands. The endless appetite for goods and services is not there; there is instead a worry that something will happen to imperil the satisfying of a far more modest hunger.

To argue that there is increasingly a limited, not a limitless, demand for material goods in advanced societies is, of course, to tell only half the story. What is equally important is that where there *is* demand for a product, be it a car or a packet of frozen peas, the new ideology of consumption predicts that it will be bought for very different reasons than those that prevailed some ten years ago. Ten years ago the prime motive for purchase was the actual pleasure of having the object, the *possession* experience. Now the trend is away from what it is to what it does, to *usage* or the pleasures you get from using it.

Possession is now no longer nine tenths of the satisfaction. With abundance of products, few producers can provide the emotional "possession" satisfaction that held sway in the early days of glossy materialism (for example, manufacturers of swimming pools still have some "possession" appeal to make). Eighty-four percent of European homes now have refrigerators, so they, and virtually all other electrical household appliances, have lost their value as status symbols (only portable color television sets seem to have this position at the moment). All that most of these objects are good for now is the freezing of ice cubes, the making of toast, and the bringing of entertainment in the evenings. To paraphrase Le Corbusier, they have become machines for living with.

One or two voices in the marketing wilderness have foreseen this change. In June 1970 the head of marketing for Lees Carpets observed: "Home furnishing customers of the 1970s will be less interested in possessing objects than in using and enjoying them." E. B. Weiss of Doyle, Dane, Bernbach has forecast several of the massive changes of heart among consumers. But most advertisers, as one will have cause to observe later, are still presenting their products to the consumer as though the consumer were still in a "possession" phase. Just how offbeam this makes the advertising message will become clearer if we look at some of the marketing consequences of this trend from possession to usage.

First, possession is measured by subjective criteria, usage by objective ones. Possession demands prestige, usage demands performance. This is even affecting the world of fashion, perhaps one of the most subjective-dominated product categories. What is happening is that it is becoming fashionable to have "usage" clothes. At an obvious level, clothes become more comfortable at the expense of style. Stiff collars are undoubtedly smarter than soft collars, drip-dry dresses don't keep the press as smartly as starched. "Performance" clothes will also tend to be fewer in number and more durable than "prestige" clothes. And it has been estimated that the value at constant prices of the wardrobe of the average Harvard student is a third of what it used to be at the end of the sixties.

The new British women's magazine *Spare Rib* recently reported from New York that "the garment industry is in big trouble in New York. That's because having discovered blue jeans and tee shirts, a lot of women here are unwilling to start spending the kind of money we all used to spend on clothes." This doesn't mean that women never want to dress themselves decorously (although there is more than a hint of functional muddiness in many of the colors). But it does mean that there is a new usage ingredient in the fashion mix that wasn't there before.

The same trend has shown itself in the world of movies. The difference between *The Graduate* and *The Sound of Music* is the difference between subjective glamor and objective reality. Film stars no longer have to have square chins, perfect teeth and blue eyes. It is the difference between Cary Grant and Jean-Paul Belmondo. Of course, there are still "fantasy" films, but the difference is that the average viewer now tends to take a more objective look at his own need for fantasy. To treat a James Bond film as a joke, albeit a very entertaining one, is to take fantasy objectively. Indeed, the fact that Sean Connery is still acceptable as 007 is of substantial significance. In *Dr. No* he was playing a part in the subjective hero mold, but in *Diamonds Are Forever* we see a different kind of hero parodying his early roles. The P.R. man who spread the word that Sean Connery wears a toupee understood the subjective/objective shift precisely. The fact that everyone knows about his toupee makes Bond's screen antics delightful when they would otherwise be ridiculous. The toupee is a larger-than-life element to remind us that we are watching fantasy, but we know that when the picture fades, our prancing hero once more becomes a balding forty-year-old with sagging stomach muscles.

Looking away from movies to the food industry, we find that the possession to usage shift shows itself again. "Possession" in food marketing is that whole range of things like the big smiles that greet every spoonful—in short, all the *nonfood* aspects of food selling. "Usage" is the nutritional side, the vitamins in the cornflakes or, for certain kinds of food, the convenience aspect.

In the mid-sixties, nutrition was not a good way to sell food. General Mills tried it with Subtract, and Carnation tried it with Instant Breakfast. It seemed then that too much emphasis on nutrition turned the consumer off. By 1970 *Advertising Age* was reporting: "The food industry is on a nutrient fortification kick that seems to be building into an important marketing effort." This verdict is confirmed by the rash of nutrition-oriented foods, culminating in General Mills' Protein Plus in 1972 with its slogan, "Protein is the name of the game."

The other usage aspect of food marketing, convenience, is also on the rise. In the European market, convenience foods often made much slower headway in the sixties than the companies marketing them had hoped they would. Instant mashed potato, the go-go product at the end of the decade, was a flop in the mid-sixties. The motivational psychologist declared that you shouldn't sell convenience foods on convenience alone because this created guilt feelings in the housewife. Hence the rash of products to which one had to add an egg, and so make a vital contribution to lift the burden of guilt.

What in fact happened was that convenience foods had been launched on a usage platform during a possession phase. At that time it *was* necessary to add possession reassurance. But then, as the consumer shifted into a usage phase, convenience foods could be sold for convenience reasons. Smash Mashed Potato openly derided the inconvenience of the fresh product ("It's good, but it'll never catch on"). And instant coffee began to wean Frenchmen away from their fresh filtered brew.

Even the $8 billion hotel industry has been shaken by the possession-to-usage trend. In the old possession days, hotels and motel bedrooms had to come outfitted with everything from cocktail cabinets to lavish décor. Now, in the usage phase, hotel people have suddenly discovered that most guests stay in motels for a couple of waking hours, and that in the dark all rooms are alike. Hence the rash of budget motels that have sprung up along America's freeways: "If Motel 6 doesn't give you a bath, just a shower," said one of the newcomers to this scene, "it doesn't soak you either."

A final example of how the possession-to-usage shift triggered a trend from subjective to objective product assessment comes from the durable-goods field. With half the population having almost a complete set of durable goods, it means that the great proportion of purchases are for replacement of an old or worn-out model. Already, for instance, 40 percent of Italy's domestic refrigerator sales are replacement units. The point is that the criteria of product choice for a replacement refrigerator are very different from those for a first-time purchase. A study done by General Electric spells this out. People purchasing refrigerators for the first time, maybe moving into their first home, took the time to stop and compare. They are building their home, so not only do they want to feel they're getting the best for the price, but the refrigerator—as part of their new home—also has some emotional significance. When this new refrigerator, after seven or so years, breaks down or needs repair, a rather different criteria of purchase are at work. First, the housewife's need is more immediate. She won't have time to shop around. She'll probably be more influenced by a point of sale than advertising (which she won't have looked at until her refrigerator breaks down, because she wasn't in the market for a new refrigerator). And—this is where we come to usage—because the old refrigerator *broke down* she will be especially concerned about quality, performance and after-sales service.

Another study found that users of a product who were replacing a similar or identical product *with which they were satisfied* generally spent little time or effort in considering their next purchase. They knew which to look for and where to look for it, and they didn't need to concern themselves with a whole mass of features and subjective attractions that weren't relevant to their particular need.

An equally important consequence of replacement purchases is that they have little—if any—of the joys that accompanied the first purchase. There are already large categories of products the purchase of which is basically an unpleasant event, since it means that something has gone wrong, worn out or run out. Light bulbs are a simple example, tires an even better one. They may even include items like suits. For all but a tiny proportion of the population, a new suit is something you buy when your old one is worn out.

The joy-through-purchase experience is thus becoming more and more infrequent, and advertisers who treat their products as though the purchase of them were as pleasurable as a night out with Sophia Loren are a very long way off the mark.

One of the attributes of a product which was thought to enhance the pleasure of possessing it was its image. By modifying the image of the brand one could—so the adherents of this doctrine believed—manipulate reality. Indeed, the image became reality. Insofar as the brand image is a *subjective* phenomenon, any brand loyalty that this creates is likely to wane as the shift to usage waxes. Loyalty in a my-country-right-or-wrong style is going out of fashion for countries and also for brands. In the German detergent market, for instance, the big three—Henkel, Procter & Gamble and Unilever—have consistently been losing ground to small independent manufacturers who make their products at a much lower price. P & G has even seen its share slump by half, to well below 10 percent of the market.

In Britain, a study by one of the country's major research companies has confirmed that the big brands' grip on the market is slipping. In 1971, the study revealed, in one third of thirty-eight key product categories, leading brands had over 70 percent of the total market. But just twelve months later, only in one sixth of these key product categories had the leading brands retained their dominance.

There are two other factors which have helped this shift away from brand loyalty. First, the growth of brand *consciousness*, a function of the information explosion. There may in fact be fewer brands of soup on the market than in 1920, but people are conscious, through the media, of more brands of soup. And the development of supermarkets with a greater number of items under one roof (the British chain, Sainsburys, has increased from 1,500 different items per shop in 1952 to 3,800 different items today) further increases the consciousness of choice. As brand consciousness increases, brand loyalty is likely to weaken, for brand loyalty partly depends upon your mentally *suppressing* your knowledge of the existence of other brands.

The second factor to weaken brand loyalty is the reduced trust in the company that makes that brand. The decline of trust for companies described in Chapter One is surely likely to have as its consequence in the marketplace the decline in trust for that company's brands. Of course, the reassurance of having a familiar face on your kitchen shelf will still prompt purchase of the well-known brand names. But even areas which have been saturated by loyalty-inducing advertising like cosmetics, brand loyalty is already looking a little like a leftover from the early sixties. An (International Publishing Corporation) survey among fifteen to twenty-four-year-old consumers found that the majority "had no usual brand" of cosmetics. One woman in six used half a dozen or more different types of eye shadow, while one woman in ten had *six* different types of lipstick.

A J. Walter Thompson study of household purchasing patterns gives this as an example that is "by no means untypical" of multiple-brand choice. Each different letter represents the purchase of a different brand of tea. And this is the sequence: BOOcGBOCOBGBGABBGBBcBGBCBBGGBBB. A total of five different brands, with even the most frequently purchased one having less than half of all purchases.

If brand loyalty is one of the casualties of the possession-to-usage shift, built-in obsolescence is the other. Built-in obsolescence worked in the fifties and sixties by giving the consumer the opportunity of a new "possession" experience every two to three years. Very often the actual *performance* of the product had no significant difference between models. The changes tended to be in the *possession* area.

But the new usage customers will not forgive a product if it self-destructs after three years. Having got over the initial excitement of having their clothes washed and dried, their food mixed and cooked, their toast toasted and dishes washed at the flick of a switch, they simply demand that their machines do these tasks reliably day in, day out.

There's another reason why the new consumers reject built-in obsolescence. Consumers who are unable to buy the same model twice increasingly feel that they are caught on an escalator of change upon change upon change. They find that the rate of change is becoming more than they can take, and suffer from "future shock." (It's the same phenomenon that torturers use to reduce their victims: a hot bath, a cold bath, light followed by darkness, silence followed by noise.) And even when the elements of change are far more benign, the consequence for the individual can be no less alarming.

Even nonworking durable goods like furniture are feeling the anti-obsolescence backlash. For instance, the president of the Stanleytown furniture company told *Business Week* that more and more young couples are buying one or two high-quality pieces and making do until their budget allows them to make additional furniture purchases. They are thus turning their backs on the old idea of buying a low-price three-piece suite, which is worn out after five years, and then having the fun of refurnishing their home.

One of the pressures against built-in obsolescence for durable goods is, of course, the shortage of people to service them. The trend to do-it-yourself is one result of this. (The expense and palaver of getting a plumber is making doing-it-yourself sensible for even the most ham-fisted.) But making products in cases where it is the exception instead of the rule for them to fall apart after five years would be another.

A logical part of any durable-goods economy would be the use of a product without ownership of that product: the ultimate consequence of the possession to usage shift. One aspect of this phenomenon (which was shrewdly observed in a series of articles by E. B. Weiss in *Advertising Age*) is the growth of rental. With rental, by definition, you can have none of the joys of ownership, only the satisfaction of use. Car-rental firms already make up a fair slice of all car sales. Office furniture (partly because of tax concessions) is increasingly rented, but why not home furniture as well? In Britain, partly because of special installment-plan controls, more television sets are rented than purchased, one reason for which is that though renting costs are higher, they spare the pains of ownership involved in servicing.

If in the fifties and sixties the consumer would often own

things he didn't use, now he increasingly uses things he doesn't own. The growth of the service industries further exemplifies this, for service industries are essentially usage: they provide service, something you use rather than something you possess. And it is this section of the economy of advanced societies that is expanding far and away the fastest. Service industries already employ two out of every three American workers (compared to one out of two in 1950). In addition to traditional service industries such as banks, there are now service companies that baby-sit, wake you up in the morning, drive you to work—even find you a new wife. And in business, companies are springing up that will plan your convention, design your products and supply you with a temporary managing director.

One extra attraction of a service is that it is effectively tailor-made to the person being serviced, while a possession tends to be mass-produced. Individualism, in fact, is the other main aspect of the new consumer's attitude toward material goods. "What does this do for *me*?" is a relevant question, rather than the old "What does this do?" Mass production of the old Henry Ford type ("Have any car you like as long as it's black) becomes a quaint museum piece from the early days of affluence. Equally *passé* is the pre-packaged consumer who had to adjust herself to fit the product and not the other way around.

The new consumer, by contrast, is highly individualistic. Ten years ago it was an endorsement for a product if the next-door neighbor used it. Now, if the next-door neighbor uses it, you probably won't want to touch it. Satisfaction is now obtained by being different from your peer group, which is now no more than a reference point for comparison. It is no longer, and this is an important point, a reference point for imitation.

Wealth, of course, finances the exercise of this sort of individuality. A poor woman may well go on using the same old cake recipe just because she can't run the risk of failure. But increased wealth makes this sort of individualistic risk-taking possible: if her cake recipe goes wrong, it doesn't mean her children go hungry. She can simply try another recipe tomorrow. And in doing this she will probably be using her consumption style as an expression of her personality. Each year St. Tropez provides an interesting example of this phenomenon. There is a basic uniform which all residents in the town wear to show that they belong to

St. Trop and aren't just passing members of a package tour. In 1970 this was a pre-faded cotton-jeans outfit. In 1971 it was an out-of-work-U.S.-Army-unit-style outfit that held the field. But despite this basic pattern, no St. Trop regular wore the same outfit as anyone else. Each outfit was in some way unique. (The move to separates in the fashion world is a move to increasing the number of options in someone's wardrobe without actually increasing the number of clothes.)

For large turnover products, instead of straightforward mass production, *differentiated* production is developing. This is a way of making a mass-produced product fit an individual's own personality. For example, the chairman of Genesco is promising custom-made suits for the masses with three-day delivery. And British European Airways Sovereign holidays began business in 1970 to move people away from ordinary package holidays to a tailor-made vacation.

Tiffany's branch in Chicago has also felt this change. In 1970 it did "unusual custom work" on one out of ten engagement rings it sold. And this in a shop where five years ago only one kind of diamond engagement ring was sold, and that on a take-it-or-leave-it-basis.

Why, apart from satisfying the personal quirks of its customers, should General Foods now offer the public sixteen different permutations of frozen peas? Yes, frozen peas.

With all this happening in the commercial field, it can hardly be a coincidence that the new religion of our day—astrology—is a religion that is customized for every worshiper. Instead of a religion like Christianity, where you have to adjust to its beliefs, here is one where the beliefs literally adjust to you, and no one— but no one—has the same *credo*.

The central core of the individualistic trend is away from the importance of the product to the importance of the individual (so making it consistent with the possession to usage shift that stripped a product of part of its appeal). In the possession phase, the product was a *substitute* for personality. You *were* your car; it dominated you and did things to you. But in the usage phase, individualism ensures that the product becomes an *extension* of your personality. You dominate it and you do things to it.

These customized consumers don't fit into any of the old pigeon-holes that used to divide the marketplace. Alvin Toffler uses the phrase "micro cosmos" to describe the network of interconnecting mini-worlds that form themselves out of the new individualistic consumers. But they *are* mini-markets, not mass markets. And it is indeed a paradox that just as we have created a mass media, the mass market disappears.

Take the youth market. Mathematically, a teen-age girl is somewhere between thirteen and nineteen. To regard that age group as one market group is foolish. All you get, in the phrase of E. B. Weiss is "demographic goulash."

The obvious result of this is that no brand today can sell effectively to the whole market, but only to certain parts of the market. A new industry has grown up to work out ways to segment the market, with things like gap analysis, contextual mapping and cluster analysis. For example, in 1962 the wrist-watch field could be broadly divided into (a) those who want to pay the lowest price for any watch that works reasonably well; (b) people who want good craftsmanship and nice styling; (c) people who want emotional qualities as well as timeless qualities from their wristwatch. By 1971, new divisions had arrived, such as a group of people who treated a watch as jewelry and regarded its time-keeping ability as almost incidental; as well as a group of people who wanted special non-time-keeping features on their watches like deep-sea pressure gauges when they never do more than jump into a swimming pool.

The result of developments like this in every market has been a brand explosion (or—as in the case of cars—an option explosion). An A. C. Nielsen report in 1967 revealed that in one supermarket chain alone there was a 76 percent increase in brands of diet food; a 71 percent in brands of soup; a 61 percent increase in brands of dog food; and so on and so forth through all the lines they held.

In all these discussions of the shift to functionalism and individualism in products, one particular three-letter word has hardly been present when you might have expected it to appear rather more frequently. The word is c-a-r.

The car has, of course, a major role in bringing about a reduced importance for material goods and in changing the shape of that modified demand. The saga of how the centerpiece of the affluent society has been knocked off its pedestal forms the next part of our discussion. Anthropologists have reported how in several primitive tribes a new god is at first welcomed, worshiped and adored. Then after a time his magic seems to weaken and he is slain. Civilized man has done the same for his four-wheeled god. Once worshiped, it has now been slain, partly to propitiate the high priests of the environment.

What new idol will replace it is one of the big questions hungry young marketing men are trying to answer.

The Sex Symbol That Lost Its Sex

●

The Kandy-Kolored Tangerine-Flake Streamline Baby isn't just a radical-chic book by Tom Wolfe. It was the apogee of a form of worship that beats anything since Aaron discovered the golden calf. How a piece of rubber and metal weighing a ton and upward and costing thousands of dollars could enter the realm of high fashion is a puzzle for historians and sociologists of the future to sort out. They will probably be as amazed as we are to think of our ancestors falling down before lumps of rock at Stonehenge.

The fact remains that ever since the 1950s, the automobile has been as much a fashion item as the little black dress or even a new shade of lipstick, commodities designed to be far less useful than this replacement for the horse. The annual-model change, with all its associated rituals, was as much a high-fashion event as the Paris shows. And as the basic structure of four wheels, an engine and seats is a bit limiting, the car manufacturers developed the concept of "overdesign" to allow them the same flexibility with metal as Balenciaga had with crepe.

Overdesigning simply means building into a mechanism more features than it requires in order to function. The American Bureau of Labor statistics reveals exactly what this means in dollars and cents. For the 1969 model change, General Motors, Ford and American Motors spent $1.5 billion. But the bureau's statistics shows a net *reduction* in performance improvements of $3 per car.

133

This means that *more* than $1.5 billion was literally spent on putting some new makeup on the old face.

This happened not so much from a desire to defraud the consumer as a direct result of the possession phase which the consumer was in. The new car did almost as much for the owner when it was sitting outside his front door as when he was being carried around by it. And it didn't just carry him around either. All the neighbors flocked around for a drive.

In 1960 General Motors' corporate car campaign reflected the spirit of the whole thing with exquisite precision. Beneath a lovingly painted picture of a huge station wagon surrounded by happy smiling children with parents proudly looking on—and done by an artist who'd managed to combine the styles of Norman Rockwell and Dame Laura Knight—was the legend that expressed the complete philosophy of selling cars at that particular moment in time: "There's nothing like a new car to enrich your family life." "Enrich" is a possession word, full of hidden undertones. And an automobile manufacturer who tried to sell cars in any other way did so at his peril.

In 1955, for instance, Ford's advertising carried the "Life Guard Design" slogan. It was a campaign to introduce safety door locks, safety steering wheels and rear-view mirrors which did not cause head wounds (this was, of course, before Nader's attack on General Motors). After a year the conclusion of the automobile industry was that "Ford sells safety and General Motors sells cars." So deep was the impact of this on Ford that thirteen years later, I discovered that Ford of Great Britain was not interested in doing a safety campaign for its cars, because the Ford people felt, after the 1955 debacle, that it wouldn't persuade the public to buy their cars.

By this time, consumer attitude toward the automobile was shifting well into the usage phase, albeit personalized usage. This shift, in fact, had been predicted by David Riesman, when he wrote in 1957 in "Abundance for What?": "It seems to us that as America becomes more accustomed to luxury, the motor car will lose some of its glamour and that eventually the cars which restore to us a sense of reality and functionalism may at least find a modest market."

The first stirring that this was so came from the massive rejection of the Edsel. After that, in Detroit they spoke of the hard sell, the soft sell and the Edsel.

An even clearer indication that consumers were falling out of love with their cars was the extraordinary success of the Volkswagen in America. Here was a modernized version of a vehicle intended by Hitler to be the people's car in prewar Germany carving great chunks out of the car market in the toughest market in the world. Volkswagen was aided and abetted in this by the development of the second-car market in America. Between 1960 and 1970 the number of cars owned by one-car families had increased by less than 2 million. The two-car families have added over 9 million vehicles to the total car population. One American home in three now has more than one car, compared to one in ten British homes. The Volkswagen presented itself as a second car that ran rings around a fat and sloppy first car. If the tide hadn't turned against those overpowered chromium-plated monsters, with their baroque décor, the Volkswagen attack would not have worked so well. How well it did work is history (the kind of history that even Henry Ford might not regard as bunk). In 1950, 350 Volkswagens were sold in America. By 1970 only one American car, the Chevrolet Impala, outsold the Volkswagen Beetle. All other models were outsold by this sparse, functional, chromeless puddle-jumper.

Volkswagen's success can't just be attributed to the exercise of greater rationality by American car buyers. For in some respects, the Volkswagen Beetle was an extremely irrational choice. Its stability at high speed, its road holding, its degree of comfort and spaciousness were all below average. And its carefully applied paintwork concealed, if Ralph Nader was to be believed, a multitude of engineering sins. To some extent, there was thus an element of irrationality about choosing a Volkswagen. It was being bought, in fact, as an anti-car: a deliberate rejection of the priorities and values of Detroit, even at the expense of some discomfort and possible danger to the purchaser. By unashamedly putting its cars on a usage platform, Volkswagen attracted the protest votes of those who had had their fill of Detroit's four-wheeled battering rams.

En passant, it may be worth noting that it wasn't only Volkswagen that presented cars on a usage platform at that time. David Ogilvy's most famous headline for Rolls-Royce was 100 percent usage (however possessiony the car itself might have been). "At sixty miles an hour the loudest noise in this new Rolls-Royce comes from the electric clock."

But even in 1970, after the usage imported cars had been giving

135

them the run-around for several years, Detroit was still pushing its own vehicles on the old possession platform. "Introducing automobiles to light your fire," said Buick. "Pontiac announces the beginning of tomorrow," said the Firebird company, with their car burnished and glistening on the glimmering water's edge. Pontiac's GTO advertisement went even further. Showing the new GTO (dubbed "The Humbler") barreling around the edge of a mountainside, it proclaimed: "Move over, mountain. This is the way it's going to be." And Cadillac with its "masterful approach to the seventies" was boasting about its "newly contoured rear-light assembly." But perhaps the best expression of the Detroit philosophy was an advertisement for American Motors: "People are demanding more 'hot' in their hot cars . . . More 'big' in their big cars, more 'new' in their new cars."

But even with these possession-oriented ads, the tacit recognition was there that the consumer had developed different attitudes to the car. The fashion accessories now had to be presented as quasi-functional items: "Gauges that gauge, spoilers that spoil and scoops that scoop," said Pontiac, to prove that its ephemera were really "usage" equipment. "A high lift cam and four barrel carburetor which breathes through real air scoops to add performance," intoned Buick, anxious to make the same point. Even Ford of Britain's Capri feels unable to simply plaster its side with dross, so the chrome panel at the back has to be dressed up as an Aeroflow ventilation outlet.

Behind all this subterfuge is the growing recognition that the car has not turned out to be quite the winged chariot the advertisers swore it was. "We were promised a machine that freed us, gave us wings," said Professor Charles Mason of the University of Southern Carolina, "instead, it turned on us, trapping us in traffic jams, polluting our air, breaking apart in accidents, and in need of constant repair."

And so the car has been relegated to a utilitarian role. Five years ago, domestic compacts and subcompacts made up only one fifth of all cars sold in the United States. By 1972 this category of cars made up two fifths of all cars sold. And the trend was still rising in 1973: in May of that year, for instance, sales of compacts and subcompacts *rose* 28 percent over the previous year, while sales of larger cars *fell* 13 percent. Of course, if the main thing you want from a car is transportation, why own the car? Why not use one only when you need it? Hence the growth of car rental and car leasing.

Looking at the new relationship of man to his transporter, you could say that the love affair with the car is over, or that it had matured into marriage (depending upon whether or not you happen to have shares in an automobile company). One of Ford's vice presidents, Donald Petersen, compared the changed attitudes to that of a man toward his middle-aged wife: "You're still in love, but you expect more. You expect her to cook." At a more candid moment Mr. Petersen expressed what is perhaps a truer reflection of the new relationship: "More and more people view the automobile as an unfortunate necessity. As soon as you are viewed more as a necessity, people are less tolerant of your shortcomings."

Studies by the Survey Research Center (some of whose funds come from the automobile industry) show the same sort of trend. They indicate that the car is increasingly becoming a means for serving important ends rather than being the highly prized possession it once was. The important ends could be simply shopping for clothes or driving for a weekend to stay in a log cabin. But as a way of revealing a man's position in society (which was the basis of car marketing in the fifties and sixties) it is not of major importance. It is no longer possible, in fact, to deduce an individual's status from knowing what vehicle he uses. A man driving a new Beetle might be a professional man or a highly paid manual worker. And the parking lots of America's richest suburbs are full of small battered old cars, so much so that car dealers in 1973 were facing a shortage of *used* cars. "We used to take nine cars in trade for every ten we sold," said one New Jersey dealer to *Business Week*. "Now we're taking in only two or three for every ten we sell."

The rise in importance of usage factors in the car market was something that Detroit was very slow to appreciate. Their tardiness in bringing out cars which satisfied the usage criteria (by being more reliable and by not falling apart so fast) is one of the most myopic marketing episodes of this decade. It wasn't until four million Volkswagens had been sold in America that Detroit brought out a serious rival. And to show the full recognition of the error of their old ways, they even started to run ads for overtly possession cars, presenting them as usage vehicles, a preposterousness that reached its peak with a headline for a Cadillac advertisement: "Surprising Cadillac, as practical as it's beautiful." The 1972-model ads (prompted by a few crisp words from General Motors' president: "I think advertising has forgotten who and what the customer is") started to tell a very different story from the newer, bigger, hotter story of the previous years.

American Motors kicked off with "If anything goes wrong with our new '72s and it's our fault, we'll fix it free. Anything." And Chevrolet lamely observed: "Many people today have changed their attitude about new cars, so we have changed . . . and only made a few meaningful improvements."

But perhaps the best example of the U-turn done by Detroit in marketing is to look at one particular car advertisement for the Chevrolet Vega and compare it with the earlier General Motors ad, "There's nothing like a new car to enrich your family life." Over a picture of a drawing of the Vega with five number plates on it, 1972, 1973, 1974, 1975, the headline says: "If you like the 1971 you'll like the 1975." This advertisement unequivocally states that the Chevrolet Vega will *not* be obsolete in four years. Any advertising agency that presented this sort of advertisement in Detroit just two years ago would probably have been fired. But this advertisement and the car it's for are the white hopes of the American automobile industry facing the onslaught of the imports. (It may be of interest that in a study of the readership of new car advertisements by the American research organization Starch, the most read advertisement was for the Ford Pinto which showed an old model Ford to point out that Pinto would not have an annual styling change: "When you get back to basics you get back to Ford.")

In its new neutered role, the car no longer generates the loving attention it did when the shape of a bumper meant as much as a curve on Marilyn Monroe. Obsessive spit-and-polishing is a thing of the past. And cars, quite simply, seem to be getting dirtier.

Instead of being interested in automobile cosmetics, today's owner is probably looking for a degree of engineering beauty that is much more than skin-deep. Remembering how the 1955 Ford safety campaign flopped, look at the results of a survey by the British motorists' magazine *Drive* to find out, apart from cost, which factors consumers considered most important in buying a new car. For one in three, *safety* was first choice, and styling was only first choice for one in fourteen. Clearly, the new safety standards for cars have widespread consumer support.

The same *Drive* survey showed that almost three quarters of motorists would welcome stricter government standards for car safety, even if that would add $100 on to the new car they bought. And a study by the Insurance Bureau of Canada showed that the same proportion of Canadian drivers would be willing to pay more for safer cars.

It's not hard to point out some inconsistencies within this new consumers' attitude toward his car. After all, if he is that concerned about safety why does he persistently refuse to put on a safety belt? And if he is that concerned about the side effects of a car's impact on the environment, why does he own a car at all?

The small car apparently offers the most accepted compromise between the need for mobility and a revulsion for despoiling the environment or oneself. The usage and individualism aspects can be seen together in the case of the jazzed-up compact cars. Air conditioning, power brakes, power steering, automatic transmission, vinyl roof: these are the embellishments to be found on the jazzed-up compacts, which in 1973 were the fastest-selling line in the entire car market. Ford, for instance, was building 25 to 35 percent of its Maverick compacts with $400 luxury décor options already tacked on.

In other advanced societies, usage cars have caught on, though in different degrees in different countries. Sweden has probably the largest following of the usage concept in cars, but the possession phase never really developed there, even in the heyday of American materialism. The greatest *change* of attitude is probably still in America. And in Europe, where many can still recall the not so distant past when they didn't own a car, it is still a more valued possession than in America.

In Germany, the car is still an object of worship. Unlike Britain, Saturday car washing is still an earnest ritual. The absence of worn-out old models is astonishing. Maybe the fact that in West Germany home ownership is rare, compared to Britain, means that a car has to satisfy the possession yearnings which an Englishman answers by treating his home as his castle. But it can only be a matter of time before the Germans begin to develop the same sort of aloof, almost hostile relationship to their winged chariots as the Americans and British are now developing (and the fact that the Germans have been first to introduce low-lead gasoline by law is an indication of things to come).

The public expression of a new view toward the automobile isn't just restricted to new types of cars presented in new kinds of ways. Government legislation, as the expression of the will of the people, may be expected eventually to reflect the demos' new views. A car, after all, is not just a vehicle. It is the expression of a particular point of view about transportation. In this sense, Ford and General Motors haven't just been selling cars. They've also tried to affect public taste so that the demand for transportation is expressed as a demand for private cars, not public buses. It is probable that in rejecting General Motors' concept of a car, the public will start to move against the General Motors' concept of transportation. Limits on the free use of the car in the city would be the consequence of this. And legislation generally restricting the use of private cars at the expense of public transportation can be expected.

Those who forecast that the car will go the way of the dinosaur are probably being too ambitious, but it has certainly experienced a profound reversal of its position in society in the space of less than a decade. One could argue that this is a healthy development.

In the role of observer, one point seems clear: if the centerpiece of our affluent society has had to respond to such a degree to changes of attitude by the new consumer, then we have at least a definite and important new trend—a trend which in the long run would have an effect on everything anyone tries to sell, be it mouse-traps or automobiles.

EIGHT

Reading Between the Lies

●

"Knowing I thought up 'Come Home to Birds Eye Country' gives me orgasmic pleasure." [Copywriter at Colman, Prentis and Varley]

If the consumer is starting to grow out of his toys, there's a fair chance that he might also be starting to grow out of his toy shop. It may indeed seem utterly elementary that once significant numbers of the consumers began to change their attitude to material goods they would also change their attitude to the things that brought them those material goods, namely, advertising and marketing. Elementary, perhaps. But judging by most of the official research produced for the advertising establishment on either side of the Atlantic, it would be wrong.

According to the British Institute of Practitioners in Advertising 1969 survey, 79 percent of the population approved either a little or a lot of advertising. That's almost eight out of ten. And this figure was only slightly less than the approval figure of 1961.

On the opposite side of the Atlantic, the position was apparently equally rosy. The 1969 Gallup study showed that two thirds of Americans were favorably disposed toward the statement that "advertising is good for keeping you informed about the things you buy." And 75 percent, according to a study done by Bauer and Greyser, had either a mixed or a favorable attitude toward advertising.

This same study also gave an analysis of people's reactions to the advertisements they paid attention to. Everyone in this exhaustive experiment was given a little counter which they were asked to press every time they paid attention to an advertisement, and every time they felt that the advertisement they noticed was either annoying, enjoyable, informative or offensive, to fill out a card saying so. Of all the cards counted, under 4 percent were dubbed annoying in the sample. And these 4 percent of annoying ads represented less than a quarter of all the advertisements to which the consumer paid sufficient attention to fill out a card.

A survey in 1969 by the Independent Broadcasting Authority on people's attitudes to television commercials reported similar glowing conclusions among the viewers, despite the fact that they were being bombarded by up to eighty commercials a day. Almost half of those interviewed said they found all advertisements enjoyable—a finding endorsed, in the IBA's view, by the fact that it received only sixty letters of complaint in 1971, and a quarter of these were about one specific television commercial.

To the reader, this apparent acceptance of the bombardment of persuasion may appear baffling. Have all our senses been so dulled that we stare with blind contentment at the advertisements, registering but the slightest twinge of displeasure, since we all know in our hearts that advertising is essential for the Free Enterprise System? To anyone who's ever been in a room full of people where the television commercials have been on the air, this conclusion must seem insupportable. Indeed, looking at all these studies, one would never be able to predict the consumer revolution as this book has so far described it. Looking at these data one would conclude that the consumer was in no important respect different from the consumer of 1950, that the wealth and information expositions had never existed, and that all that separated this decade from the last one was the passage of ten years.

But what are these conclusion-shaking data based on? They are simple *quantitative* data: you ask people a straight question with a limited number of options for answers. It's the sort of survey which is beloved by statisticians who believe that when scraping off these surface opinions, they are in fact "measuring" something. Even if something is actually being measured (and a later chapter will probe this sort of research technique more fully), it is undoubtedly true that this particular technique is very slow to sense trends and undercurrents.

Probably a better guide to what people really think is provided

142

by *qualitative* data. This doesn't involve asking direct questions with limited options for answers. It means not so much taking measurements as *soundings*. Qualitative data are often provided by group discussions in which up to a dozen people meet to discuss, under the supervision of a psychologist, some broad general issue which gradually focuses itself, through group participation, onto the topic you want discussed. It's true that such data don't fit onto slide rules so easily, but it does provide a far more sensitive measurement of what people feel.

With this in mind, six group discussions with cross sections of consumers in the Greater London Area were organized with a view to finding out if their in-depth feelings tallied with the results of the other data. The result was something of a shock. The degree of hostility to advertisements that surfaced was quite out of line with the contented smiles the other surveys had led one to expect. A few quotations from the tapes will give the flavor of the discussions.

"I thought they were trying to treat you as a very young child."

"They try to make their products seem better than they are."

"It absolutely irritates me, it's so corny."

"I must say I resent buying magazines full of advertisements . . . I'm the one who's really paying for them."

"At first the commercials are just silly, but when you see them time after time they really annoy you."

"As soon as the commercials come on the air I leave the room."

"You know that all the people giving testimonials have been paid."

"What really makes me boil is when they use children in television commercials."

The phrase that was repeated again and again was "It's only advertising." Clearly, for these consumers, advertising had entirely ceased to be a useful source of information in making product choices, something that isn't useful, but to which you are continually and forcibly exposed.

The other point which emerged was the difference in attitude toward advertisements and advertising. The clean bill of health that the other studies gave was in fact for *advertising*, and the consensus of these in-depth discussions also was that advertising in principle was, if not a "good thing," at least as central a part of life as the car.

When the talk changed from principle to practice, from advertising to *advertisements*, a very different view predominated. The attitude of the consumer to advertising is, in short, very similar to the attitude of a white supremacist Southerner toward an Eastern liberal. In principle, he believes in a free society and the right of others to hold different viewpoints. But in practice he would probably like to have the liberals' guts for garters.

Is it possible to reconcile the earlier data with these more pessimistic conclusions (which common sense would have predicted anyhow)? For a start, it's worth pointing out—if a trifle churlish—that all the figures I quoted earlier were from studies commissioned by bodies with a vested interest in giving advertising a clean bill of health. One of the IBA's jobs is to keep a shine on advertising's public image in Britain. The Bauer and Greyser study was sponsored by the American Association of Advertising Agencies, so it would have been a surprise if their overall conclusions had been vastly different from the expectations of their sponsors. And the IBA has the job of making sure that only appropriate advertisements get onto the television screen, so their standpoint cannot be unbiased.

This is not to say that the researchers who carried out these studies actually fudged their statistics. But if you find, as did the IBA, that 44 percent enjoy television commercials, do you express it in this form (implying all is well) or do you say a minority of television viewers actually enjoys television commercials, an equally accurate version from the evidence? Or take the Bauer and Greyser figure that "only" 25 percent of advertisements to which consumers paid attention were found annoying. On one premise, that would be interpreted as meaning that people have basically a favorable attitude to advertising. On the other hand, once you find—as the group discussions showed—that consumers seem to have a far less favorable attitude, then an alternative interpretation of this same statistic makes more sense. And the 25 percent annoyance level starts to look *high*, not low.

It is reasonable, after all, to expect the brain's filtering mechanism to admit only that information which, on an unconscious level, appears useful to it. Assuming that the brain is an efficient filtering apparatus, one would expect the major portion of advertisements to which a consumer paid attention to be something that he or she found useful or enjoyable. On this basis, every percentage point of disapproval for an advertisement by a consumer represents a degree of disappointment in finding that the message she admitted to her consciousness was not of any use to her. Bauer and Greyser found that one out of four advertisements to which a consumer paid sufficient attention to not only press a hand trigger but also fill out a card came into this category. To have one advertisement in four disappoint the consumer in this way must be a source of great irritation, even more so if one believes, as common sense suggests, that one percentage point of disapproval probably carries more weight than one percentage point of approval, in the same way that discomfort is a stronger sensation than comfort. In fact, if one looks at other parts of the voluminous Bauer and Greyser survey, figures arise from the morass of statistics that cast grave doubt on the overall favorable impression implied.

They have, for example, a table of "top of the mind sources of annoyance." This was established by putting this question: "Everyone has some things that annoy them, like health, money and other people. Aside from that kind of personal problem, what four or five things annoy you most?" Excluding the personal sources of annoyance, like the inconsideration of your neighbor hanging up her washing just before your friends are coming in for coffee, the main percentages of spontaneous mentions of annoyance were as follows:

Noise	13%
Things relating to advertising	9
Government and government policies	6
Traffic	4
Weather	4
Breaking down of machinery	4
Politics and politicians	3
Housework	1

The fact that one American in ten finds advertising a source of everyday annoyance is serious enough news for the advertising community. What is even more revealing than the absolute measurement is the ranking of advertising. It received as many *spontaneous* mentions as a source of annoyance as the whole apparatus of government, government policies, politics and politicians, and it is *nine* times more annoying for most Americans than the everyday drudgery of housework.

This table was not referred to in either of the two leaflets prepared in Britain by the Institute of Practitioners in Advertising for public consumption, although it *was* mentioned in an IPA document, marked "Strictly Confidential," published in September 1967.

The figures in this table have extra significance in view of the fact that Bauer and Greyser also found that advertising wasn't very "salient" to people's lives. Three times as many people mentioned the federal government, rather than advertising, as something they talk about most. Yet despite the fact that advertising is not at the forefront of people's consciousness, it is still one of the main public sources of annoyance.

Even in 1964 (when the research on which these findings were based was carried out) one sixth of Americans felt that advertising needed immediate attention and change. (Please note that 1964 was before the arrival of Ralph Nader and before the growth of the consumerist ground swell described in this book.) As recently as 1970 Dr. John Treasure of J. Walter Thompson felt confident enough to issue a report on public attitudes to advertising, basing several of his conclusions on the optimistic interpretation of these 1964 Bauer and Greyser data. It is no wonder that many admen gravely underestimated the hostility they faced.

In fact, the warning signs—as the Bauer and Greyser figures show—were clearly there. But either the measuring instruments were too insensitive to pick up the tremors, or if sensed, those interpreting the data mistook the evidence.

Even in 1972, when the IPA in Britain published the greatest assessment of public attitudes toward advertising, its conclusions were overall optimistic and it advised policy makers not to be "misled by the clamour of a tiny and unrepresentative anti-advertising lobby." Yet within the pages of that same report were figures showing a 30 percent slump in the number of people who approved strongly of advertising in just three years. Such is the power of selective perception.

On those rare occasions when the advertising establishment in a moment of weakness was persuaded to concede the existence of some hostility toward advertising, they always added a proviso. They argued that this hostility was purely an educated middle-class quirk—"a small percentage of narrow, ascetic or clannish people," to quote Mr. John Hobson, chairman of the Advertising Association—and that among the bulk of the marketplace there was still a benign tolerance for the advertising practitioner, whose excesses are allegedly taken with no more than a pinch of good-humored cynicism.

This belief is similar in pedigree to the idea that consumerism is a strictly middle-class kink. In a formal sense it may be true. Few working-class wives have a coherently worked out position to justify their feeling of hostility toward a majority of advertisements. But you don't need to be able to justify a feeling in order to have it. And the evidence of all the in-depth discussions was that the hostility toward advertising spreads right across the class scale. The fact that working-class papers as well as professional media run Nader-style exposés of advertising and its related arts surely confirms this. Anyone who believes that a docile proletariat exists happily lapping up the jingles has had his senses numbed by too many dry martinis.

The development of hostility among the workers is worrying enough for the hidden persuaders. What is as alarming is that the business community is also growing hostile toward advertising. Businessmen wear two hats: they're both consumers and advertisers. And if this group is starting to bite the hand that allegedly feeds them, the ulcers of Madison Avenue have good reason to twinge. A study in the *Harvard Business Review*, carried out by Steven Greyser, found that "Businessmen today take a somewhat more critical stance than they did nine years ago." He found, for example, that a majority of the 2,700 businessmen interviewed thought that—compared to nine years ago—there was a greater proportion of advertisements which insulted the public's intelligence, which insulted their own intelligence, and which were irritating. A similar picture emerged in Britain. A National Opinion Poll there revealed that only 1 percent of the upper-income groups thought advertising was a worthwhile career. After the Watergate affair, where several of President Nixon's staff who testified before the Senate committee had previously worked for J. Walter Thompson, advertising can expect a similar rejection as a career option in America.

The most extraordinary aspect of this reaction against advertising was not that this ill feeling should exist, but that the advertising industry should believe that it didn't, or if it did, then only in forms and in areas that were so tiny or so limited as to be of no practical significance. Very few admen sitting down to write an advertisement believed that they were addressing an overwhelmingly hostile audience. It is rather as though a Democratic politician were to address a meeting of staunch Republican party supporters with the same speech and in the same way as he would address a rally of Democratic party faithfuls.

That enormous companies entrust equally enormous sums of money and their reputation to people with this degree of foresight may surprise the reader. We shall save our explanations of this for the following chapters, where the curious theory of how advertising works will be explored. But first a more pressing question demands an answer: If it is accepted that the majority of the population was far more hostile to advertising than the advertising industry had led itself to believe, can the industry still be blamed for this hostility? Hasn't enough already been said in this book about a revolt against authority, about a more educated and sophisticated consumer, to show that this hostility is simply the backwash inevitably produced as our great society sails farther and yet farther forward?

It is a plausible argument—not the least because it is partly true—that the structural changes within affluent societies in the last twenty years *have* created conditions within which hostility toward advertising, as the torchbearer of a way of life increasingly under attack, was likely. But that is not to say that such hostility was *inevitable*. It was not inevitable that advertising should generate nine times more hostility than the drudgery of housework (which is also resented by the modern woman). It was not inevitable that advertising should generate as much hostility as the whole apparatus of government, government policies, politics and politicians (also resented as the concept of authority begins to crumble). What has happened is that the advertising industry has willfully lit fires which are now threatening to roast it alive.

The first of these generators of hostility is admittedly something not easily within the control of the adman himself: the sheer volume of advertising. Apart from selflessly cutting back his own budget, there may be little an individual advertiser can do. That the whole industry is so helpless to restrict the volume of its own outpourings is not quite so obvious.

In fairness, it should be said that the growth of advertising is just another dimension of the information explosion mentioned earlier. Malcolm Muggeridge has coined the phrase "newsak" to describe the information pollution that harries him when he seeks peace and quiet in his car or in his bathroom. The total volume of this is reported by Alvin Toffler to be ten to twenty thousand words of printed material and twenty thousand words of radio and television material "ingested" per day.

Although the editorial side of this information input is huge, it is at least something which the consumer has chosen to look at. She turns on the television set to watch *Ironside* or *Bonanza*. She opens the paper to read the news. But the battery of advertising messages has no such invitation. Very few people actually open a paper or turn on the TV set to see the advertisements.

Estimates of the number of these uninvited intrusions into the consumer's day vary from about 500 (based on a calculation done by a marketing director of General Foods) to 305 a day for women and 285 a day for men (based on a recent study by BBDO, New York). Even at this lowest figure it still represents an orgy of abrasive sound and sight all designed to induce the consumer to do something he or she might not otherwise do. And all the time this din is getting louder. The American semanticist S. I. Hayakawa has calculated that by the age of eighteen, the modern American child has watched 350,000 commercials. In Britain in 1952, for example, £126 million was the total expenditure on advertising. By 1969, at 1952 space rates, this had grown by *two and a half times,* to £315 million (or £535 million in actual money). The growth of "invisible" (as opposed to conventional display advertising) classified advertising accounts for some of the increase. But this "invisible" advertising still had no higher proportion of all advertising in 1969 than 1952. In America in 1970 there were 31 percent more minutes of TV commercials transmitted than in 1960; there were 79 percent more commercials than in 1960; and 133 percent more network commercials per month than in 1960.

A chart in the Bauer and Greyser study (p. 298) shows that advertisements for the six most heavily advertised product groups were thought to be *twice* as annoying and almost *half* as informative as the advertisements for the remaining (and less advertised) product groups. On this basis, the more you spend, the more hostility you risk creating. Extra hostility also comes from the fact that so much of the advertising for these heavily promoted product categories appears to be for virtually identical products. Indeed, adman Al Ries has calculated that a *quarter* of all American advertising is between virtually identical competitive products, so the uproar becomes even less justified from the consumers' standpoint. The result is that advertising is now widely regarded as being as much a pollutant as the fog and filth that choke our cities.

Of course, it is not just the volume of advertising that has caused this; the *content* has quite a lot to answer for as well. The deluge of persuasion might be *just* acceptable if like the clergyman who knocks on your door, it were polite, respectful and truthful. But on the grounds of truthfulness alone, advertising is found seriously wanting.

The *Reader's Digest* Survey of Europe showed that only 37 percent of people were either partially or generally favorable to the statement that "In general, advertising presents a true picture of the product advertised." In Britain and America, *two thirds* of the population disagreed with this statement, and disbelief in advertising is growing. The biggest single shift, measured by Steven Greyser in his *Harvard Business Review* study comparing businessmen's attitudes to advertising in 1962 and 1971, was in this area. He found that the proportion of businessmen who believed advertising presented a true picture of the product had slumped by 24 percent. By 1971 the proportion of businessmen who believed that advertising told the truth was even *lower* than the proportion of the general public that did. And businessmen, as clients of the advertising agencies, are the ones who ought to know. On the other side of the Atlantic, a study by the International Publishing Corporation found that 42 percent of young consumers thought all advertisements were misleading. About the same number told the IBA's researchers that television commercials weren't to be trusted. So if you put all the various statistics together, you have half at least the population believing that despite the rules and regulations advertising isn't truthful.

Again, the *more* you advertise the *less* truthful your advertising appears to be. Bauer and Greyser found that among five of the seven top-spending advertising categories, "informational failure" (a polite way of saying that the advertisement was judged by the consumer to be untruthful in some way or another) was often *double* the average of the lower-spending product categories. This is probably a measure of the degree to which big advertisers have continually succumbed to the temptation to stretch credulity further and further in order to add to their sales points. But all that has happened is that their advertisements are taken with approximately larger pinches of salt by the consumer. According to Professor Galbraith, the consumer has now developed a mechanism for dealing with these untruths. He writes in *The New Industrial State*: "Because modern man is exposed to a large degree of unreliable information, he establishes a system of discounts which he applies to the various sources (of information) almost without question. This discount becomes almost total for all forms of advertising." It's a rather chilling thought for anyone whose livelihood depends on his ability to make consumers respond to the advertising messages he creates.

Brian Young, director general of the IBA, doubtless wouldn't agree with this. He told a gathering of London admen that "If there is a problem, it is not a question of deception. It's a question of disbelief." In other words, though advertising has been telling the truth, the complete truth and nothing but the truth, a cruel and cynical public persists in disbelieving it.

A behavioral psychologist could tell Young that this disbelief is no more than a conditioned reflex as a result of continual disappointments after taking advertisements at their word. And if one looks at "The Effects of Television Advertising on Children and Adolescents" (a million-dollar study prepared with the aid of a U.S. government grant by the Marketing Science Institute), one begins to see how distrust for advertising develops even before a child can fully understand the advertisement itself. Kindergarten children, according to this study, had "virtually no understanding of the purpose of the commercials." Yet what did a kindergarten child answer to the question "Do you think commercials always tell the truth?": "Nooooo!"

By the age of *seven*, children have a "clear recognition that advertisements were intended to sell" and "semi-recognition of the advertisers' motives." For example, Question: "What are advertisements for?" Answer: "To make you buy [products]." Question: "Why do they want you to buy?" Answer: "So they can get more money and support the factories they have." All from a seven-year-old.

This "cue to manipulative intent," to use the psychologist's jargon, has somehow been learned by the child. Maybe by watching his parents' reaction to television commercials, he has already grown this membrane of skepticism. But from then on, the mere

151

act of selling to him will put his psychological bristles up and trigger off the Galbraithian system of discounts.

But it's not just something he has learned from his parents or teachers. "Second graders," says the study, "indicated concrete distrust of commercials *often based on experience of advertised products*" (my italics). "Fourth graders exhibited mistrust of specific commercials and tricky elements of commercials, and sixth graders exhibit global mistrust." "Global mistrust" from a boy whose voice hasn't even changed.

And the number-one reason behind this generally contemptuous attitude of American children? A further study showed that products are "not like the ads say they are" was the reason given.

Any adult who has ever seen a commercial for toy racing cars that makes it seem as though they're selling high-power dragsters (like the Johnny Lightning script quoted earlier) or watched a dancing-doll commercial that suggests you're really buying a syncopated robot that frugs like a sixteen-year-old, can understand the disillusionment of a child. No wonder, then, that the London *Financial Times* reported from the Brighton Toy Fair that retailers were now disenchanted with hard-sell television advertising. Even though the manufacturers had jacked up their expenditure on television by 20 percent, it didn't work as effectively as the previous year. After reading the U.S. government–Marketing Science report, the reason for this failure in Britain is surely clear: the children had learned to disbelieve the exaggeration of the advertisements and weren't going to be taken in a second year running.

Up to this point, the assumption has been made that the consumer *requires* an advertisement to be truthful, and if it isn't, he places a black mark against it. But is this correct? Or do consumers grant poetic license to the practitioners of commercial verse?

In one sense, the discussion is an old one: "Doth any man doubt," asked Sir Francis Bacon in his essay on Truth, "that if there were taken out of men's minds vain opinions, flattering hopes, false valuations, imaginations as one would, and the like, but it would leave the minds of a number of men poor shrunken things, full of melancholy and indisposition and unpleasing to themselves?" Four centuries later came Harvard's distinguished Professor Theodore Levitt to press the same case for advertising. "I shall argue," he wrote in the *Harvard Business Review*, "that embellishment and distortion are among advertising's legitimate and socially desirable purposes." For advertising, like art, achieved its effect by being larger than life. Moreover, echoing Master Bacon, "without distortions, embellishment and elaboration life would be drab, dull, anguished and at its existential worst."

Whether the exaggerations and distortions of advertising do in fact act like a ray of sunshine in the gray little lives all of us lead is something the reader must judge for himself. Certainly, a claim that is obviously not meant to be taken too seriously and is perhaps treated humorously (like "The disadvantages of smoking Benson and Hedges 100s") may come into the category of accepted embellishment. But do the whiter-than-white soap operas have the same charm?

The trouble with any argument that advertising is entitled to the same illusions as literature is that it forgets that literature declares quite openly that it is an illusion. Advertising generally does not; it hides this fact for nakedly commercial reasons. While Keats' "Ode on a Grecian Urn" may be embellishing the truth, it is intended to uplift your soul, but an ode to a new cake mix is intended only to uplift the sales graph.

Those who declare that the two situations are the same must answer for part of the credibility gap that now separates advertising from its audience. Is it any wonder that many consumers now believe advertising is simply lying raised to the heights of respectability when the admen are given this sort of encouragement to gild their lilies?

A cartoon in one of the American advertising papers indicates the path to which a less than scrupulous regard for truth leads. It shows a round-table meeting of advertising executives, with one of them saying: "Seventy hospitals tested our product and found it completely ineffectual. But we can still advertise it as 'hospital tested.'" This, of course, is a joke, but it betrays the core of cynicism about the value of verity that is alarming. Few who have worked even for a short time in an agency can have failed to be infected (and the present writer does not claim immunity) by the open acceptance of the stretching of truth which is the *practical* consequences of Theodore Levitt's philosophy. It has led to the advertisers' belief that they have a license to exaggerate. Hence the chorus of unsubstantiated superlatives which, even if not taken at face value by the public, serve to still further debase the coinage of advertising.

Even those carefully checked television demonstrations can be guilty of creating a false impression in the eyes of the consumer. For instance, a British paint company trying to demonstrate the covering power of its paint showed a brush overpainting a black-and-white checkerboard with remarkable effect. What wasn't shown was that when this paint dried, the black-and-white checkerboard showed through the dry film of paint. Sometimes the misleading impression comes about through unintentional mistakes. Lever Brothers discovered in Britain that though laboratory washing of clothes did indeed produce the whiter-than-white results shown in the television commercials, the public wasn't skilled enough or didn't have the right laundry equipment to get the same results. A collection of towels washed ten times by housewives with the same powder used in the television commercials ranged from white to very, very dirty-gray.

But whatever the reason, the loss of credibility for advertising moves remorselessly onward and will continue to do so until admen recognize that their license to exaggerate has expired and—in the current consumer environment—is not renewable.

Disbelief in advertising has led, naturally enough, to disbelief in the mouth that apparently utters these not so magic words: the advertiser. A study by the Supermarket Institute of America found that only car salesmen were thought to be lower in credibility than advertising executives, and government officials were regarded as being *forty* times more credible than advertising executives. The position, in a phrase, is that the advertisers are now regarded as compulsive liars, people whose job of selling products makes them almost incapable of telling the truth.

In Victorian times it probably was possible for the untruth of advertising to be tolerable in the same way that someone always telling tall stories is tolerable (and sometimes amusing). You know that you're listening to a fib, so you don't take it too seriously. But how would you feel if this compulsive liar burst into your living room every night and pestered you with fibs and half-truths? Would you still smile as you did when Beecham's told you its pills were worth the (preposterous) sum of "a guinea a box"? It is this barging in without even bothering to knock, the intrusiveness of the new advertising media—television—that has eroded still further the consumer's tolerance of his persuaders.

Reverting once more to our faithful friends Bauer and Greyser, one finds that when asked why they found certain advertisements annoying, consumers mentioned "intrusiveness" *even more often than* "informational failure." In other words, the sheer act of having something rammed down your throat is as unpleasant as its bad taste. The "intrusive" medium is, of course, television, even though "involving," not "intrusive," is the word Marshall McLuhan would use to describe the electronic medium.

Perhaps the point is that television, which should be a very low-pressure, open-ended medium, has been used by advertisers as a high-pressure huckster. In McLuhan's terminology, they have treated a cool medium as though it were hot. The fact that most television commercial jingles are nearly always used as radio commercials as well shows how the advertiser treats television as though it were no more than "radio with pictures." You only need to look at the special television stars like Johnny Carson, Dick Cavett or Mike Douglas and compare their *style* with the style of the advertisements that slice up their shows. What has happened is that advertising has used the undoubted power of the television medium to *force* attention, when perhaps it should have used it to *invite* involvement and participation.

In printed advertising, advertisers can get away with this practice without being quite so irritating, because it is easier not to look at the ad. Being still and silent, it is less obtrusive. And even more important, there is alternative viewing matter while you are being exposed to the advertisement. This is not true of a television commercial. On television your program is interrupted by an advertisement in a way that your newspaper is not. The consumer still has a whole battery of defense mechanisms to keep out the television intrusion. But it is the fact that he has to work so hard not to pay attention to something he doesn't want to look at that is the source of irritation.

A 1969 British study, prepared by J. Walter Thompson for the IPA, gives the scale of this compulsory exposure to advertisements for products in which the consumer isn't even interested (however brilliant the commercial). In the first six months of 1969 the males who watched television most frequently saw over 200 detergent commercials, 125 margarine commercials and 120 toilet-soap commercials. Female viewers had the pleasure of seeing 125 draft-beer commercials and 100 razor-blade commercials. It is no wonder that television advertising was shown in the same study to be ten times more annoying and ten times sillier than press advertising. Five times as many people said they'd be happy to see television advertising done away with compared to press advertising.

The truth is that the very reversal is happening in many countries. Twenty years ago in Britain, for example, there was no advertising on television. Since the introduction of commercial television in 1955, the proportion has steadily risen until today more than £ 1 in £ 4 spent by advertisers is spent on television. For the really big advertisers the proportion was even higher: fifty-seven of the top one hundred British advertisers spent more than half of their budget on television.

But even if the total level of television advertising were not rising, the way it was spent could still make the *amount* of this intrusive form of advertising appear to increase. In America, for example, the shift from 60-second to 30-second commercials helped to cause a 50 percent increase in the number of commercials transmitted on the network from 1964 to 1968. They shot up from 1,950 a month to 3,022 a month. Despite this growth, even American television at the heaviest peak of advertising has no more than 27 percent of television time devoted to advertising (which is one of the highest figures in the world). The average magazine or newspaper carries, proportionately, a great deal more advertising than this. Few advertising managers feel satisfied unless they have sold 40 percent of the total space in the paper to advertisers. Clearly, then, the same amount of money spent in the press would generate far less hostility than that amount spent on television. The following table makes the point that in Europe at least, the more minutes of television advertising which are allowed, the greater the hostility toward advertising.

In some of these countries there are extra restraints which would reduce still further the irritating impact of television commercials. In Italy, for instance, a television commercial can't be repeated more than five times; it has to be changed, thus saving the viewer from the endlessly repetitive bombardment common in other countries.

COUNTRY	MINUTES OF TELEVISION ADVERTISING ALLOWED PER DAY	PERCENTAGE FAVORABLE TO ADVERTISING*
Holland	10	79%
France	13	72
Switzerland	15	61
Germany	20	51
Austria	20	64
Italy	27	61
Spain	60	42

* *Reader's Digest* Survey.

There is one final aspect of the intrusiveness of television advertising which merits some consideration. The move to television in countries like Britain and America has shifted the brunt of advertising down the class scale. Printed media, by virtue of the fact that they require some effort, are read most by better-educated people. Television, because it requires less effort, is watched most by the least educated. Workers in Britain, for instance, watch 31 percent more television than business executives.

Moreover, given the extraordinarily irritating nature of television advertising, one has here a further explanation of why, in Britain, consumer power has been provoked into existence in the working class as well as the middle class. Contrary to a view popular in certain advertising agencies, the working classes are not simply the middle classes with less money and less brains; their structure of life is profoundly different and one of the key differences concerns the role of the home. The home for the affluent white-collar worker, already regarding himself as middle-class, is a place to which even distant friends are invited. It is not a holy of holies reserved only for kin and very close friends, which it is for the blue-collar worker (as Goldthorpe and his colleagues discovered). It is into this very private sanctuary that the advertisers send their television commercials every night. To a middle-class home, which is not such a closed environment, these uninvited incursions into the living room are bad enough. But for the working-class man, his privacy has been shattered in a quite different sort of way.

When the advertiser opens his mouth to actually deliver his sales spiel, he generally does it in a way that alienates his audience still further. The blame for this lies with the various philosophies of

157

advertising that lie behind the sales messages. If one looks at these it becomes clear that the way advertisers have chosen to speak to their public has had the effect of rubbing salt into the already open wound. Of the five main philosophies of advertising, four must be regarded as profound irritants to the consumer.

If we take a thirty-five-year-old housewife of today we can trace over her lifespan a variety of theories of communication that have been practiced on her, whose net effect has probably been to make her not so much think more of the product as to think less of the advertising. At the time this thirty-five-year-old was born, Claude Hopkins was waging war on the fierce style of advertising that had held sway between the wars. Hopkins, who wrote "Washed in live steam" to make Schlitz the best-selling beer in America (earning himself a salary of over $1 million a year at today's rate), had no time for such pleasantries. "The average person," he wrote, "is constantly choosing between ways to spend his money. Appeal for money in a lightsome way and you'll never get it. Nobody can cite a permanent success built of frivolity. People do not buy from clowns." This joyless doctrine, which eventually led to the view that if consumers actually liked your advertisement there was probably something wrong with it, runs like a thin thread of gloom through many of the subsequent theories of advertising.

Immediately after the war a man named Rosser Reeves put on Hopkins' mantle. By then it was clear that the natural state of products in a mass-production society was similarity. Some people write as though this were a recent phenomenon. But ever since Henry Ford got his Tin Lizzies rolling, it has been normal for the actual differences between competing products to be small. Of course, each product tended to be different in some way, but the difference was strictly marginal.

It was out of these marginal differences between brands that Rosser Reeves believed the admen should construct his own Unique Selling Proposition. The "uniqueness" of the proposition was just as likely to result from making a unique claim about an otherwise homogenous product as it was from having a unique product itself. But having got your U.S.P., you then hammered those few magic words into the consumer's skull in the same way that a carpenter bangs a nail into a plank, and very often with the same result: the recipient got a severe headache.

Some of the better-known U.S.P.s include Colgate's, "Helps

158

stop bad breath, fights tooth decay" (which had been running at least as long as Agatha Christie's *Mousetrap*); M&M's, "Melts in your mouth, not in your hand"; and Fairy Liquid's, "Hands that do dishes can feel soft as your face."

In fairness to the U.S.P., it should be said that in the postwar economy, when consumer goods were in short supply and where the media environment was less saturated, this approach made some sort of sense. Judged by the agency's own standards it certainly worked, but by the late fifties, as both wealth and education levels rose, some practitioners of the art began to feel that making major claims out of marginal product differences was no longer sensible. "Let us remember," pontificated David Ogilvy, "that it is always the total personality of the brand rather than any trivial product differences which decides its ultimate position in the market." In short, forget the quality, feel the myth. This was the theory of the brand image. Ogilvy became amazingly successful thanks to his ability to put his client's products on a pedestal and worship them in magnificent English prose—like Hathaway shirts, Schweppes tonic water and Rolls-Royce cars.

But though this sort of advertising (which, by the way, was an addition to, and not a replacement of, the Hopkins/Reeves school) *did* create less hostility, in the sense that it was less prone to driving sales points into consumer's skulls, it created another sort of irritation instead, for the image of the product that could satisfy all the dimensions of the consumer's personality was far from the truth—and consumers knew it.

The other sort of irritation that resulted from Ogilvy related to the language he recommended that admen use. Although he was the man who said, "The consumer is no moron, she is your wife," he was also the man who suggested a basic vocabulary for the would-be successful advertiser of twenty-five key words, such as *new, free, important, sensational,* etc., without any qualification as to how relevant they might be to the product concerned. Perhaps it's revealing that in none of his best advertisements did Ogilvy fall back on the formula he so keenly recommended to others.

After the publicity Ogilvy gave to brand imagery, it soon ran out of control with motivation researchers rushing in to discover that everything was full of hidden meaning. Even eating your breakfast cereal meant a lot more than simply filling your stomach. In the words of the high priest of motivation research, Ernest

Dichter: "Breakfast, or breaking the fast, has an interesting psychological role. The greater the fighting attitude people have towards the struggle of the day, the more they seem to be insistent on consuming a good breakfast. This is one of the reasons why mushy soft cereals are rejected." When it didn't stray over the lunatic fringe, most of this so-called motivation research was just sound common sense. But in the hands of an American professor of journalism called Vance Packard it became something else. Admen were "hidden persuaders," and consumers were mere lumps of clay to be molded and shaped to the ends of big business.

Whether or not this is how advertising works is something to be discussed later. But the important point to be made now is that all this research persuaded many advertisers and their agencies that they possessed semimagical powers, and that image-rich, motivation-inspired advertising ruled the world. This was the period when glossy materialism received its greatest promotion. The fact that many consumers were already falling out of love with it was something that most of the admen overlooked.

The lone voice in the wilderness was that of Bill Bernbach, who in 1948 had helped start an agency called Doyle, Dane, Bernbach. Rather than hero-worshiping the product, he treated it as an anti-hero. Like the consumer, he took a slightly irreverent view of the product. He admitted that not every product was perfect (remember the advertisement showing a picture of a shining Volkswagen with the word "Lemon" underneath?). He recognized that for the consumer, "biggest" didn't always mean "best" (remember Avis' "We're number two" campaign?).

Unfortunately, Bill Bernbach wasn't as vigorous as Ogilvy or Reeves in selling his philosophy. For example, the other two wrote books to explain their beliefs, but Bernbach made no such missionary efforts for his particular cause. The result was that his view of advertising, which *could* have defused a lot of the hostility that has since built up, remained a minority cult. The new clean-limbed graphics of the Bernbach school were certainly widely adopted, but for the most part they were just new clothes for the old thoughts of Reeves and Ogilvy.

One extraordinary fact about advertising techniques is that since 1960 there has been virtually no new thinking of the advertising basics. The industry is still shuffling the pack of the pre-1960 ideas and coasting along on the dynamism of times very different from our own. This fashionable, highly paid, fast-talking profession seems to have run out of ideas (as opposed to glib headlines). And they are now, by and large, selling to Mrs. 1974 in *basically* the same way as they sold to Mrs. 1954. If you strip their handiwork of the slick graphic and look at the central core, it isn't a lot different from the ads of yesteryear.

The only exception to this intellectual sterility has come from someone who is in no way part of Madison Avenue hurly-burly— Marshall McLuhan. McLuhan's particular style of writing is to throw out a barrage of ideas and ask the reader to sift the good from the bad: "probes," he calls them. Some of McLuhan's "probes" about advertising are just what one might expect from an ex-Wordsworth scholar who wanders lonely as a cloud to be suddenly confronted by a field of plastic daffodils (free with Tide). For example, he describes puns as one of the highest forms of advertising because they act as a decoy for the brain's rational defense mechanisms. While the consumer is occupied unraveling the pun, the subjective imagery of the advertisement rushes with electronic speed into her cranium to manipulate her as the advertiser wishes.

The sad point about McLuhan's impact on television advertising was that he did have some important things to say, particularly about the impact of nonverbal, unfocused advertising messages on people, and the right and wrong ways to use television as an advertising medium. But as the line of his argument ran directly counter to the practices of the admen, it tended not to be identified.

So there we have it: Rosser Reeves, David Ogilvy, Ernest Dichter, Bill Bernbach, Marshall McLuhan—the stuffing that the hidden persuaders are made of.

If we go back to the American study of television advertising and children, an interesting parallel emerges between the assorted techniques of the admen and the cognitive development of a child. The authors of this part of the study (Blatt, Spencer and Ward) put together the work of educational psychologists on a child's cognitive development and deduced from that the sort of advertising appeals that would be most appropriate at each level. The first level of a child's development, at the age of five, is where he is impulsive, self-protective and submissive. "At this level viewers respond principally to basic needs and fears and tend to be most receptive to commercials which demand, threaten or use hard sell." And "advertisements aimed at this level can be blunt, direct and concrete." Cast your mind back to the Reeves/Hopkins school of advertising and you see that it will work like clockwork on a five-year-old.

Level two, according to this study, is characterized by "intentional self-interest." "Viewers at this level are most susceptible to appeals to 'hedonistic' personal desires, 'mastery' and 'power.' Themes which appeal to self-image . . . and sexual identity."

So by the age of six to seven, the child has outgrown a susceptibility to Rosser Reeves's techniques and has become susceptible to what amounts to brand-image advertising *à la* Dichter and Ogilvy. The power of this sort of appeal lasts through level three (the eight-year-olds), when conformity is the order of the day. "Viewers at this level are most susceptible to 'other-directed' appeals—comparisons with others, themes based on an individual's need for social approval, popularity and status." This, in short, is brand-image advertising that recognizes the influence of others in addition to the influence of self (of level two).

But by the time level four (aged ten) is reached, the child is no longer under the influence of such spells. Now "conscientiousness' is part of a child's mental development, so the viewer responds to appeals to duty, functional utility and rational role requirements.

Level-four appeals, says this study, tend to be objective and factual—which, of course, is almost a blueprint for Bill Bernbach. By the age of twelve, a child has started to outgrow even this higher level, for the final level identified is what is called "social utilitarian integrative and self-actualizing." "Viewers at this level respond preferentially to aesthetic, altruistic moral social concern appeals: buy this and you'll improve society while attaining your own highest potential." This is the level that advertisers have not yet reached.

The advertiser continually and persistently insults the consumer's intelligence, first by promoting trivia as though it were God's gift to humanity, and second, by talking to consumers as though they belonged to a school for backward children.

If the advertising were selling something important (like health insurance, for example), hollering and shouting might be tolerable. But to simply dispose of what may be regarded as the flotsam

162

and jetsam of the industrial state, the bombardment of persuasion is just too much. It isn't only the screams that upset the consumers, it's the way the advertiser always seems to be talking about things that are meaningless to the consumer, and talking about them in a way which gives the product a ludicrously overimportant role in somebody's life. The detergent (Daz) that will make the neighbors think more of you when they see your nice white washing on the line. Or in America, Fab, the detergent "that will help these girls to get married" (a detergent)? The bedtime drink (Horlicks) that can turn a Weary Willy into a superman by the quaffing of flavored malted milk every night. And always there is the suggestion that by swallowing some chemical you can solve the sort of problems that would have baffled Freud.

But the fact is that these roll-on fairy godmothers exist only as a figment of the advertisers' fevered minds. Face creams don't subtract years from the face. A cigarette isn't the peak of a relationship that two people can reach (even when it is mentholated). No detergent, even when it's called Fab, can transform a crumpled thirty-five-year-old housewife into looking like "a bride every time." "It's no surprise that the satisfactions offered in advertising are mainly marginal," said the Advertising Association in its statement on "The Social Contribution of Advertising." No surprise, at least, to everyone but the creators of the advertisements, for the satisfactions are normally presented in a way which suggests that they are very far from marginal.

Believe it or not, there are people who turn out this sort of advertisement every day and who seriously feel that in doing so they're adding to the sum total of happiness in the world. As a copywriter at McCann-Erickson explained: "If you have 'all day freshness' and a 'ring of confidence' and you stopped making those 'simple mistakes in everyday English,' you must be a better person for it."

Must you? The new customer as we have described her just doesn't think like that. The less she worships the 1950 concept of materialism, the more she declares its gods are false. And to suggest that a mere dollar-fifty product can perform any of these quasi-spiritual functions for her is to betray a lack of respect and understanding for Mrs. 1974. She doesn't believe that the sum total of happiness is clean clothes, clean breath and (nowadays) a clean vagina. Fullfillment for her is not just a matter of showing her husband and their 2.4 children how much she loves them by the brand of soup she chooses for them.

This yawning gap between the values of the advertiser and the values of the consumer shows up sharpest in the so-called slice-of-life commercials. It's a slice that nobody lives—not the advertiser, and certainly not the consumer. Even the businessman who pays for the advertisements "don't think that people in advertisements are pretty much like the way people really are" (according to Greyser's *Harvard Business Review* study). After all, how many times has your next-door neighbor rushed in to talk to you about a new lavatory cleaner? It may hurt the sales manager's feelings, but these products just aren't that central to people's lives. Compare the dialogue of the top British TV program *Coronation Street,* with the language of the commercials in the middle of it. One is about real people, the other is about cardboard figures that even an avalanche of glistening adjectives and a coating of North Country dialect can't bring to life. Or take the new slice-of-life films and compare them to the advertisement. *Midnight Cowboy, Easy Rider, Tell Them Willie Boy Is Here* are just three of the new realistic (usage) movies. Compared to the slice of life that such films betray, the resemblance in advertising to any person living or dead is purely coincidental.

Talking to people who don't exist with words that don't mean anything is one way for the admen to keep themselves out of the consumer's heart. An equally good way is to trivialize important emotions and feelings by trying to link them to their products. Like Greens of Brighton, which ran an advertisement for its *cake mix* with the headline "How to be the best mum in the world in 30 minutes." The rationale behind this has been provided by the British adman Ronnie Kirkwood, who believes that today's woman "is positively interested in any product that can make her a better wife, a better mother, a better cook." All this from a can of beans or a bottle of bleach?

The emotion which has been most used by the admen as wrapping for their products is, of course, sex. Ultrabrite is a toothpaste with sex appeal. Certs breath mints ask, "If he kissed you once, will he kiss you again?" Even gravy mixes are apparently aphrodisiac potions. The recent King Beef commercial on British television showed a young permissive wife mixing the King Beef gravy mix for the young trendy husband and ended with the memorable lines "King Beef . . . it makes everything between us better . . . well, almost everything" hint, hint.

A Tokyo psychiatrist, Dr. Solichi Hakozaki, kept a "sex in ads" check over a seven-year period. He found sexual expression in about 30 percent of the advertisements he monitored.

But how can the use of something which consumers are so fond of, sex, be a cause of consumer irritation when the advertiser uses it to tart up his wares? First, because the relationship is normally a phony one. Second, because it's debasing an important emotion by putting it on the supermarket shelf. The actual way the advertiser talks about sex is a further example of the distance that separates the audience from the advertiser. The coy sexual innuendo is right off key for a twenty-five-year-old girl to whom sex is something in the open, rather normal, and altogether very different from the leering wink that the wet-dreaming adman sends her as his mistaken impression of the real thing.

Presenting trivia as important, suggesting that this same trivia can do important things, and trivializing important emotions in the process are all different features of the same phenomenon—a belief that the consumer is dumb. Nothing else can explain the extraordinary achievement of grown men in trying to get consumers to buy their wares. Marshall McLuhan opined that because reading an advertisement aloud made it sound ridiculous, it must be targeted not on your conscious but on your subconscious. A more reasonable explanation, though admittedly less exotic, is that the advertisement is simply laughable.

Martin Mayer reports this delightful conversation between an advertising man and his young son in *Madison Avenue, U.S.A.*: "The other day the kids were watching television and one of those cartoon commercials came on. It showed two big wrestlers in a ring, one with the label 'pain' on his robe and the other with the label 'ordinary pain killer.' The 'pain' then threw 'ordinary pain killer' out of the ring. Then another wrestler climbed into the ring with this brand name stenciled onto his robe, and he threw 'pain' out of the ring, knocking him out completely. My own boy called me aside and said, 'Dad, am I to understand that a bunch of grown men sat down and said that was a good idea, and another bunch of grown men went to all the trouble to make a movie out of it?' "

No wonder that over a third of the adolescents covered in the U.S. government–Market Science study of the effect of advertising on children criticized commercials because they are "stupid . . . and insult the intelligence."

As has been shrewdly observed, the only person nowadays with a mind of a thirteen-year-old is a six-year-old. Yet the advertisers have completely ignored this. Just pick up any women's magazine, for example, and compare the editorial on beauty or the editorial on dieting with the advertisements for products in either category. The beauty editorial deals factually and simply with how to cope with real problems, accepting as it must that not all its readers look like Elizabeth Taylor. But the advertisements? Listen to this piece of copy for a Revlon ad: "Hear it crashing now, on the softer shores of chic. A new wave of shimmer shades. Sun glistening. Sea cooled. Trembly with the frost. The Seafrostlings." And the dieting editorial recognizes that dieting is a long, slow, hard business. A very different impression from the quick, easy and painless ways offered by the advertisers to lose inches and wipe off pounds: "I cut down starchy foods, refused sweets and biscuits, did exercises every morning. And still I bulged out of my swimsuit! Then I started using Saxin and those extra inches soon began to go." Over half of all women believe they are overweight, and most of these have tried to diet and failed. They know that there are no easy solutions. So why do the advertisers try to kid them?

The advertising industry has developed a respectable theory to justify their assessment of the backward mental age of their audience. They argue, as did Colin Goodson and Burkard Frobenius in the British publication *Admap*, that as the communicators and the communicated-to have different linguistic and comprehension levels, "familiar" concepts in advertisements are better than "original" concepts. In short, be childishly simple because you're dealing with nincompoops. "Original" thoughts, i.e., those involving pleasing, entertaining ideas, will only confuse the wretched fellow.

The evidence for the "low comprehension level" of the consumer was simple. The researchers simply asked various consumer groups whether they understood certain phrases. For instance, 79 percent of the top occupation group understood what was meant by "sterling area," whereas only 9 percent of the lowest occupation group understood this term. That's certainly proof that if you talk about "sterling area" in your advertisements and you're aiming at the lower income group, you're likely to be disappointed. But it's not proof that you have to baby-talk to women when you're talking to them about something they fully understand, such as detergents or frozen peas.

The key to the talking-down problem lies in the sort of people who work for advertising agencies. There are basically two types: first, the ex-prep-school, forty-year-old gent; second, the thirty-year-old-or-under working-class kid who has "made it" into advertising. This second group went into advertising as a conscious act of climbing onto an escalator that could take them away from their proletarian backgrounds. Consequently, they tend to adopt middle-class camouflage, like joining smart clubs and living in WASP ghettos.

The key point about both the natural-born and adopted members of the middle-class working in advertising is that they are fundamentally alienated from their audience. Through all the promotion of miracle this and amazing that, through the talking and the trivialization of values, runs a thin—but persistent—vein of contempt. The adman finds it difficult to create advertisements that respect his audience's intelligence because fundamentally he doesn't. He has persuaded himself that he has in his hands a tool with which, without too much difficulty, he can more often than not persuade working-class people to do what he wants. No wonder, then, that he flaunts the symbols of the middle class at his working-class audience. No wonder that he crudely and unsympathetically spreads the gospel that cleanliness is next to godliness, and parades scenario after scenario of suburban bliss, so that those less fortunate souls living on the wrong side of the track are in no doubt as to what they're missing. And all the time with a sneer on his lips.

The extraordinary truth is that these middle-class admen are singularly unsuccessful in doing what they believe they are doing, for not only is their handiwork profoundly irritating to those whom it is intended to influence, it is also extremely unpersuasive.

What the hidden persuaders have been best at hiding is the severe limitations of their persuasive powers. Many of the advertisers themselves have recovered sufficiently from their double Chivas Regals and their expense-account lunches to realize that they're the ones who've been sold, rather than their beloved products. The following chapter will show why the day of reckoning is at hand.

The Witch Doctors Who Lost Their Magic

●

Once upon a time there was a lion tamer who, though he was a very clever man, wasn't very clever at taming lions. But because he was such a clever man he discovered a way to make the circus audience believe that he had actually tamed the lions. Every time the lion climbed onto the tub in the center of the ring, he cracked his whip. Then, when the lion roared, he cracked his whip twice. And because he was so clever, he managed to crack his whip at just about the same time as the lion performed all these things, so everyone thought that the lion had climbed onto the tub and then roared because the lion tamer had cracked his whip. Then one day the lion decided to show the audience who really controlled whom. So he ate the lion tamer.

The moral of this sad little fable is, hopefully, clear for all to see. Whether you regard the advertising industry as fraudulent lion tamers or unmagical witch doctors doesn't really matter. What is important is how the advertising industry has so long managed to conceal from itself and its clients its very real failure to deliver the goods on anything approaching the scale that has been promised. That this industry, alleged to have its hand firmly on the pulse of its audience, should have allowed itself to suffer such delusions of grandeur is folly enough. That in doing so it should provoke the ire and contempt of those it is trying to sell to resembles nothing so much as the self-destructive urge of the lemmings as they plunge into the cold waters of Canada.

The most extraordinary point about the story to be told in this and the next chapter is that every key fact about the way communication *actually works,* as opposed to the way the communication experts *say it works,* has been published (some facts were even available twenty years ago). Yet for all this time the vast majority of advertisements have been constructed in a way which pretends that none of the developments in social psychology or communications theory over the last twenty years have taken place. As Harry Henry, elder statesman of British market research, has seen fit to observe: "Most of the contributions that have been made by me or my contemporaries during the past two decades might as well have been written in water."

Before looking at these contributions further, it would be as well just to recall the way in which advertising has managed to win golden opinions for itself.

It was in the years between the wars that advertising made its rise in the eyes of business—from being just a huckster selling quack medicines to becoming something else: a process with the power to persuade people to do as the advertiser said. The credit for this change belongs not so much to any new inventory of skills that the admen developed as to World War I. This was the first war to be fought with words as well as bullets, with the use of recruitment and anti-German propaganda, and it was here that the foundation of modern advertising was laid.

By the end of the 1960s J. K. Galbraith could observe without provoking too much dissent that "It is an everyday assumption of the industrial system that, if sales are slipping, a new sales formula can be found that will correct the situation." If you *do* wish to dissent, the Harvard professor will ask you why, in that case, the largest and most successful companies in the world keep coming back for a second helping of this wonder drug. But there have been few dissenters, and hardly more when Vance Packard took a Cook's tour around the research departments of a handful of advertising agencies, emerging to dub them the "hidden persuaders": "Americans have become the most manipulated people outside the United Kingdom." And so, for example, you find a marketing man like Ralph Glasser declaring in *The New High Priesthood*: "All he [the consumer] can do, and it is indicative of his weak position as a buyer, is to be guided by what he is told in the advertising." And why this total submission? Because of motivation research: "The greatest breakthrough in modern persuasive skills is the discovery of how to peep behind the screen that a person's consciousness erects before the world and use that vision to fix upon the thoughts and designs one is most likely to tempt with successfully."

But despite all these claims that the admen now have the power to see into men's souls, the evidence tells a different story. It shows how advertising has very often oversold its powers and underdelivered its promises.

For a start, consumers only pay conscious attention to seventy-six advertisements a day (according to the indefatigable Bauer and Greyser, who asked their equally indefatigable sample to press a hand counter every time they noted an advertisement). Whatever figure you accept for the total number of advertising messages to which a consumer is exposed in a day, seventy-six is a small proportion of the total.

That, in view of a consumer's defense mechanism, isn't so surprising. What *is* surprising to those anxious to protect the laurels of Madison Avenue is that consumers find 85 percent of the ads they note neither enjoyable, informative, annoying nor offensive. They are merely indifferent to them.

In 1967 an enterprising Dr. Charles C. Allen set up an apparatus called a Dynascope in a sample of American homes. This enabled him to record what the people in the room were doing while the television set was on. Going through Dr. Allen's film must have been like looking at some of the Masters and Johnson clips, for he reported: "Adults eat, drink, play, argue, fight, and occasionally make love in front of their televisions. Sometimes these activities are coextensive with viewing." Clearly, their minds would be on things other than the amazing flavor of Morton's cranberry pie.

And so we find that statistics confirm what common sense suggests: only a very small proportion of advertisements are remembered. According to Gallup and Robinson, the average for the "featured idea" being retained for *twenty-four hours* was *under* 10 percent for TV-set advertisements, tire advertisements, after-shave and insurance advertisements (down to 2.6 percent). A survey in America by Quaker Oats among viewers of six popular television shows revealed that only 3 percent could remember the brands they had seen advertised. A study for Coca-Cola found that only 1,400 out of 13,000 people polled could remember the company's Hi-C Fruit Drink campaign. And only one out of those

1,400 professed to believe the claim that Hi-C was "the sensible drink."

Alas, worse is to follow. For if the ad is looked at, and if the claim is remembered, it is now *more* likely to be attached to the wrong brand than to the right brand. In just twelve months, from 1969 to 1970, there was a 70 percent drop in the percentage of commercials that were attached to their correct brand.

Or take the admen's great love: slogans. American Airlines spent $15 million telling people it was the "airline built for professional travelers." But after the company had spent all that money, only one consumer in five could link that slogan with American Airlines, so four fifths of the benefit went to airlines other than the one that had paid the bill.

This, in fact, is happening every day on television in America. A vaginal deodorant, Pristeen, actually had *more* viewers associating the advertisement with its main rival, F.D.S., than with itself. And Excedrin, with its David Janssen commercial, actually had *twice* as many viewers associating the advertisement with its biggest rival, Anacin, rather than with Excedrin itself.

The lesson from all these studies is that the effect of mass media is far less than is generally imagined. The facts again are at hand, and have been for several years, to confirm the limited, short-term impact of advertising. First, a study by J. Walter Thompson, the biggest advertising agency in the world, recorded what a sample of consumers bought over a nineteen-week period and compared it to the advertising they were exposed to. One can summarize their key finding in this way: imagine a group of people, some of whom use Brand X and some of whom don't. Then expose the *whole group* to two commercials for Brand X. The result is that these people are only 5 percent more likely to *start* to purchase the brand than to *stop* purchasing the brand after being exposed to two commercials. To get this number of exposures to a television commercial *between* each purchase for three quarters of all housewives for something that's bought weekly (like butter or coffee) would in Britain cost £750,000 (over $1.5 million) a year in television time alone. There can hardly be a dozen brands with that money to spend.

The second study was directed by Leo Bogart, executive vice-president of the Bureau of Advertising of the American Newspaper Publishers' Association (an extremely kosher outfit anxious to prove the efficacy of advertising). This study was designed to find out the effect of just one advertisement. Averaging out the effect of twenty-four advertisements for twenty-four separate brands of package goods, one average advertisement certainly has some effect. Instead of 0.44 percent of the population buying it, 0.50 percent bought it. But the way these ads worked seemed to be by making some customers purchase the brand a day or so before they would have purchased it anyway. Was it for this that the copywriter toiled and the art director sweated? Or, for that matter, that the client forked out his dollars?

The third study was a complete book, written over ten years ago by a Harvard professor, J. B. Stewart: *Repetitive Advertising in Newspapers*. This studied the impact under carefully controlled conditions over a twenty-six-week period in Fort Wayne, Indiana, of the advertising for two products: a bleach called Lestare and a frozen food, Chicken Sara Lee.

The town was divided into areas that were exposed to the advertising and areas that weren't. The conclusion for the Lestare advertising was that by the end of the test period more housewives had bought Lestare in the areas where the advertising *had not* appeared than in the areas where it had. This led to Professor Stewart's view that "beyond any doubt some advertising is not necessarily better than no advertising."

You can understand why the advertising industry has ignored this conclusion from one of the most carefully controlled field tests of advertising effectiveness, for the basic *assumption* behind every advertisement is that it is better to run it than not to run it. *How much better* is a matter for argument, but the other assumption has never, to my recollection, been questioned by any advertising agency (and quite understandably).

The effect of the Chicken Sara Lee advertising was a fifth better than that of Lestare, though still not much more than marginal.

Both these case histories relate to new products, and the launching of these is one key task entrusted by the advertisers to their agencies. It is this same area that Galbraith uses to make his taunt against those who put forward the Edsel as proof of the limited power of advertising: "Its notoriety owes much to its being exceptional." But the evidence is that precisely the reverse is true. Starting with the automobile field, very few cases suggest a power of mass persuasion that Galbraith's "demand management" implies. For example, the Maxi failed at its first launch. The new Cortina at first only got half the initial market share Ford had planned. The Classic failed almost totally. The Pinto and Vega sold almost half the number that Detroit had *publicly* announced they would sell.

Outside this particular product category you see further testimonials to the limited power of advertising. Heinz Happy Soups, Knorr Dry Soup Mix, Cue Toothpaste, Reef Mouthwash are among the 7,500 new products that flopped in America in 1969. And in Britain the roll call of distinction includes Unilevel (with three Spree Squash Concentrate and Lyril Soap), Beecham's (Water Lily Shampoo, Mark Vardy Toiletries), Nestlé (Nestea), Cadburys (meat), Rank (Bowling), General Foods (Jell-O and now freeze-dried coffee).

The point has already been made in an earlier chapter that many of these new products were rejected because the housewife was fed up with the new improved way of doing something that she wasn't interested in doing. But, and here's the crunch as far as the efficiency of advertising is concerned, bad advertising was found to be the reason for failure *three times* as often as bad product performance (according to *Advertising Age* columnist Ted Angelus, who looked at the American flops). So the failures then are with "successful" products.

How about the long term (by this is meant the period outside that which immediately follows the running of the advertising)? Doesn't advertising give "added value" to a product by draping it with feelings and qualities to make it more desirable to the consumer?

There is certainly quite a lot of evidence that something of this nature happens. The story of Andrex toilet paper versus Delsey toilet paper in Britain is a case in point. What appears to have happened is that Andrex, by continuing to advertise heavily over a ten-year period, became a brand that was "more highly valued by consumers than Delsey" (which after six years stopped advertising), so that relative to Andrex, "people value Delsey a little less highly" (both quotations from a J. Walter Thompson case history on Andrex).

Or take another case of a well-known food product. When one

sample of consumers were asked to try this product and its main competitor in *a situation where the identity of the brand was not revealed*, consumers split 51 to 49 in favor of Brand A. But when another sample did the same test, this time *with the brand identity* revealed, Brand A was preferred 67 to 33—a 32 percent increase in preference for one product just by identifying which brand people were eating.

There are other studies which may be cited to show the longer-term success of advertising, including the ones carried out by the Television Consumer Audit of Great Britain. Its study of fruit squashes, toothpaste and heavy-duty detergents suggests that brand loyalty to the major brands was supported by media advertising and actually eroded by promotional expenditure, particularly among the heavy buyers. Much evidence has certainly emerged to show that money-off's and deals only create a temporary upward kink in the sales curve, caused by consumers' increasing their stock of the product at the special-offer price, followed by a sales decline as consumers use up the extra stock. It shows that brand advertising is better for the brand than money-off's.

But even the more optimistic case histories about the long-term effect of advertising don't always show that advertising was a *cost-effective* way for the company to have promoted its product. If, for example, you had spent £300,000 to launch a dry cat food in the English market (as did Carnation Foods for their Go-Cat) and you achieved a one-third market share, that might seem like a substantial success until you realize that the total value of the dry-cat-food market at that time was barely £2 million a year. Ergo: £600,000 of sales for £300,000 worth of advertising. Or take the case of Lucozade, a fizzy glucose drink used by people recovering from minor illnesses. Lucozade's marketing director revealed to the *Admap* World Advertising Workshop that increasing the advertising expenditure by 46 percent raised the sales level by 9 percent. And when the advertising expenditure on Ribena, its sister product, was increased by 25 percent, sales actually *declined* by 6 percent. Maybe sales of Ribena would have declined more without the advertising, and maybe sales of Lucozade wouldn't have increased at all without advertising, but this isn't the sort of stuff that would persuade me if I were a Beecham shareholder to endorse my board's expenditure of £1,021,000 in 1971 on advertising these two brands.

174

Or take the case of gasoline marketing. *Management Today* magazine, the prestigious British management monthly, carried an article in December 1971 that should have caused at least some tremors to be felt in the advertising industry. This was a report of a study carried out by the University of Louvain in Belgium analyzing data on gasoline markets for a seven-year period for a representative sample of European countries. The data included sales volumes, market shares, outlet shares, short-term innovations, promotional campaigns, and measures of advertising pressure on the marketplace by the brands concerned. The conclusion of this study, as it was reported in *Management Today,* was: *"In all the cases studied, there was no economical return on the advertising budget."* It is true that this study has been fiercely attacked in private by both the advertising and petroleum establishment. But until it is adequately rebutted it remains as further evidence that the value of advertising to a brand is certainly not something that can be *assumed.*

Cigarette advertising tells a similar tale. Between 1954 and 1965 the British tobacco barons increased their annual advertising expenditure from £1 million a year to £16 million a year. But despite this sixteenfold increase in the weight of advertising, they were unable to persuade a higher proportion of the total population to take up the habit. Since then, of course, they have used this inefficiency to justify the continued advertising of cigarettes after the cancer scare, saying the advertisements are only designed to sell their own particular brand and not to expand the market by selling the idea of smoking. Even if one accepts this spurious plea, the fact remains that the relationship between the brands' share and the advertising expenditure is equally tenuous. Three brands, Embassy, Filter, Benson and Hedges King Size, and Piccadilly No. 7, all spend roughly the *same* amount on advertising. But their market shares were 19.6, 6.6 and 0.4 percent, respectively.

Even in the case of the "relatively" successful Sara Lee campaign studied by J. B. Stewart, he was forced to conclude that "the advertising efficiency in this experimental campaign [was] barely enough to justify the expenditure." If this marginal benefit is the return on a "successful" campaign, the return on an average campaign could even be negative. The most recent study of the effects of advertising is the result of a ten-year study carried out by a team at Columbia's Graduate School of Business. The full study has yet to be published, but one of the project leaders, Professor John Howard, summarized his findings as follows: "Advertising makes a difference, but it is a weak signal."

What all this shows, as much as the limits to the skills of the agencies, is the unmalleable nature of the consumers to whom they are pleading. Far from the only option being to do what the advertiser tells them (as Ralph Glasser suggests) or to become more malleable the more affluent they become (as Galbraith suggests), consumers are showing that they are becoming *less* persuadable than ever before.

Social psychologists have done quite a lot of work on this particular point, and the evidence is clear. The people who are *most persuadable* are those who feel inadequate (Klapper, *The Effects of Mass Communication*), who lack confidence (Secord and Blackman, *Attitude Organisation and Behavioural Change*), and are less intelligent (Hoveland, Janis and Kelley, *Communication and Persuasion*). There is also the finding that women tend to be slightly more persuadable than men (Whitaker, *Cognitive Dissonance and the Effectiveness of Persuasive Communication*). And the *least* persuadable, according to the same authorities, are the more intelligent and the more extroverted, the most confident and those with the highest self-esteem.

If we relate all this to the way consumers and patterns of consumption have changed, all the developments—from the emergence of individualism in product choice to the increased role of men in the purchasing of everyday items—they all point to more and more consumers having the sort of characteristics that will make them less persuadable. Although this fact is recognized by very few agencies, it is being appreciated by more and more advertisers, for the advertiser is also a consumer. He knows that he's not persuaded by the vast majority of advertising, so why should the consumer he's currently trying to win over to his product be any more persuadable?

This is just one more question mark to be placed against the value of advertising by business. The rush into consumer promotions in the last few years (the money-off's and free pantyhose) was really a way of the companies' saying to their agencies that they had lost faith in the advertisements themselves.

The fact is, the only reason why many companies advertise is

176

because other people do. A study by the Marketing Communications Research Centre found that top industrial executives advertised "out of fear of some nebulous, possibly dire, consequences if they discontinued or dramatically cut their advertising while their competitiors continued." No surprise then that barely more than *a quarter* of the business executives in the *Harvard Business Review* study agreed that most of the money allocated for advertising was well spent. The president of General Motors even publicly pointed out that whereas it would cost him 45 percent more in 1970 to run the same amount of advertising as he ran in 1960, the average price of his cars had gone down in that time by 2.5 percent despite an 82 percent increase in labor costs.

If industrial productivity could increase so much, why was advertising productivity so stagnant? In fact, individual advertisements differ enormously in their productivity. In America it can cost as little as 0.8 cent to get one message to one person who can correctly identify the commercial as yours. Or it can cost as much as 2.8 cents, the extra 2 cents being the price of bad advertising. Even taking a less extreme maximum/minimum position, the difference in readership between the *average* full-page color advertisement and the best-read color advertisement is 136 percent.

Although reading and noting down scores are not the most useful measure of advertising efficiency, the wide variation in one suggests an equally wide variation in the other. And all for the cost of the same media space. The crucial point is that the advertising agency is probably no more able to pick an advertisement for the client that will help his sales than is a pin. Leo Bogart reported in "What One Little Ad Can Do" (*Journal of Advertising Research*, August 1970) on whether the advertising experts' ratings of advertisements tallied with the performance of these advertisements as measured in the marketplace. Their predictions of "recall" were no better than you get by tossing a coin. And the odds were sixteen to one *against* their picking the advertisement that could get the best sales result.

Hell may have no fury like a woman scorned, but business has no fury like an advertiser misled by his agency. The resultant night of the long knives struck blindly and almost unselectively through Madison Avenue (and to some extent through British and German advertising as well). Just when Bill Bernbach's ideas were about to win out by showing the power of "creative" advertising, "creative" suddenly became a dirty word. "Creative" was the trend, and just because the clients were getting uppity (particularly under the influence of the slump), the industry had to drop *whatever* trend they were currently running on and pick one up that would be sure to mollify the irate advertisers. "Look," they said, "once we get those long-haired creatures out of our office, once we stop being cute, once we get back to the sort of ads that really shifted product, then all will be well." So public executions of the leading "creatives" were arranged. Even the head of Young & Rubicam, Steve Frankfurt, a former art director, was dutifully axed. The example was sufficient *"pour décourager les autres."*

One of the early disciples of creativity, Mary Wells Lawrence, went over to "product oriented advertising." (Compare her original Braniff campaign with her latest Alka-Seltzer advertisements and you will see that the smart lady believes that her bread is now buttered on a different side.)

The ill wind also blew on the British side of the Atlantic. One of the earliest creative agencies, Collett, Dickernon, Pearce and Partners started getting cold feet. Geers Gross, the people who dreamed up delightful ads, started to churn out the sort of advertising that would have done credit to any of the flat-footed advertising giants. And these people were right, of course. The business was turning away from "creative" just when "creative" was on the point of making business flow.

Doyle, Dane, Bernbach, uncompromising as ever, actually *lost* billing (overall) in 1971—an unheard-of phenomenon. Its London office made so little headway that it had to spend a small fortune buying up a rival agency called Gallagher Smail that had found success by doing the sort of advertising that normally gave Bill Bernbach nightmares.

The irony of this switch back to the old safe principles of the fifties and sixties was twofold. First, in the words of *Ad Daily,* the New York news sheet on advertising: "The creative revolution brought honesty . . . believability . . . relevance . . . originality . . . drama . . . respect . . . authority . . . and excitement to advertising. Stuff that it seldom demonstrated before and it sold things like crazy—Alka-Seltzer . . . Braniff . . . Benson and Hedges . . . the original Contac . . . Fresca . . . Volkswagen . . . Polaroid

. . . Clairol . . . Diet Pepsi . . . North East Air . . . *Forbes* magazine and a hundred more."

Second, even if these enthusiastic claims weren't true, even if "creative" advertising had been as much a flop as its detractors claimed, going back to what might have worked ten years previously was no solution. In that time the consumer had transformed herself into something else, and it made no more sense to talk to the 1970 consumer like the 1950 one than it would to talk to a twenty-year-old girl like a ten-year-old one.

Nevertheless, it is onto these "tried and tested" principles (principles that have done much to creat the yawning gap between the advertiser and his audience which this book has described) that advertising has now retreated. It is almost as though an aging comedian tried to make a comeback using the style and the jokes that brought him success in his golden years. The old formula no longer gets them rolling in the aisles or, for that matter, rushing along to the cash register. Indeed, when one examines the admen's supposedly "successful" magic formulas it appears that when their ads *did* seem to work, it was largely because of the dubious way their effect was measured, as the next chapter will reveal.

Putting Advertising on the Psychologist's Couch

●

If you asked almost any one of the hundred thousand people involved in advertising in America exactly *how* the process of advertising works, you would find them less forthright than members of other professions talking about their specialties. Doctors understand the physical properties of the body, engineers understand the processes of physics. Yet the process of communication is hardly discussed within the industry that spends billions of dollars every year to communicate.

The annals of social psychology—rich sources of knowledge for those anxious to influence human behavior—remain largely untapped. Instead a folklore (and it is no more than that) has grown up about how advertising, as it is practiced, works. It is a folklore that is enshrined in a series of principles that stands—implicitly or openly stated—behind the bulk of advertisements on both sides of the Atlantic:

First, "hard sell" is better than "soft sell."

Second, the more you repeat your sales point, the better.

Third, overclaim or exaggeration is a sensible advertising practice.

Fourth, you should aim for high recall of your advertising message (i.e., the more people who can remember your jingle, the better).

Fifth, if you can get people to look at your advertisement and understand it, your job's virtually done.

Sixth, the greater the change of attitude you can measure about your product, the more your sales are likely to rise.

Seventh, if you do get more sales, it's because of the advertising.

These principles have the advantage of being so simple and straightforward that even a second-rate advertising manager can understand them. The seven assumptions convert into a simple model of advertising theory that is also straightforward and common-sense.

Claim
↓
Repetition of Claim
↓
Recall of Claim
↓
Attitude Change
↓
Behavior Change
↓
Sales

The procedure works as follows: first you make your claim, then you make sure it's attended to; then you repeat that claim as often as your budget allows. You repeat that claim to get it into people's memories (which you measure as "recall"). You do this because you believe that if you've got your powerful claim into someone's head, there's a fair chance he'll be more favorably disposed about your brand. And if he is, that someone is more likely to buy your product.

The important point about this model is the suggestion that there is a simple, direct link between the advertisement and the sale. So if you manage to steer your claim through stages two, three, four and five, then six *will* happen.

Consistent with this, those who live by this theory of persuasion also believe that the *more* advertising you feed into the top in terms of money spent on buying space, the more you'll get out of the bottom in sales, so that a $500,000 campaign is ten times as effective as a $50,000 campaign.

This particular model of the persuasion process is not one you'll find in any serious study of social psychology. You won't even find many believers of it in the research departments of the advertising agencies. Why? Because over the last twenty years each of the relationships in this model have been shown to be false, and that the way a claim "works" on people is not in any way as simple as the flow of arrows suggests.

Even without looking at the research evidence that follows, simple mathematics suggests that this cannot be the model of Galbraith's "demand management," or Orwell's "Big Brother," or Packard's "hidden persuaders," for each step in the chain can only happen if the previous step has occurred. While probability values decline as probabilities are multiplied, even this simple six-step model is extremely tenuous. If, for example, each step had a 50–50 chance of happening, then when all the probabilities had been multiplied together, you find that the chance of a "claim" leading to a "sale" is 50–1 against.

With this background, let us wend our way through this model and see the snares and delusions. To begin with the claim, this is the kernel of any advertisement: what you say to the consumer to persuade her of the merit of your case. It can be a Unique Selling Proposition *à la* Rosser Reeves, or a brand-image claim *à la* David Ogilvy.

There are two key points about the kind of claims that charge at you from the newspaper page and television screen. First, they tend to be formulated as though they were trying to persuade a nonuser to start using a product. Second, the weapon in aid of this conversion process is *either* anxiety arousal (B.O. being the classic) *or* overclaim ("whiter than white" being the classic of this).

† The notion of converting people to become users of your product has, like the model itself, the blessing of common sense. But that is all, for the fact is that for nearly all mass-market low-cost items, like detergents or baked beans, your proper audience should be the *existing* users of your product.

Take the frozen-pea market. Most consumers will be "users" of all the major brands. The examples given about the lack of brand loyalty in Chapter Seven have, as their corollary, multiple brand usage. In fact, if you forget for a moment about the amount of product that people buy, the actual *number* of users of a brand varies only slightly over a year. According to J. Walter Thompson's Advertising Planning Index, there is only a 1 percent change in the number of users of a typical brand in a year, and the number of first-time users of a brand is rarely more than 3 percent per year for an established product.

Of course, for some people this average brand will be purchased once a year, for others once a week. But the task of advertising is still to make it as frequent as possible for both types of purchases. This may involve encouraging *usage* of the product rather than *purchase* of it (i.e., eating the can of baked beans off your shelf rather than being persuaded to buy another can in the super-market).

The heavy users tend to be the guts of a brand's business. If you look at virtually any mass-market low-cost product you will find that about half the sales volume is consumed by about one fifth of the users. Discovering what it is that shifts people into this category and what stops them from shifting out of it are relevant questions to the advertiser. But judging by the large number of advertisements that seems to be trying to talk you into *trying* the brand as though you'd never bought it before, it's not a question the typical advertisement is tackling.

The fact that the target of our advertisement is also the user of the product, albeit a light user, is of immense significance. It is also of immense significance that she is probably also a user of the product we're competing against.

To see how this affects the process of claim→sale, we must dig into the annals of social psychology to discover that the consumer who is receiving our claim is not in any way a *tabula rasa*, an empty tablet on which to imprint our U.S.P. On the contrary, she has a whole set of feelings, beliefs and thoughts in her head, many of which are born out of her experience of our own and competing products. All these feelings, thoughts and beliefs are mutually consistent and in balance with one another. A simple example of this internal self-consistency is that often someone who regards a certain brand of beer as "manly" will also think that the beer itself is stronger. Or a detergent that is advertised on a efficiency platform will also be thought of as not being gentle to the hands. One half of the attitude naturally follows from the other, even if it's not overtly expressed.

Now, if we confront our consumer with a piece of information—say, an advertising claim—that is out of balance or inconsistent with the contents of her mental dossier, we have created a stress-causing situation for her. The feelings we're offering her about the brand are out of balance with her own feelings about the brand. The theory of social psychology that predicts what happens next in this situation is Leon Festinger's theory of cognitive dissonance, which sounds frighteningly complicated but actually is beautifully simple. (Festinger is the author of *The Theory of Cognitive Dissonance*, which is the standard work on this particular subject.) "Cognitive" relates to the knowledge in your mental dossier, and "dissonance" simply means unbalance or inconsistency.

The theory is that when a piece of information is put into the consumer's mental dossier which is "out of balance" with other information already in the dossier, then she will modify her attitudes and behavior in such a way that the two conflicting "cognitive elements" are brought into balance. More than this, the theory also states that she will actively avoid situations which might lead to "out of balance" pieces of information coming into her mental dossier.

For example, if you have just bought a new car, it's probable that the car you chose *not* to buy had *some* attractive features that the one you chose hadn't. The cognitive-dissonance theory predicts that you will therefore find large numbers of new car purchasers reading the advertisements for that car *after* they've bought it, as part of the process of seeking information to buttress their choice. And this, in fact, is precisely what occurs.

Apply the cognitive-dissonance theory to testimonial advertising, and you have a neat ethical problem. If the *normal* response after purchase is to modify your perception of the product so you can persuade yourself that you made the right decision, then to tell a nonpurchaser that a purchaser finds that a product does all that the advertising says it would is—arguably—exploiting the purchaser's need for self-consistency to the possible detriment of the nonpurchaser.

How does the dissonance theory affect the claim that we fired at the consumer? It simply means that the consumer is equipped with a large number of mechanisms to make sure that our claim *doesn't* create any psychological stress by becoming out of balance with any part of her mental dossier.

The first of these is *selective exposure*. This may mean that the mind simply does not receive a message that doesn't fit in

184

with the recipient's mental dossier, in the same way that a lock will not admit the wrong key. For example, twice as many non-smokers as smokers look at antismoking propaganda. For the nonsmoker, it fits in with his view of the world *as a nonsmoker,* but for the smoker it creates tension and stress as the propaganda is in conflict with attitudes and feelings within his mental dossier. So the watchdogs in the brain will pounce on any antismoking propaganda as it comes in, and try to kick it out before it creates any stress. This is why the people you may want most in your audience often are least likely to be there.

After this first filter, which can stop our claim from getting through, comes the second. A certain kind of message may be so powerful (for example, some television commercials) that it actually manages to batter its way past this first line of defense. If the claim cannot be accommodated into the mental dossier, it is then dealt with by the process of *selective retention*, and promptly kicked out of the brain.

The third watchdog protecting the consumer's mental dossier is *selective perception*. Instead of not admitting or throwing out out-of-balance material, the *incoming* material is recast until it fits in with the consumer's existing attitudes. This can take the form of "ego defense mechanisms": denying a communication that threatens some aspects of your ego structure (e.g., a smoker saying "It can't happen to me"). Or it can work by an ordinary denial, saying that the relationship of the out-of-balance attitude that's causing stress doesn't really exist (e.g., denying that there is a link between smoking and cancer).

This was actually measured in a study in Minneapolis after a news release about the relationship of smoking to health. When asked whether they thought the relationship had been proved, 29 percent of nonsmokers said yes, compared to only 7 percent of smokers.

Or selective perception can also work by balancing the stress-causing incoming attitude with something that makes it acceptable (e.g., smoking may be unhealthy, but it does make me relax). Or, finally, the incoming material can be split into bits, one of which fits in with the consumer's mental dossier (e.g., smoking may be unhealthy, but filter cigarettes are not so unhealthy).

So the simple act of "making a claim" for the product really isn't anything as simple as the current consensus of advertising practice suggests. Before our poor little claim has even reached the stage of repetition, it is pounced on by a pack of watchdogs that just aren't allowed for in the theoretical model. Let us see how these watchdogs treat some of the typical forms of claim that try to gain admittance by the consumer.

Let us suppose our claim is an *overclaim*, i.e., typical of the exaggerated puffery that the advertising industry produces. More precisely, let us suppose that you are an advertiser making an "overclaim" for your detergent called Tode. What you might say is that it would get my clothes "whiter than white."

If I am a typical user of your product, I not only use Tode but have also used most other brands of detergents at some time or another. I am thus well aware of the differences between the brands. There could be any of a dozen reasons why I am using Tode at the present moment, but let us say that I find it gets my clothes satisfactorily clean and the box I bought happened to have 10 cents off. But I certainly wouldn't agree with your claim that it got my clothes "whiter than white." There is thus an imbalance between my attitude toward Tode (gets my clothes clean) and the attitude your advertising is asking me to accept (gets clothes "whiter than white").

Dissonance theory predicts that I will have to modify one of these two attitudes to avoid creating stress in myself. As the "whiter than white" claim is coming from such a low-credibility source as an advertiser, I will tend to reject that one and buttress my own attitude toward the brand. Hence, by overclaiming on me in a situation where I had an easy way of verifying the claim (i.e., I used the product), the net effect was to make me think less of the advertising claim and to rank advertising as a lower credibility source than before. This means that the next time around, maybe when the manufacturer of Tode offers me a new product, I will have an extra special reason for rejecting his claim.

Let us now make another supposition about Tode—that Tode is a good product and cleans my clothes efficiently. So why should I stop using it? Maybe my laundry needs will increase, so I might even use more of it.

In short, even though I have *rejected* the "whiter than white" claim, I may very well continue using Tode. This is particularly likely to be true if, as has been suggested by H. A. Simon in *Models of Man*, I am not so much trying to maximize as "satisfize": that is, I have an idea of what is "good enough" in detergents, and one that "satisfizes" these criteria, as does Tode, is fully qualified to receive my money.

This fact, however, goes right to the heart of one of the central doctrines of modern advertising: if the consumer is misled once, he won't come back and purchase the product again, but if the product "satisfizes," he may well come back. However, if you are the advertiser working on the simple claim→sales model and observe that I haven't deserted your brand, you will deduce that I have accepted your claim and that it is this claim which has motivated me to buy Tode. You will therefore repeat this claim again and again, and the whole business of processing your claim in such a way that it fits into my mental dossier (i.e., by rejecting it) will also repeat itself. So the spiral of overclaim gradually winds its way upward into cloud cuckoo land, where the gap between claim and reality grows wider and wider.

This particular communication structure may well be the typical way an overclaim affects a consumer who is already a user of the product. But even a nonuser could respond in this way, because he has his own *expectations* of how the product will perform. For instance, the car that suggests it'll make you the biggest draw for the girls since Marlon Brando may still be bought by a consumer who has rejected that claim and is buying the car on the grounds of its superior road holding. As long as the product *does* "satisfize," then the overclaim won't—at least not in the short term— make the product less appealing to the consumer. It will only make the overclaim less appealing to the consumer.

There is just one question mark which you are bound to put against this argument. Is a "whiter than white" claim really sufficient to create the sort of stress that'll bring all these fancy balancing mechanisms into play? Research studies (see Festinger, or Halloran, *Attitude Change*) show that the *higher* the ego involvement of someone in a particular situation, the *greater* will be the tension caused by introducing an out-of-balance belief. Which detergent I use, it might be argued, is hardly a very ego-involving situation. It certainly shouldn't be, but the whole weight of advertising for all these trivial products is to try to make them ego-involving, to make which detergent, which aspirin, which toilet paper I use an important part of my life. To the extent that they succeed in this, these trivia do become important to the consumer's

187

ego. To the extent that they fail, then the advertisement, as the source of a rejected standpoint, sinks even lower in the credibility stakes, so either way, the overclaim gets rejected.

Even though rejected, the overclaim can, in the long run, still have one remaining effect on the consumer. By continually being told that Tode gets my clothes "whiter than white," I eventually become disappointed that my clothes are merely clean (even though I may still go on using Tode). This means that the normal overclaim, as it works on the typical consumer, is creating not sales, but simply dissatisfaction. And if one is looking for a reason why consumers are now becoming more demanding—the "phenomenon of rising expectations," as it has been called—one reason at least is that they are simply demanding what they have been promised.

Little of this, however, crosses the mind of the advertiser who is instructing his agency to say his product is the greatest thing since sliced bread. "Are you ashamed of our television sets?" a client once asked me when I was reluctant to say that its fabulous woodprint cabinet would be the pride and joy of every home.

The effect, then, of the first type of claim that is in everyday use—the overclaim—is to lower still further the credibility of the advertiser even though the advertiser believes it is in fact moving his product off the shelves at the speed of light.

The second typical sort of claim, the *high anxiety appeal*, has scarcely more success in crashing through the consumer's defense barriers. Whether the anxiety invoked is by suggesting that you might smell bad; that your neighbor thinks your child's white clothes look off-white; that you ought to buy insurance, since danger could strike at any moment; or just that smoking will kill you, the principle is the same. And the evidence of how the watch-dogs respond to this sort of appeal is that the *stronger* the fear invoked by the advertiser, the *less effective* the advertisement.

First of all, these anxiety-arousing appeals cause too much stress in the poor old consumer's mental dossier, simply because they contain many elements out of balance with the consumer's own feelings. So the fear tends to be processed in such a way by the brain that the threat to the consumer is *minimized*. The Tavistock Institute (a British psychiatric research unit) found this out when it did some research in 1957 on road safety: the mind simply switched off when confronted by anxiety-provoking situations.

A classic study by Janis and Fesbach ("The Effect of Fear-Arousing Communications," *Journal of Abnormal Social Psychology*, 1953) shows the differing impacts of a mild fear appeal with a strong fear appeal. A fifteen-minute illustrated lecture on dental hygiene was prepared in three different forms for three groups of students. The strong fear appeal contained a powerful emotional appeal emphasizing the serious consequences (including cancer) of not brushing your teeth. The mild fear appeal simply gave a "minimal" appeal which didn't dramatize the consequences of tooth neglect at all but gave advice about dental hygiene. The third appeal, a moderate one, was somewhere between the two. The result was that the minimal factual appeal persuaded *twice* as many students to follow the advice given (which included going to a dentist for a checkup) than the strong fear appeal. In fact, *fewer* students in the latter group actually looked after their teeth properly after the strong appeal than before.

This is really an example of what is called "the law of reversed effort"; namely, the more frightened people become of the consequences of an action, the more they may be impelled to continue or even increase committing it. This certainly appears to be the case with the British antismoking campaign. Using strong fear appeals, its greatest impact seems to be on the bodies who hand out advertising awards. According to Action for Smoking and Health (ASH), just as many cigarettes are now being smoked as before the campaign. In fact, the likelihood is that a high fear campaign would *increase* the level of smoking. The effect of this sort of advertising would be to increase tension among smokers; they would be more aware of the dangers of smoking but unable, because of the addictive power of nicotine, to give it up. And to relieve the extra tension this would cause, they probably smoke more cigarettes.

So, to revert to our claim→sale model, if a fear appeal is to get anywhere, it needs to be the very opposite of what the advertising agent tends to make it: it needs to be a *mild* fear appeal which can be relatively easily absorbed into the consumer's mental dossier without causing too much mental upset. Partly as a result of the overclaiming, and the high anxiety, the sort of claim that spins off the standard claim→sales model is also one that tends to be actively disliked by consumers. This is not a matter of concern for the majority of advertisers. They are not in the business to

189

make friends, so goes the argument, but to make sales. "If there were any correlation between liking and effectiveness in advertising, Procter & Gamble would not be the great marketing company it is today," said the head of research in the London office of the BBDO agency. However, as we shall see in a moment, the main measurements made by Procter & Gamble are not with effectiveness but with the extent to which their commercial has been *remembered*, and the relationship is that the most remembered commercials are *either* the most liked *or* the most disliked.

In the same way that you'd be more likely to buy from a door-to-door salesman with good manners and a friendly smile than a rude man who bellowed at you from the doorstep, it would be natural to expect the same to be true of advertising. It doesn't take much of a search of the literature to find evidence for this. As long ago as 1949 a study for NBC by Thomas Coffin among 1,600 people in New York found that "those who saw and liked a commercial advertising a product were found to be more apt to buy the brand than those who saw the commercials but did not like them." There has also been no shortage of studies to show that communicators are more effective when they are "liked" by their viewers. Dr. John Treasure and Timothy Joyce in *As Others See Us* (written for the Institute of Practitioners in Advertising) found that almost eight times the percentage of people who liked a commercial a lot shifted brands after seeing it, compared to those who disliked the same commercial a lot. (But despite this, they finally concluded that liking and effectiveness were not related in any simple way.)

The detergent companies have a great mass of evidence on file on the subject of liking and effectiveness, and the commercials that are made on the basis of it are prima facie evidence that in the selling situation, liking and effectiveness are *not* twin brothers. Even supposing that this is correct (and the theory of cognitive dissonance suggests that you will be less willing to look at an advertisement which you dislike than one you like), the question remains as to *why* liking and effectiveness have become such a discussion point among admen. Is it the suggestion that in order to sell something, the price you must pay is to be disliked by the person you sell it to? What has surely happened is that admen have neglected the finer feelings of their audience in a way that would shame a common street peddler, and they have *then* set out

190

to justify this dislike on the grounds that their product is still selling. Maybe it is. Maybe you can bully, cajole and nag people into buying your product. But why do this when you can influence people by winning friends just as easily?

Besides an unconcern with dislike, the advertiser working on the traditional claim→sales model also feels he is immune to any bad effects that might arise from the consumer's disbelieving his sales message. Faced with the massive incredulity that confronts the agency's handiwork when it reaches the marketplace, the "irrelevance of belief" is the only response the agency can logically offer to its client to persuade him that its advertisement is doing a good job for him: "If the consumer says your advertisement is completely believable, it probably means you have nothing in the advertisement which will get him to try your brand" (Nahl, *Journal of Advertising Research*).

Going even further than this, the motivation researchers have developed an approach to the subject of belief which is accepted with apparent alacrity by Professor Galbraith when he observes: "Failure to win belief does not impair the effectiveness of the management of demand for consumer products. Management involves the creation of a compelling image of the product in the minds of the consumer. To this he responds *more or less automatically* [my italics] under the circumstances where the product does not merit a great deal of thought." In this model, an ounce of powerful fantasy is worth a pound of circumstantial evidence of the truth of the claim.

If all this is correct, advertising has a good deal less to worry about as a proven low-credibility source than the earlier discussion of the growing disbelief in advertising implied. But the believers in the unimportance of belief still owe us an explanation of why, contrary to the impression given by Galbraith and others, most advertisements don't normally work in the way their creators had intended. Does disbelief really have no part to play in this?

Of course, the less rigorously you define "advertising working," the easier it is to show that it works either in conditions where people don't consciously look at it or where they don't consciously believe it. For example, the head of research at General Electric in America, Herbert Krugman, has written about advertising "working" in the sense of "being repeatedly learned and repeatedly forgotten and then repeatedly learned a little more." This process over a very long period of time can alter the way you think about a brand in a manner that "may fall short of persuasion or attitude change." Learning without involvement" is the way Krugman describes the process whereby this can happen. Belief isn't important because you're not sufficiently involved with the message to either believe or disbelieve it. The question simply doesn't arise. (A humbling side discovery by Krugman was that the "learning curve" for advertising resembled almost precisely the "learning curve" for nonsense material.)

If most advertising restricted itself to being this sort of low-profile, nonchallenging "mental wallpaper" (which, as we shall see, has quite a lot to commend it), then maybe belief wouldn't be important. But most advertisements *do* try to smash into the consumer's consciousness, and they do so by arguing vigorously for *belief* in their proposition ("Builds strong bodies 12 ways") Sweeps as it beats as it cleans," etc.).

There is also the interesting halfway point between belief and disbelief called "curious nonbelief." Here uncertainty is aroused in the consumer: "I wonder if that *would* be a better product, after all." This uncertainty creates a type of imbalance within the mental dossier, and to restore the situation the consumer may well try the product as a form of "tension reduction." Such claims would need to be verifiable by consumer experience of the product. Like "End scuffed-up floors," "The margarine that spreads even when ice-cold," "The dog food that ends dog odor"—all of which arouse considerable "curious nonbelief" but apparently improve sales.

But the paper that developed this concept (J. C. Maloney, "Curiosity versus Disbelief in Advertising," *Journal of Advertising Research*, 1968) also stated quite categorically, if circuitously, that a *disbelief* response was "generally predictive of inhibited consumer interest to interact with the product advertised." The simple explanation of this goes back to the concept of the mental dossier. A claim you "disbelieve" is simply one that doesn't fit in, so to reduce the tension that its arrival creates, it will either be processed in such a way that it can fit in or simply be rejected.

Funnily enough, it is this same mentality which, working on the advertiser, persuades him that disbelief of his message won't harm its sales impact. Fortified by a conviction of the massive power of advertising (which is quite at odds with all the studies of the impact of mass communication), he is convinced that advertising, like Fantastik, works wonders. So logically it *cannot* matter that the claims aren't believed, nor can it matter that the advertisement is fear-arousing, overclaiming or disliked. The advertiser finds these notions uncomfortable, so he is not prepared to countenance them. Until he begins to question the fact that advertising has the sort of strength that Galbraith's "demand management" implies, then these huge hurdles to persuasion seem to be no more than bumps in the pathway to success.

If but a shadow of doubt creeps over a client's face, and if a good dinner can't wipe it off, the instrument that keeps the tottering edifice in the upright position is "research." "Well, we did research it" is a phrase that an adman will use to justify the latest irritating inanity which his agency has just spent half a million dollars exposing to the public.

This extraordinary process of the measurement (and justification) of the claims produced by the traditional advertising model requires a little analysis. Most admen will admit that they know very little about how the process of communication works in advertising. There is no general theory which satisfactorily explains the various stages of the mental processes that are involved. Faced with the odd situation of believing that their advertising works but being unable to say much about *why* it works, the admen have chosen to build a series of stages between claim and sales which act as mileposts along the route. These show how far the "message" has gone toward its ultimate destination of getting those cash registers ringing. If you don't accept the simplistic claim→sales relationship, then the intervening process of measuring to see how far you've got can be of very little interest. But the advertising industry as a whole has accepted all or most of them without substantial reservation. The conclusions it draws from the investigations it makes into the campaigns it runs for its clients are treated with the sort of statistical lunacy you might expect from a computer gone berserk. One particular formula, developed by Warren Twedlt in 1952 to predict advertising readership went like this: Advertising readership $= 10{,}456 + 8.2$ (size of advertisement in pages) $+ 3{,}869$ (number of colors) $+ 0.181$ (square inches of illustration).

The slide-rule worship that produces this sort of mathematical monster is reared on the erroneous belief that if you express something in statistical form, then you are "measuring" it. But Stanley Pollitt of Boase Massimi, Pollitt publicly conceded, when discussing the sort of research techniques that the advertising industry used: "We are not dealing with something which is at present just a little bit imperfect, or with existing techniques not working properly, *but of them not working at all.*"

To begin with, the testing situation is normally so remote from the real buying situation as to make assessments in the former of dubious application to the latter. Those sessions where they test television commercials bear little relationship to the environment in which you normally watch television commercials, stuck between boiling the kettle and going to the john.

Forgetting even the technical inadequacies of this and other types of research, there's another sort of bias which is involved, the bias of the agency which prepared the advertisements and which tries to show the client that it's working like clockwork. A sad example of this occurred during the FTC hearings on Firestone tires described in Chapter two. A study by Firestone's agency, Campbell-Ewald, was cited during the hearing; it reported that 81 percent of consumers had got the impression from the advertising that Firestone tires were safer than others. But another study, done by Hans Zeigel, professor of sociology and law at the University of Chicago, told a rather different story: only 15.1 percent of consumers had felt that Firestone tires were absolutely safe after seeing the Firestone advertisement. Professor Zeigel dubbed the Campbell-Ewald study "the sloppiest type of survey," and when asked by one of the attorneys why advertising agencies spend so much money on this kind of worthless research, he replied, "You and I know the answer."

Even if the environment of testing were realistic and the motivation were pure, the techniques of measurement just don't stand up to serious examination. The first of these are the measures of how much of the claim (for all its exaggeration or anxiety-arousing qualities) has been attended to. The way of assessing the extent to which an advertisement is consciously attended to ranges from watching people look at test advertisements to observing how much their pupils dilate when exposed to the advertisement.

After you've done a fair number of these studies, you can deduce the general principles that will get your advertisement a high "attention score"—babies, dogs, naked ladies, big pictures generally covering three quarters of the page, shortish headlines, and so on. The net result is a whole string of advertisements which look like a 1960 Ivy League student (well-groomed but dull), for the art of getting attention is no more prone to such simple formulas than the art of writing sonnets. In fact, the key variable in attention—if you want to measure it—is the number of people who use your product already. These people will wish to read your advertisement in order to reassure themselves that they are buying the right product. Despite this fact you never find in the Gallup reading-and-noting studies (one of the most popular tests of attention) any index of the market shares of the brands whose ads were checked and so make their data in any way meaningful. Add to this the problem that many of the people who say they look at your advertisement don't actually do so, and you can see the sort of problems that face even this fairly basic sort of measurement.

Is it worth all the palaver? Certainly, the more people out of your target audience who attend to your advertisement, the better. But the very careful study by Leo Bogart found that "*sales results have only a chance relationship to the advertisement's ability to win attention.*" Yet this factor with the chance relationship to sales is the object of more veneration within the advertising industry than any other single measurement.

If one does want to find a relevant measure for the persuasive impact of an advertisement, it's not attention or comprehension that is the key, but the *credibility* of the source of the message (and this has been known for twenty years). For instance, in one carefully controlled study (by Hoveland and Weiss, and reported in *Public Opinion Quarterly*, 1951) where precisely the same communication on four topics was used, first when linked to a high-credibility source (Robert J. Oppenheimer) and then to a low-credibility source (*Pravda*), the identical text was judged almost twice as convincing for Oppenheimer as for *Pravda*. There was no correlation between the attention to or comprehension of the message with persuasiveness.

This being the case, you would expect the advertising industry to look for ways to raise the credibility of itself as a source of information. You would expect it to discuss some of the different credibility levels of the various media in which it can place its advertisements. In one sense, for example, television should be credible because it is "now," but it isn't because most commercials are prerecorded. Most important, the rhubarb noises that greet the commercial provide group pressures which reduce the credibility of this information source still further. The effect of group viewing by an audience is something that can reduce the credibility of an advertisement in a way that the private viewing of that same message when reading a printed advertisement or a poster would not. The group situation provides the social support for distrust that isn't present in the private-viewing situation.

Even within the same type of media there can be differences in credibility. The so-called "presenter effect" is a direct descendant of the difference between having your message delivered by an Oppenheimer and delivered by *Pravda*. One study showed that an advertisement for Armstrong cork floors was 27 percent more persuasive in the London *Sunday Times* magazine than in *Ideal Home*, and that a television commercial with the same message was 10 percent less persuasive than the advertisement in *Ideal Home*.

Before moving away entirely from the matter of whether it's right to look at the measures of credibility instead of the measures of attention and comprehension, the "sleeper effect" deserves an airing. You may recall that the "sleeper effect" was used by SOUP in developing the "rotten-apple concept," whereby an advertiser was said to receive some benefit in year four from the advertisement in year one. Technically speaking, the "sleeper effect" is the phenomenon of forgetting the source of the message over a period of time, and if the source is a low-credibility one, it may mean the message will actually be more persuasive eight weeks after it was delivered than when it was delivered. This was apparent when during the last war researchers who had shown American troops a film about the Battle of Britain (in an attempt to make the American troops believe their British allies) found that nine weeks after the showing of the film it had *increased* in persuasiveness. If you apply this to advertising, you have a mechanism that might suggest that Professor Galbraith and his allies are right in saying that belief isn't important, for eight weeks after you've run your advertisement the consumer has forgotten *where* the message came from, and will then lap up your opinion like a cat taking to cream.

The only snag with this argument is that advertising, by the way it functions, makes it very hard for an audience to forget that the source of the message was a low-credibility, highly despised advertisement. After all, quite a wide range of people might have spoken to the American troops about the Battle of Britain following the film. They could even have chatted among themselves about it, read articles in the newspapers, etc. Gradually the exact source of any particular attitude could have become fuzzier and fuzzier until the message remained alone, unsullied by its carrier. But in the case of advertising, there aren't many alternative sources for the information that Tide has the whiter white. You know that any message you have stored in your brain about the whiteness of Tide *must* have come from an advertisement because nobody else talks about such things. Just to make sure that we don't "disassociate the source from the message," the advertiser is continually repeating his claims, continually reminding us that the "whiter-white" message is coming from a low-credibility source.

This isn't a new point. In 1953 Hoveland, Janis and Kelley showed that while, with a high-credibility source, the effect of reminding the recipient of the message after three weeks *added* to its persuasiveness, the effect of "reinstating" a low-credibility source was simply to wipe out the "sleeper effect." Once more the message was *reduced* in impact because of the low credibility of the source (namely, an advertisement).

It's perhaps worth inquiring why the advertiser is so resolved to destroy any possible benefit he could receive from the "sleeper effect" by persistently repeating his message. It is because he has resolved to get the maximum "recall" for his sales message. He has been persuaded that the purpose of advertising is "to make the consumer learn and retain the association between the two elements of an advertisement—the product and the brand name" (Rabindra Kanungo, *Journal of Applied Psychology,* 1969). If that brand name comes wrapped in a snappy phrase like "The Esso sign means happy motoring," and then is further encapsulated in musical form (otherwise known as a jingle), perfection is nigh. The more he repeats this memorable expression of his product's virtues, the more virtuous the product will appear to become. Just how persistent this belief is, is demonstrated by the fact that the jingle is just about the most common form of television message. Almost the only reason for using a jingle is to make your sales message so "catchy" that it will be self-repeating, i.e., every time you hum "Schaefer . . . is the one beer to have . . . when you're having more than one," you're giving the advertiser a free showing of his commercial inside your cranium.

"Recall measures" are thus a measure of the extent to which, through repetition, you have got your parcel of information about the products safely delivered into the consumer. Those who believe in using repetition for this purpose ought to study the psychological concept of "semantic satiation." The standard way of arousing annoyance in an audience for experimental purposes is to repeat the same word or phrase twenty to thirty times over a brief period. The psychologist's tool for creating annoyance is the advertiser's tool for creating sales.

However, even if you manage to embed your claim in the consumers' memory with parrot-like repetition, it probably won't make you richer. There is much evidence to show that there is precisely no relationship between whatever measures of recall you take and whatever measures of attitude and behavior change that you make. The parable of the three mirrors, as told by researcher Alfred Politz (*Journal of Marketing*, 1960), explains why. One of the mirrors was cracked, the second was perfect and had a beautiful gilt frame, and the third was perfect but unframed. These faced an open window and a visitor was asked to look at the mirrors on the wall and tell what he could see. Of the first mirror he said, "I see an old cracked mirror." Of the second, "I see a mirror in a beautiful frame." Of the third, "I see a beautiful view out of an open window." The third mirror was Politz's description of good advertising: reflecting the product favorably without drawing attention to itself. "Recall" may be likened to paying attention to the frame instead of looking at the view through the window.

But whatever recall of sales points may correlate with, it isn't sales. For example, though the higher the recall does *not* mean the higher the attitude change, recall *is* highest for those who have shown the greatest attitude change. This is the result of the consumer's mental dossier looking for pieces of information which buttress its current position. That being so, the greater the proportion of the market, the higher will be that brand's recall scores. Once your client's brand has obtained a hefty share of the market, then you can "prove" how good your advertising is, just by show-ing him the high recall scores which it is achieving.

With this built-in bias for the larger-brands advertising, it's understandable that the agencies handling these brands have stuck with recall measures. Sophisticated agencies like Ogilvy & Mather and sophisticated clients like Procter & Gamble still chase high recall scores like Sir Lancelot seeking the Holy Grail.

Agency documents abound with boasts about high recall scores, and case histories use recall measures to prove the "success" of the campaign. For example, the 1971 IBA Annual Report com-mented on the Scottish antismoking campaign: "The campaign . . . has pleased the unit as regards public response, and a recent survey carried out by the University of Strathclyde ascertained that the advertisement had reached and stayed in the minds of nearly 70 percent of the I.T.V. audience in Glasgow."

One reason for all this emphasis on recall is that throughout David Ogilvy's book *Confessions of an Advertising Man*, there are continual admonitions to do things like using captions under photographs or using large type for the first paragraph of the copy in order to push up the *readership* by x percent, or mention-ing the brand name in the first ten seconds of a television com-mercial because it increases the *recall* score by 14 percent (this last suggestion by the head of Ogilvy's agency in Canada). The only thing this leads to is a crazy numbers game with all these figures being used as fodder to keep the client happy.

Of course, information may have a big role in an advertise-ment, but you can't measure how much of that information has been *communicated* by asking someone to parrot it back at you. Of course, an advertisement has to be looked at if it's to affect a consumer, but that doesn't mean the most looked at ad is the most effective one. However, the belief that in parroting there is com-munication and in readership there is riches are two of the founda-tion stones of modern advertising practice.

Another central belief is that the more I can make you change your attitude in favor of my product, as measured by various techniques, the more likely you are to buy my brand. The classic study on this subject (almost twenty years old) is the Janis and Fesbach mentioned previously. It involved testing different sorts of appeal to persuade people to clean their teeth. You may recall that it was the strong (horror) appeal which got the least behavior change, and the minimal (factual) appeal the most, but in terms of *attitude* change the result was exactly the other way around. While the *factual* appeal got 79 percent more behavior change than the horror appeal, the *horror* appeal got 64 percent more attitude change than the factual one. Since this discovery a lot more evidence has emerged to suggest that there is not *necessarily* a relationship between favorable attitudes and purchase.

In 1965 Dr. Anthony Greenwald reported in *Journal of Public Opinion* that he could get junior-high-school children to change their beliefs about the importance of learning vocabulary, but still not get them to change their behavior (by doing difficult vocabulary problems). This occurred when the children had previously stated they were antivocabulary. The effect of this "prior commitment on behavior change after a persuasive communication" also worked in reverse. An antivocabulary child could be persuaded to learn more vocabulary with a "behavioral incentive" (e.g., giving him money for extra words learned), but that didn't stop him from having an antivocabulary attitude. This second point helps explain why "behavioral incentives" to buy groceries, e.g., 10 cents off, don't do anything to strengthen a brand's image.

The first point is also demonstrated in the way people respond to propaganda about wearing seat belts in their cars. For manifold reasons, some to do with the fact that wearing a seat belt is to deny your masculinity, less than one driver in six wears a seat belt *despite* the fact that five out of six drivers believe they could well be involved in a serious accident at some time. The propaganda has persuaded them that they might have an accident, but it has still not persuaded them to wear their seat belt.

Even without a "prior commitment" operating, there can still be a change of attitude without the expected change of behavior. I may have a favorable attitude toward wearing trendy clothes, but it may be that my wish to dress as others expect me to keeps me wearing pin stripes. Or my wife may have a favorable attitude toward a brand of soap but actually buys another brand which she feels less favorable toward when her mother-in-law visits, in her desire to conform with what she believes the mother-in-law expects to find.

In both these cases, simple prediction of how one would behave based upon attitude measurements would have proved wrong. An additional reason for such predictions proving wrong in the case of advertising is that there is normally quite a gap in time and space between the attitude measured and the behavior expected.

Some time ago RCA did a survey which demonstrated this exact point (cited in *Madison Avenue, U.S.A.*, by Martin Mayer). People who thought they might buy a television set within the next twelve months were asked to state which set they liked best or were most likely to buy, and rank other sets in order of likelihood of purchase. Later on, the interviewer returned to these homes to see which make was actually bought. Twenty-two percent had bought one of the four brands they had listed as possibilities, but 59 percent had bought a brand which they had marked in the first interview as being most unlikely for them to purchase. It could be argued that all that had happened was that these consumers' attitudes had changed after the first interview. However, as long ago as 1954 a study by Du Pont among 5,200 women showed that only three out of ten actually purchased the brand they expected to buy before they entered the store, and that seven out of ten changed their minds in the store.

An ingenious theory which explains this phenomenon has been developed by Dr. Herbert Krugman of General Electric. He suggests that the supermarket provides a catalyst which brings out all the potential shifts of attitude that have been accumulated up to that point by the consumer even though nothing could or would be verbalized prior to *that* moment if the consumer was asked about his attitude. The attitude change that results *after* this purchase would be twofold: first, bringing into balance the expectations of the product and the reality of the product's performance; second, the balancing of the act of purchase with other elements in the mental dossier (rationalization).

Interestingly, Dr. Andrew Ehrenberg has shown ("Towards an Integrated Theory of Buying Behaviour," *Journal of the Market Research Society*, October 1969) that once you know the penetration of a brand into a market, you can with uncanny accuracy predict the likely response of consumers to most attitude questions. But researchers are still having great difficulty in making the prediction in the other direction. And the fact that it may not be possible to predict choice of brands or type of product purchased, even knowing a consumer's previous habits, beliefs or attitudes, is a fairly tough nut for the crystal-ball gazers of the market research industry to crack.

The full impact of these theoretical doubts has not yet come home to the mass of the advertisers and their agencies who, for the most part, are still merrily measuring people's attitudes before exposure to the advertisement, measuring the attitudes after exposure and deducing from that the sales effectiveness of the advertisement as if the past criticisms of this approach had never been penned.

The only real alternative to measuring attitudes as a predictor of behavior which has emerged is to measure what is called the "behavioral intention." This tries to shift the moment of measurement much closer to the act of purchase. For instance, if you asked a woman who was standing in front of the soap section of the supermarket which brand she was going to buy, your correlation with behavior would probably be much higher than if you asked the same question just after she had seen a commercial for your brand of soap. But despite the brave hopes of the supporters of this notion, it doesn't at present amount to a lot more than saying, "Once you know what someone's going to do, you know what someone's going to do." This leaves the poor advertiser stranded like a whale on a beach. He has spent his huge advertising budget. His agency has told him that the recall scores are tremendous. But then he learns he can't believe in recall scores, so the agency tells him that the promotion produced a tremendous shift in attitude by consumers in favor of the product. Now he learns that this doesn't mean that they will also be buying his product in droves. How, then, can he go to his managing director to justify the expenditure of this enormous sum, when all the other departments in the company can't wait to get their hands on what they regard as a conspicuous way of throwing money down the drain? In this situation he will fall back on the final link in the chain. "Well," he can say to the board, looking the R. & D. man straight in the eye, "your wife may think our commercial stinks, and maybe I haven't got any convincing research measures to prove the ads were right. But I can tell you one thing"—he pauses here—"*it sells.*"

These two little words have been the justification of much of the advertising that has helped build up the consumerist backlash. (Perhaps one should add that the relationship is expressed slightly more subtly: if sales go up, it's because of the advertising, but if they go down, it's because of something else.)

Every advertiser who visits a new agency will be told about the campaign that raised sales 40 percent or of an advertisement that took this brand out of the ashcan and turned it into a brand leader. Isn't this a fair measure of an advertisement's success? As we shall see, the proper function of an advertisement may well be to create sales, but sales are not normally a proper measure of how well that function has been carried out.

For a start, there are a huge number of other variables, many of which the agency has no control over, such as the efficiency of the sales force, the company's track record with the trade, the price of the product, its distribution, the packaging, the quality of the product, the competitors' share of the market, the competitors' activity in the market, the consumers' attitude toward the product itself. But more than this, the way cognitive-dissonance theory suggests that people respond to overclaim shows how—despite total *rejection* of the advertisement—sales of a product may still go up subsequent to the claim, even when all the other variables are held constant.

A case in point is Fairy Liquid (Britain's answer to Ivory Liquid). The in-depth interviews reported earlier on people's attitudes to advertising also showed that these commercials were irritating. (These commercials involved children playing with bubbles and their mother cooing to the accompaniment of a choir singing the "hands that do dishes can feel soft as your face" jingle.) To this, many of the consumers I spoke to replied, "Children don't behave like that," and "It's silly to make such a song-and-dance over washing up," etc. Yet the product is a brand leader, despite having entered the market later than its main rivals.

Can the undoubted sales success of this product be attributed to its hard-sell advertising? Well, the Fairy Liquid company, Procter & Gamble, had a lot going for it—like an ultra-tough sales force and a good track record with the trade. But they have also had flops in their time, so these alone couldn't explain the success of Fairy Liquid. What *is* revealing, however, is to look at the actual performance of this product against other brands of dishwashing liquid. The British Sunday paper *News of the World* did a study, for example, which showed that because Fairy Liquid contained the highest proportion of "active ingredients" (i.e., the

203

solvents that get rid of grease), it gave 20 percent more "washing-up power" than the next major brand. And a study by *Ideal Home* found that compared to the retailers' own brands, Fairy Liquid could absorb three to four times as much fat before the dishwashing water went flat (you'd need four drops of a retailer's own brand of detergent to get the same sudsing power as one drop of Fairy Liquid). In short, it is Fairy Liquid's *performance* in cleaning dishes that probably explains its success. Many consumers perhaps tried a retailer's own brand because they have a low price, but after finding that they actually worked out more expensively, they could have returned to Fairy Liquid.

What is certain, however, is that the housewives are not buying Fairy Liquid because they believe the advertising claim that "hands that do dishes can feel soft as your face with mild green Fairy Liquid," for even if they tell the researchers from Young & Rubicam, Fairy Liquid's advertising agency, that they think the product is amazingly mild, they are voting with their hands to show they think nothing of the sort: in Britain, 57 percent of all housewives use rubber gloves regularly for dishwashing (according to London Rubber Industries, which makes Marigold gloves). Unless all the non-rubber-glove wearers veer toward Fairy Liquid, this fact can only mean one of two things: that the mildness claim is not relevant, since housewives use rubber gloves because of the effect of water on their skin, or that, since Fairy Liquid is such a strong detergent, they need rubber gloves for protection. (However, Procter & Gamble was unable to supply any evidence that Fairy Liquid is as mild as the advertising claims.) All of which makes the link between Fairy Liquid's advertising and the success of the brand an extremely tenuous one. Nevertheless, this case history is often used in the advertising industry as proof that schmaltzy hard sell is the thing that moves mountains of groceries.

Does that mean that Fairy Liquid would have been just as successful as a brand without the many million pounds in advertising that were spent telling people about its mildness? It's not impossible.

In the case of the world's largest pet-food producer (Ralston Purina, advertising played an insignificant role in its success in the British market. The company launched its Seanip dinners into the British dry-cat-food market in 1968. Within three years it had over a third of the market nationally and half the market in the key London area, but it achieved that without spending a penny on advertising (even though at the same time Purina's main rival spent over half a million pounds on advertising). If, however, Purina had appointed an agency and if that agency had spent large sums of money running commercials for Seanip, the company would have pointed triumphantly to the 30 percent market share as indication of the cost effectiveness of its advertising.

This naïve *post hoc, ergo propter hoc* relationship is not only misleading, it is very dangerous for the advertising industry itself, for once a company starts to judge its advertising by a measure that may well be a false one, then the agency is in trouble if it dares to adopt a new approach to its advertising.

Suppose a big agency, recognizing the scientific reality, decides to dispense with recall studies, throw out attitudes measures and concentrate on some of the techniques of persuasion which are described in the following chapter, it becomes very vulnerable if it is being judged on sales alone. Sales may go down or they may rise less fast than previously, and for no reason at all to do with the advertising (in the same way that their earlier rise may have had very little to do with the advertising). Then the client will be complaining that the advertisements "aren't working" (as happened, in fact, when several agencies tried to move toward the so-called "creative" approach). In short, the advertising industry is hoist by its own petard. It can't change its ways easily because it has chained itself to a method of judgment that makes any innovation, even if it is an improvement, vulnerable to attack.

The other reason why the advertising industry finds it hard to change, even though most of its measures have been found to be built on sand, is that it has nothing else to fall back on. If a manufacturing company decides to write off some capital equipment because it doesn't work properly, it can simply dispose of it by putting in new capital equipment instead. But the advertising agencies can do no such thing. Remove the data bank of twenty years of recall studies and they have nothing. Rob them of their pre- and post-exposure attitudinal measures and they are naked in the boardroom. And it is not always just the agencies that feel the need for props. A company like Procter & Gamble finds recall studies useful as a management tool to keep its brand managers up to the mark, quite apart from any marketing importance it might have. Take all this away and the advertising industry is left with a whole battery of techniques for selling products without any method, which any professional scientist could accept, of measuring whether these techniques function as their makers claim or not.

It is this tremendous void that advertising has to fill quickly if it is to avoid becoming no more than a memento of the golden days of the sizzling sixties, a not-so-glorious future where little children ask their fathers, "Daddy, what was a commercial?"

As Not Advertised on TV

●

Is it really so fanciful to suggest that signs carrying the words of this chapter heading should spring up in the shop windows of affluent societies? Already the degree of consumer hostility that exists seems to make the mere act of advertising a product a black mark against that product. "If it's so good, why does it need to advertise?" has increasingly become the reaction of many consumers.

What has happened is that because of the sort of things they talked about and the particular way they talked about them, most advertisements have become for the new consumer less and less useful as a guide to deciding which product to choose. In a study by the British Bureau of Television Advertising, for instance, 96 percent of car purchasers didn't think advertising was very important in guiding their choice of car. As one of the main reasons for the existence of advertisements—to help consumers choose products—such a figure suggests that the advertising industry is in serious danger of going out of business.

Once upon a time, though frequently reviled and sometimes persecuted, the advertising industry was believed to be in possession of strange powers. Now a consumer environment has developed which shows up these powers for exactly what they are: modest rather than magical, sometimes useful rather than always essential, and—above all—sullenly resented by those to whom they are directed. This is not to say that there isn't a role for advertising in keeping consumers aware of the available choice in the marketplace, but because the information provided by advertisements has proved so unhelpful, alternative information systems have developed to answer this need.

Editorials in fashion and automobile magazines have been around for some time, but now their role has changed, from being outlets for companies' P.R. releases to being well-informed aids to product selection for their readers' benefit. And they are quite prepared to go out and openly attack their advertisers in a very tough way. Now *Car* magazine can run a major issue largely devoted to exploding "the Cortina myth," Ford's biggest-selling British car, and actually go through a whole Cortina advertisement sentence by sentence, paragraph by paragraph, making raspberry noises.

In addition to new editorial attitudes, there are new kinds of editorials. Shopping advisory columns abound, on food, furniture, domestic appliances, houses, insurance, garden equipment, vacations—they cover an area as wide as the spectrum of advertising itself. Although the space these columns occupy is still small, their impact is substantial. A mention in just one paragraph is probably equivalent in sales power to a substantial advertisement in that same paper, and every fashion manufacturer knows that the fashion editorial sells far more clothes than the fashion advertisements.

Technology is likely to add to this alternative information system. There is no technical reason why a "dial-a-product" information service shouldn't exist, to give plus points and minus points on a brand-by-brand basis. The Home Communications System (Homecom) which has been developed in America could take this idea a step further. With Homecom a cable-television receiver and keyboard transmitter in every home would enable you, for example, to see a visual display giving details of the special offers in various supermarkets before you even left home. Linked to a computer, Homecom would enable you to give your shopping list to the computer and then get back from it the name of the shop where these particular items can be purchased most cheaply on this particular day. Even without this elaborate technology, it is clear that product information can, and is, being distributed without recourse to the admen. Both contraceptives and marijuana became mass-market products without mass advertising, and a quarter of a million people went to a pop festival in Woodstock with only the tiniest advertising budget being used to woo them.

In this situation, the marginal promotional dollar is less and less likely to be allocated to advertising, and more and more likely to be spent in some other part of the marketing mix. All this may bring a profound sense of gloom to smart New York advertising agencies (and to the smart New York restaurants who live off them), but it also brings a rather surprising opportunity—an opportunity, please note, which carries with it the chance to help the consumer as well as the manufacturer.

The most neglected portion of the whole marketing mix is the area of finding out what the consumer needs and wants, and then actually doing something about it. Most of the research effort goes into monitoring the market and product or advertising testing. Much of the supposed consumer-oriented product development is designed simply to find out, for example, if the consumer notices the fact that his cigarettes are a fifth of a millimeter shorter.

It is into this arena that the admen can step. Instead of concentrating all their attention on an area of activity where they are becoming less and less helpful to their clients, they can tackle the task of adding value to the products. This is essentially the same function that design engineers are engaged in, be it drawing up a new car design or reformulating an instant coffee. But while the design team tends to use science-based skills, the adman in his role as a consumer engineer will use his communication skills.

In one sense, "adding value" to the products is what admen have claimed to be doing for some time. A bar of soap was more than the sum total of its molecules, and the personality that the advertiser provided increased the pleasure of washing. But more and more, as has already been argued, the kinds of values that are attached to products are increasingly thought to be phony. Values like sex appeal, personal acceptability, esteem by neighbors, personal self-confidence are felt less and less to come with a stick of deodorant.

The new role of an advertising agency as consumer engineers will be quite different. It is to become a *"social information broker"* which tries to act both as a *sensor* in the marketplace, picking up tremors (like the man who saw people mixing vinegar and oil to stop sunburn and then himself brought out a commercial suntan oil), and also as a *modifier* of products based upon these soundings. The acronym C.O.N.T.A.C.T. (Consumer Oriented New Thinking And Communication Techniques) summarizes this function.

Arguably, it is a function which ought to be within the capacity of the innovatory client company itself. But the evidence of Jewkes, Sawyer and Stillerman in *The Sources of Invention* suggests that the process of innovation works rather inadequately in large corporations. Admittedly, the innovations studied there were technical, like the Moulton bicycle, the Wankel engine and the Hovercraft. But the blocks to this sort of innovation—pyramid structure in the company, employing the wrong sort of people for innovation, having the wrong environment for innovation, being too far away from the consumer—would also inhibit the less technical sort of innovation as well.

Some work on the C.O.N.T.A.C.T. philosophy is already being done by existing agencies within their new-product workshop, such as the development of US, the Unisex deodorant, and Quaker's raspberry-flavored porridge. But most of these workshops are simply mechanisms for checking out innovation rather than developing it.

The C.O.N.T.A.C.T. approach, however, implies a greater change of role than can be found in new-product workshops. For example, C.O.N.T.A.C.T. would have discovered that a supermarket or a food manufacturer could use the concept of open dating or unit pricing as a profitable marketing tool *before* the consumer lobbyists used these issues as canes to clobber the manufacturers with. C.O.N.T.A.C.T. would have also developed a new type of car guarantee and car servicing control *before* consumer journals lambasted the car companies, which only then—after denial and protest—came up with their own proposals.

C.O.N.T.A.C.T. is thus working to find a new coincidence of self-interest between the consumer and the manufacturer through carrying out a social information broker role.

A few companies are already operating on some of these principles, and though they are exceptions, they prove the practicality of the concept as well as its profitability. TWA's million-dollar service scheme, Whirlpool and Travelers Insurance telephone "Hotlines," Ford's "We listen better" scheme, Braniff's painting of their planes (C.O.N.T.A.C.T. doesn't rule out trivial ideas if they are judged pleasing to consumers), Monsanto's Wear Dated scheme, American Motor's special car guarantee. Even Lever Brothers offered (in one American state) to donate 2 cents for every box of detergent purchased to a university extension program on improving water quality ("Let us put in your 2 cents for clean water"), and this is a move in the right direction.

Quaker has even incorporated on the back and side of its *Life* cereal boxes a preschooler learning program. Each box will have a four-part lesson, and there will be six lessons in the series. Without changing the product at all, the role of the product in the family's life style is thus instantly changed.

The company that has probably gone furthest with this approach is Hunt-Wesson. In 1970 they began their "We'll help you make it" program to assist families with a low food budget to live healthily. They invited housewives to write, giving the number and age of the people in their family and the amount of their weekly food budget. The housewife then received in return a personalized letter plus a special computerized print-out of menus for her family for the entire month, carefully tied to her budget (as well as the recipes for preparing the dishes on these menus). Over 1.4 million housewives have already sent in for their menus so far.

C.O.N.T.A.C.T. does not dispense with the agency's job of creating advertisements. It merely makes it the last thing an agency thinks about, rather than the first. But in view of the havoc wrought by the consumer revolution, even with sound C.O.N.T.A.C.T. concepts, advertising is at present unable to credibly communicate them.

The alternative information system may step in here. On the other hand, there is the opportunity for advertising to drastically change methods and—as a social information broker—become a useful information source (even though an information source that is known to be biased). This will require profound changes to both the structure of the advertising industry and the techniques of the admen themselves.

The first change that is required to ensure the survival of this species is that it recognize the types of change among consumers which have occurred over the past ten years. They don't worship materialism in the way the advertisements suggest. Housewives don't worship housewifery, and a new ethos is growing up among the under-twenty-fives, who wonder why so much money is being spent on selling trivia when half the world is dying for a meal.

If the admen can appreciate all this, they will soon see that they are living and behaving in a way that is quite out of keeping with the times. If, as seems likely, the advertising industry is still unable to lead the parade of reform itself, then it will have to be dragged along behind.

Too many of the rules controlling advertising on both sides of the Atlantic have a laxness that is unacceptable in the age of militant consumerism. No advertiser, for example, should be permitted to make a claim (even a trade puff) unless he can fully substantiate it. And the judgment of the claim that has actually been made should be based on communication research (which actually measures what people get out of an advertisement). This would both allow those humorous claims that aren't really claims, as well as eliminating those claims which cunningly use verbal hairsplitting to get themselves on the air but are actually implying a lot more than they're saying.

The restrictive practice of not allowing comparisons between yours and rival products should be dropped. Strangely enough, the prohibition of comparisons is strongest in Germany, where otherwise advertising controls tend to be in the best interests of the consumer. The only restraint on comparisons should be the laws of libel. The same rules that govern television advertising should also govern all other sorts of advertising. A dual standard of truth is not acceptable any more.

Remembering how much lower the hostility to advertising was in those countries where there was less television advertising, it would be in the advertising industry's interests to reduce the amount of television advertising. A lower figure of the minutes of television advertising per hour is required, and commercials should not be allowed to interrupt programs, as this is one of the major causes of hostility.

The loss of revenue that this would cause the broadcasting companies could be replaced by increasing the rates at which they sell television time to advertisers to a level where the total revenue obtained was the same as previously. The price elasticity of television time is probably sufficient to allow this increase of price to be made. By making companies pay a lot more for their advertising, it would also serve to make them think much more carefully about the efficiency of the way they spent it. If raising the price was insufficient to bridge the income gap caused by the reduction in advertising time, tax concessions to the broadcasting companies might be used as compensation.

The final Draconian measure that would actually be helping

the advertising industry is a maximum-budget level for advertisers. The fact that cigarette sales were maintained both in Britain and America after banning the advertising of cigarettes on television suggests that a lot of advertising expenditure is simply self-canceling. A high proportion of the $500,000 I may spend to advertise my brand is canceled by the $500,000 my rival spends (and my expenditure also serves to cancel a lot of his). Although the advertising may have been neutralized in a commercial sense, from the consumer standpoint there is still a great deal of unpleasant noise going on around him. If a maximum ceiling were placed on advertising budgets (and I can see that it would be difficult to arrange), it wouldn't stop new companies from coming into the market (though it would discourage the build-up of monopoly positions by the established companies), but it would slice off the top end of the giant advertising budgets and so eliminate some of the self-canceling advertising.

These measures would start to restore to advertising a modicum of tolerance from the public. They would also, by eliminating most of the puffery and unrelated comparatives, help to turn advertising from a flabby amalgam of words and pictures into an effective selling tool. But in order to regain the respect of their clients, two further reforms are necessary.

First, agencies should endeavor to have a slightly higher standard of whose account they will handle. They should ask potential clients questions about the satisfactory performance of the product, the safety of the product, and the value of such a product in a consumer society. They should refuse to take on products whose companies cannot give satisfactory answers to such questions, instead of the current practice of jumping into bed with virtually anyone. If agencies are ever fussy, it is more often because they're worried their customers can't pay the bill than because there is anything wrong with what the customer has to offer. To have no higher standard of client selection than a common prostitute is not the way to obtain the respect of the business community.

Second, the 15 percent commission payment system for agencies should be ended. This is a system where for every $100 of media space an agency books, the media only charge $85—though the agency bills the clients for the full $100. Besides restricting competition between agencies by fixing the price at which an agency sells its services, this system concentrates the agency's attention on that stage of the communication process from which it receives remuneration. Activities that do not provide any media revenue (such as suggesting instead of advertising that the client should spend his money on some other form of promotional activity) actually cost the conventional agency money and is therefore not encouraged by them.

The net result is that the brain power of the advertising industry is concentrating its attention on an arena of activity which is becoming of less and less importance to clients, of less and less usefulness in adding value to products. Dismantling the commission system, and replacing it with a fee system, would probably be the single most important structural change that would enable agencies to reorient themselves to the new consumer environment in which they have to survive.

Changing the techniques of advertising, as opposed to the structure of the industry, is a rather more substantial task. Perhaps the possibility of extinction will persuade admen to pay attention to the discoveries of social psychology and advertising research over the last twenty years.

For a start, a more realistic assessment of the relationship of advertising to sales is long overdue. The following model on consumer behavior, which owes much to the work done by Francesco Nicosia ("Consumer Decision Processes in the Behavioural Sciences," 1966) and Johann Arndt ("Advertising—to a Problem-Solving Consumer," *Admap* magazine, October 1969) shows the many intervening processes between making a claim—even a claim deriving from the C.O.N.T.A.C.T. approach—and the act of purchase.

In the New Advertising, even though advertising is not conceived of as the prima donna in the marketing process, it still has a role to play in the drama of consumer choice. Its prime job is to help consumers solve problems in the consumption area. The problem-solving consumer is an intelligent animal who is faced with needs to fulfill. He seeks out as much information as seems to him necessary (i.e., more information for buying a car than for buying a pack of chewing gum) and relates this information to the purchasing problem. The flow-chart model shows, conceptually at least, the various stages he will go through in making a product choice.

To pass each of the hurdles, the advertising message will have

214

The complicated relationship between ... no. 3 and 4.

Consumption

Purchase Action

Stage in decision process.

| Aware-ness | Know-ledge | Evalua-tion Attitude | Intention to buy |

SA Satisfaction

Defence mechanisms
Selective exposure
Selective perception
Selective retention

Subjective need for information

Predispositions

	Economic variables
Ability to buy	Needs physiological psychological social
Willingness to buy	General attitudinal structures
	personality factors
Information variables	Stored information
	Information routines
	Media habits

Product attributes
Price
Service

Information	Advertising
Commercial sources	Store personnel
Neutral sources	Consumer reports etc.
	Word of mouth advertising

Source: Arndt

to be constructed in a way that is quite different from the typical hard-nosed, hard-sell U.S.P. (which is quickly chewed up and spat out by the watchdogs, selective exposure, selective perception and selective retention).

Instead of overclaiming, underclaiming offers the advertiser a better chance in the seventies. In some ways similar to that much maligned concept "soft sell," underclaiming is an analytical response to a particular communication situation.

Underclaim, to revert to the theory of cognitive dissonance, creates the minimum amount of cognitive dissonance necessary to persuade the consumer to act as you suggest. Just enough to get the "curious nonbelief" described earlier, but not too much to get rejected because the claim doesn't tally with what she knows to be within the realm of possibility.

There is considerable evidence, including one bizarre experiment trying to persuade American soldiers to eat grasshoppers, that this sort of minimal appeal is more effective. One amusing, if unscientific, anecdote of the success of underclaiming is reported in Sam Baker's *The Permissible Lie*. He relates the tale of a New York department store which couldn't sell a consignment of green neckties. They tried every advertising gimmick, even cutting the price by $2, but nothing worked. In the end the celebrated retail-store advertising personality Ira Hirschman tried an ad with the headline "Our buyer made a bad mistake." The copy told what had happened and concluded: "If there are 207 men who'd like a green tie, you can get these magnificent $7 imported ties for $5 because very few men like green neckties." The ties sold like hot cakes.

Volkswagen ads generally use underclaim. So do the Campari ads that run in America with the headline "9 out of every 10,000 Americans prefer Campari" to present it as a status drink instead of using the photograph of a room full of (unbelievably) smart people drinking (unbelievably) nothing but Campari. Or take Ronson in Britain, which ran an ad for its new hairdryer with the headline "Ronson announces a slightly better hairdryer." No nonsense about a new-improved-hairdryer-with-30-percent-more power. Just the truth. Because not only is honesty the best policy in the seventies, it is probably the only policy for an advertiser trying to sell things faced by the new consumers' defense mechanisms.

In the same way that underclaiming is a stronger claim than hard-selling in the new consumer environment, admitting that there are two sides to the story you're telling can make your advertisements more effective. When your audience initially disagrees with you or when it's probable that they will hear the other side from someone else (as is generally the case with advertising), a two-sided argument will stand you in better stead. Better-educated men, in particular, are more influenced by two-sided communications. Probably because they feel that as there must be two sides to the point in question, a one-sided presentation is treating them like nincompoops.

In one study in America, one-sided and two-sided commercials were made for cars, gas ranges and floor waxes. They were tested on five hundred people, and it was found that the two-sided commercials produced significantly more attitude change in favor of the product. (One has, of course, reservations about this sort of measurement, but still, it may be revealing something.)

Another study (A. Mcniven, *Persuasion*, 1966) on Marlboro cigarettes also confirmed in practice what communication theory had suggested in principle. In this case the researchers produced advertisements which gave the standard one-sided version available in most printed ads, saying that Marlboro cigarettes were the mildest, best-tasting available. They also produced advertisements which said that everybody knows a filter cigarette can't be as nice-tasting as a plain cigarette. But Marlboro is still the finest-tasting cigarette you can get. The second appeal was clearly negative, as it admitted that filter cigarettes didn't taste as good as plain, but in discussions it emerged that smokers responded better to the two-sided argument. "He's giving us the straight scoop" was one typical comment.

All these forms of underclaiming take into account, in a way that current advertising practice does not, the low credibility of advertising as an information source. And the evidence of social psychologists (as well as common sense) is that the lower your credibility and the more you attempt to influence people, the greater will be their resistance.

Strangely enough, the advertiser receives one-side benefits from being such a low-credibility source. Raymond Bauer of the Harvard Business School has found that the best defense against counter-propaganda is a low-trust, high-competence source. So if you make your advertising very factual and informative, then just because you are a low-credibility source the consumer will tend to think the matter over carefully rather than simply accepting at face value the facts from a highly credible source. This process of weighing the pros and cons serves to inoculate the consumer against the rival advertising counter-propaganda.

One implication Bauer draws from this is that if you are selling something where the decision to buy is made over a long period, like a car, and the rival brands are coming in with counter-messages to your own, this inoculation procedure can be used to help you. However, if you borrow "a high-credibility source," then this source, though excellent, is more vulnerable to the counter-propaganda (because the consumer has taken the word of the source and not thought the matter out for himself).

On the other hand, if you are selling a near impulse-purchase, maybe hiring a high-credibility source to deliver your message would be sensible. Certainly, the Norman Ross discount chain found it successful in Australia. They signed up three clergymen as pitchmen for their commercials, all of which ended with the same words: "The offers of Norman Ross are genuine. I wouldn't do their commercials if they weren't." And then, superimposed on the screen, was the following message: "Norman Ross discounts pledge 2 percent of net profits to the Aid of Humanities Foundation."

Besides renting clergymen, another way an advertiser can raise his credibility is by presenting his message before revealing his identity as a low-credibility source. This doesn't mean hiding your advertisement in an editorial style, which may only irritate the consumer, but it does suggest that a client who insists that his agency stick an enormous logo in the advertisement, dominating the whole page, is actually making the agency's handiwork less effective.

The advertisement also needs to take into account its audience, in a way that is rather different from the conventional aiming of the message at "young marrieds with 2 children." You can classify differences in your audience on the basis of their defense mechanisms, on how close they are to a purchase decision, on what they think about the brand. Each of these different segments may need a different sort of message. Then, as the consumer "progresses" from one segment to another, you will need to modify the type of advertising that now reaches him. What this is effectively doing is making your advertisement fit your target consumer's predispositions. There is plenty of evidence to show that if, for example, the advertiser expresses some views that are also held by his audience, he'll find it easier to persuade the audience toward his viewpoint on another (and maybe quite separate) issue.

As an alternative to making your proposition acceptable to the consumer by adjusting it to him, you can also tailor a message by constructing it in such a way that the consumer adjusts himself to it. This is something that goes back to McLuhan and the participatory nature of television. Applying this thinking to advertising he observes: "The need is to make the ad include the audience experience." One way of doing this is to leave the message incomplete, like just saying, "You can take Salem out of the country but . . ." Or you can make your claim incomplete by leaving the brand name out, as in "I'm only here for the beer." This encourages the consumer to complete the phrase or add the brand name; by involving himself in the message, it becomes more acceptable than if it were thrust upon him in a complete form.

What you are encouraging the consumer to do by leaving the message incomplete is simply to improvise. And improvising is, again, a proven way of increasing the persuasiveness of the message. In one study (by B. D. King and I. L. Janis, "Comparison of the Effectiveness of Improvised versus Nonimprovised Role Playing in Producing Opinion Changes," paper presented for the Eastern Psychological Association, April 1953), two groups were shown a script. Those in one of the groups were then asked to read the script out loud, while those in the other group had to present the contents without relying on the script. It was this second group that were most persuaded by the arguments in the original script. They had been forced to "hand-tailor" the message to fit themselves, so they were more influenced by it.

In fact, one of the latest research measurements tries to assess a number of "connections" a consumer makes with your advertisement. Developed by Dr. Herbert Krugman of General Electric, it suggests that the more "connection" a consumer makes, the more unstructured is the advertisement, and the more unstructured the advertisement, the more the consumer can fit himself into it— and so, the more persuasive it becomes.

All these techniques (and I don't say "new techniques" because many of them have been lurking in the annals of social psychology for some time) are no more than a better way of doing the traditional advertising agency job. But if they were part of the deeper reorientation implied by the C.O.N.T.A.C.T. philosophy, then they would be not only acceptable in the new consumer environment, but also useful and profitable to businessmen.

Of course, all this is only part of the reorientation that business will have to make toward the new consumer, as a company discovers that social responsibility is no longer an optional extra but a standard item for any company that wants to do business in the seventies.

In the business of advertising, the C.O.N.T.A.C.T. philosophy perhaps represents a change of heart that is too much to ask for from the old men ending their days as wheelers and dealers. But if the philosophy were to grow, and not be trampled underfoot by the gray-flannel men with minds to match, then the advertising industry has a possibility of a useful future.

It can cease to be the irritator, the deliverer of half-truths, the un-informer, the disrespecter of persons, the social blackmailer. Instead it can become a problem solver for consumers, a bridge between consumers and manufacturers carrying two-way traffic, and a way of adding genuine, not phony values to its clients' products.

Despite all its failings, blindness, folly, ignorance and stupidity, advertising still has one more chance, for the Consumer Revolution is not vengeful. It does not demand the death of the old and fraudulent magicians. It merely wishes to turn them into useful human beings.

INDEX

"Abundance for What?" (Reisman), 112–13, 134
Action for Smoking and Health (ASH), 17, 189
Ad Daily, 178–79
Adler, Alfred, 88
Admap (magazine), 166, 214
Admap World Advertising Workshop, 174
Advertising Age, 39, 40, 42, 68, 69, 77, 80, 114, 124, 128, 173
Advertising Association, 7, 146, 163
Advertising Association Conference of 1971, 7
"Advertising—to a Problem-solving Consumer" (Arndt), 214
Advertising Standards Authority, 56
Advertising in the Twenty-first Century, 107
Agnew, Spiro, 93
Aid of Humanities Foundation, 218
Allen, Dr. Charles C., 170
Alyeska Pipeline Service Company, 79–80
America, Inc.: Who Owns and Operates the United States (Mintz and Cohen), 9
American Advertising Federation, 67
American Airlines, 171
American Association of Advertising Agencies, 53, 70, 144
American Bar Association, 21
American Bureau of Labor, 133
American Business Council, 66

American Can Company, 72
American Management Association, 67
American Medical Association, 43
American Motors Company, 133, 136, 138, 210
American Newspaper Publishers' Association, 171–72
American Standards Association, 13
Anadin Company, 61
Anderson, Jack, 17
Angelus, Ted, 173
Ariès, Philippe, 97
Arndt, Johann, 214
Arnold, Dr., 88
Article 8 (American Advertising Code), 37
As Others See Us (Treasure and Joyce), 190
Ashby, Sir Eric, 29
Aspirations and Affluence (Katona), 88, 112
Association of National Advertisers, 41, 42
Atomic Energy Research Establishment, 108
Attitude Change (Halloran), 187
Attitude Organisation and Behavioural Change (Secord and Blackman), 176
Avis Company, 76, 160

Bacon, Francis, 152, 153
Baker, Sam, 216
Balenciaga, 133
Banzhaf, John, III, 16–17, 30, 38

224

227

229

ABOUT THE AUTHOR

ROBIN WIGHT has worked as a copywriter at major
advertising agencies in London. In 1969 he was
awarded the Designers and Art Directors Association
prize for the best-written campaign of the year. In
1970 he won the British Electrical Appliance
Manufacturers Association prize for the best campaign of the year, and in 1971 he received the Rizzoli
Diplome d'Honneur. In New York in 1972 he won
a silver award at the "Creativity '71" exhibition,
and in 1973 Mr. Wight was presented with the
Punch "Humour in Advertising" award. He is a
regular contributor to *Campaign* and the London
Financial Times. He is now Creative Director at the
London office of a £21 million European agency.
He is married and has one son.